MRS. PENN-LEWIS

A Memoir

By
Mary N. Garrard

*He that believeth into me, out of the depths
of his life shall pour torrents of living
water. This spake he of the Spirit...*
John 7:38–39 (Old Syriac)

Kingsley Press

Shoals, Indiana

Mrs. Penn-Lewis: A Memoir

Published by Kingsley Press
PO Box 973
Shoals, IN 47581
USA

Tel. (800) 971-7985
www.kingsleypress.com
E-mail: sales@kingsleypress.com

ISBN: 978-1-937428-45-7 (paperback)
ISBN: 978-1-937428-46-4 (ebook)

Copyright © 1930 Overcomer Trust
First printed in 1930 by Overcomer Book Room
First Kingsley Press edition 2014

This first Kingsley Press edition is published under license from The Overcomer Trust, 10 Bydemill Gardens, Highworth, Wiltshire, SN6 7BS, United Kingdom.

Contents

Publisher's Foreword

The life story unfolded in the following pages is quite amazing and unique. It demonstrates what can happen when a life is completely yielded to God, emptied of self, and filled with the Spirit's power. Hopefully, the careful perusal of these pages will leave every reader with an intense desire to plunge, as Mrs. Penn-Lewis did, into the depths of Christ's redemptive work in such a way as to become a channel through which his power and glory can flow out to others.

This biography was originally published in 1930 by the Overcomer Book Room. A second edition was printed in 1947. An edition by Sentinel Publications appeared in 2002. This Kingsley Press edition is based on the second edition of 1947 and is complete and unabridged, though some very minor spelling and other improvements have been made. We would like to express our sincere thanks to Michael Metcalfe and the Overcomer Trust for granting permission for this reprint.

May God bless the republication of this rich biography to the inspiration and spiritual enrichment of many hungry hearts.

Edward Cook
Kingsley Press
June 2014

Jessie Penn-Lewis.

October 1925

Photo by Stuarts, Richmond

Foreword to the First Edition

This book is largely compiled from diaries and notes collected by Mrs. Penn-Lewis with the intention of writing her autobiography, and placed at the disposal of the council of *The Overcomer Testimony* by her literary trustees. Much that was only stored in a retentive memory must now remain untold, but the author has linked up the material available as simply as possible; and the council, at whose request she has acted, believe that this life story will be of service to others desiring to follow the same pathway of devotion to God and love to his people. It is the spiritual history of one suffering under great weakness of body, to whom God taught the deep lesson of life out of death—the lesson of the "grain of wheat" given to death in its sowing, that by the reproductive power of the life of God, life more abundant might spring forth in others.

In spite of her great natural gifts of mind and personality, the frailty of her body was such that, but for the strengthening power of God, much that Mrs. Penn-Lewis was enabled to accomplish would have been physically impossible. Her almost childlike confidence, too, in the love and loyalty of her fellow-workers was not invariably justified, and this also drove her more entirely upon the divine resources. The story of her life, like that of every saint, is the story of her Lord's sufficiency. Only those who have known her longest and most closely can fully appreciate how strongly their friend influenced much that was deepest in the evangelical life and thought of her time. They too will realize most readily the assured place that is hers in that succession of "honorable women" who in all ages have been accounted mothers in Israel. Surely such a blessed succession ends in those upon whom was promised, in these latter days, the outpouring of the Spirit of God.

May one who was honored by Mrs. Penn-Lewis' friendship only toward the end of her life give thankful expression to his sense of such a privilege, and the hope that this book will convey something of the inspiration of personal intimacy to that wider circle who for so long knew and loved her, both as speaker and writer?

It remains for me to express the grateful thanks of the council to their colleague, Mr. J. Gordon Logan, for so kindly advising on and reviewing the manuscript before going to press, as also for his selection of quotations from *Thy Hidden Ones* at the beginning of each chapter.

Bernard W. Matthews
Parkstone
June 1930

Foreword to the Second Edition

When I received the invitation to write a foreword to the new edition of the life of Mrs. Penn-Lewis I responded very gladly, for much blessing had come to my own heart through reading a previous edition. Hardly had my letter been posted, however, before I regretted what seemed to be a presumptuous action; for I greatly feared, and the fear is now strong within me, that I should fail in the proper discharge of my task. A foreword, I imagine, is designed to attract the attention and hold the interest of the reader to whom the contents of the book are unknown, in the hope that the reader will be encouraged to press forward through all the pages. Lest therefore I may fail in my task, let me at least say that a blessing direct from God awaits every reader who gives prayerful and serious thought to what is now presented.

As a Christian, Mrs. Penn-Lewis sought hard after God's best. She was not content to be saved; she was eager to enter into heavenly experience. She believed the blessing was a reality, that is to say, not an emotion of the being but an action of God upon herself. She had faith to receive it and she was prepared for any price to the flesh involved in the priceless blessing of release to her spirit. Upon that experience, not as an end in itself, but as an essential equipment for the fulfillment of the purpose of God, her whole life turned. No doubt specific characteristics that make up our varying personalities will exercise their influence in the receiving of the blessing. We need not suppose, therefore, that we are to experience precisely that to which Mrs. Penn-Lewis bears testimony; but we must surely believe that God has his own precious blessing for us, a blessing that sets us free for the doing of his will and becomes the opening of the door into fellowship that is heavenly indeed.

It has been said that she had a tendency to trust other folk too much. That, I think, must have been a weakness of the heart, for these pages bear witness to her powers of insight. Certainly in matters of truth she was endowed with a fine penetrating insight that not only exposed the wrong but with unerring judgment of the spirit provided the remedy.

It is twenty years since she died and the world has changed. We are in the era of vast organizations methodically engaged in the suppression of the significance of the individual. That, however, is not the divine intention or even permission. Here is a woman, weak in body, enriched and equipped of the Spirit, bearing aloft the word of truth whose life surged in her slender frame. May we not fervently pray as we draw near to the close of the fifth decade of this century that God will be mercifully pleased to raise up men and women of like spirit who know their God, who are filled with the Spirit, and are sure of the purpose of God in his Son.

Theo. M. Bamber
15th March, 1947

Introduction

The Current of the Spirit's Leading and its Conditions[1]

There is a COURSE prepared for each believer from the moment of his new birth, providing for the fullest maturity of the new life within him and the highest which God can make of his life in the use of every faculty for his service. To discover that course and fulfill it is the one duty of every soul. Others cannot judge what that course is. God alone knows it, and he can make it known, and guide the believer into it, as certainly today as he did Jeremiah and other prophets; Paul and Philip and other apostles.

This principle is clearly seen in the lives of the servants of God recorded in the Scriptures. Take Jeremiah and his call and commission. The Lord said to him, "Thou shalt go to all that I shall send thee, and whatsoever I command thee, thou shalt speak" (Jer. 1:7). "I have this day set thee over the nations ... I have made thee a defensed city ... they shall fight against thee, but they shall not prevail ... for I am with thee ..." Jeremiah then spoke as he was given the word of the Lord, and in the midst of personal conflict and suffering and the giving of messages rejected—and in his lifetime, on the whole unfulfilled—he completed his work. *He did not plan or choose his service.* He was chosen for the service and the service chosen for him. He had to fulfill it whether it was acceptable or not (Jer. 1:17–18), for the messages were filled with the word AGAINST, as he declared all that God was AGAINST, even to this day.

We find the same principle in the ministry of Ezekiel. He was called, commissioned, and empowered for a definite service

---

1   Extract from an "Autobiographical Sketch" written by Mrs. Penn-Lewis for *The Overcomer* in 1914.

11

(Ezek.1:1, 2:1–10, 3:1–17), and however much he suffered (Ezek. 9:8) his work had to be carried out, and family and home held subservient to the command of God (Ezek. 12:3–6, 14:16–18). His messages too were filled with the perpetual word AGAINST, as God placed on record, by his servant, his attitude to the evil of the world.

In the New Testament we find exactly the same personal choice (John 15:16) of God's servants; the same personal commission, with a personal course of life and work ordained and revealed. First in the life and ministry of the pattern servant of Jehovah, the Lord Christ—God himself in human form. All through the life of the Lord we see that he *knows* his commission and his course and will not be diverted from it by ties of affection (cf. Luke 2:41–52), the scorn of brethren (John 7:5–9), or the voice of the crowd (John 6:15). He knew when he had *finished* his work in one district (Mark 1:37–38) and left for another; he did not go beyond the limit of God in the work of healing, which had primarily the purpose of fulfilling prophecy concerning him (Matt. 8:16–17). He worked the works of him that sent him, not his own will or personal desires (cf. John 4:34, 6:5–15).

The same clear fulfilling of a course is seen in the apostle Paul, with the personal guiding and restraining of God. Paul is *chosen* (Acts 9:15) for specific service, which costs him great suffering; chosen to be the apostle to the Gentiles with a message which even the chief apostles were not given to proclaim.[1] The apostolic council at Jerusalem is in frequent storms and trouble through him, through his "new message"[2] and the fruits thereof. But he knows his *commission,* even though "they of repute" do not share it, and he must be faithful to his trust. He must fulfill his part in God's great plan for the church and his dealing with the world. He *knows* by the Spirit where he is to go and what he is to do;[3] when he is in the stream of the Spirit in staying in a place, by the unction on the message (Acts 14:3); he knows when he

---

1   Cf. Gal. 2:9.
2   Acts 15:6–12; 21:18–20.
3   Acts 8:2–4.

is restrained from a certain course (Acts 16:7), and when he is being sent of God on another errand (Acts 16:10); when he must go forward even though it means death (Acts 20:22); when he has finished his work in ministering to believers who loved him (Acts 22:25); knows that the "wolves" will break in among them after his departure (Acts 22:29)—*knows it all in his spirit,* and by the Holy Spirit—and through all he watches only to "finish his course." Wolves or no wolves, the testimony at *Rome* must be given, even though they break in to the flock he leaves behind, whom he calmly commits to God.

This brings me to my own course, which illustrates the principle referred to in the lives of the servants of God as recorded in the Scriptures... For the help of others who would know the conditions upon which such a leading of God becomes possible, I must refer to two outstanding characteristics of this path of service, which bear witness that it was the fulfilling of a course planned and guided by the Spirit of God.

The first is, that from the time when the baptism of the Spirit came and thrust me out into unpremeditated service in 1892, every "open door" in my path was set before me, unsought, unthought of, and unplanned. I then saw that I was in a current of the Spirit which would lead me on into all the plan of God for my life, and that my one business was to make sure of being in the will of God and, being sure, to keep myself free to carry out his will. This brought about deep rest of heart and simplicity of purpose. It eliminated all planning and troubling about the future. "Am I in the will of God *now?*" was the question, "then he will reveal whence he leads tomorrow."

But the conditions of knowing the will of God were: no bias to any path, however pleasant or apparently "good for the kingdom"; no double motive, however good, e.g., policy for the "good of the kingdom"; no personal aim, however justifiable, e.g., the electing to take a voyage on the Lord's service, and—the good of myself as part of the motive!

The voyage might be good for myself and the work's sake, but that must not deflect the compass needle of the soul seeking to know the will of God.

The second characteristic of the path of service I have outlined was that as God opened the doors, so he provided financially, and otherwise, all that was needed to enter them; and this he did apart from all councils and committees. In apostolic fashion he moved his own hidden saints to "set forward" on her journeys his messenger in a manner "worthy of God." In land after land, as door after door opened, the supply never failed. Only one condition was necessary on the messenger's part—to *keep free to follow the will of God, and that only.*

Set apart … for Himself

—Psalm 4:3

"Set apart"—a chosen vessel
To the King of Kings,
"Set apart," for ever severed
From all earthly things.

"Set apart" to bear the fragrance
Of his blessed name,
And with him to share the sufferings
Of a cross of shame.

"Set apart" with him to suffer
O'er a world undone,
And to stand in fiercest conflict
Till the fight be won.

"Set apart"—an earthern vessel,
Empty, weak and small,
Yet the treasure that it beareth
CHRIST the Lord of all.

—Freda Hanbury Allen

From an original poem written as a
birthday message to Mrs. Penn-Lewis

Chapter 1

The Preparation of the Vessel

1861–1891

Childhood surroundings and formative influences—Early beginnings in Christian work—Real conversion—Richmond and consecrated service—The river of life "ankle deep" (Ezek. 47:3)

I was born on the 28th of February, 1861, in Neath, south Wales. My father was a civil and mining engineer, my mother the daughter of a business man who married a girl of gentle birth who had been adopted by a wealthy uncle. I was the second daughter, the first having died before I was born. My father's father was the Rev. Samuel Jones, of Neath, an eminent minister of the Calvinistic Methodist Connection, whose service was for the whole Principality, north and south, going on preaching tours as colleague with the leading divines of his time. His main ministry was the building up of believers, and his favorite theme was the atonement. He was said to be the most metaphysical preacher of his day in the C.M. Connection, and was associated with a group of divines who were the leaders in Wales at that time: Charles of Bala, Henry Rees of Liverpool, Matthews and others.

My father's house was a rendezvous for the leading ministers of the Connection as they passed hither and thither on their master's business, and all my childhood's memories are gathered round the great meetings of the Sunday schools on the first Sunday in May, and the constant coming and going of ministers at our home. I was brought up, therefore, in religious surroundings and in the lap of Calvinistic Methodism.

My mother often told me in later days that she had given me to God before I was born. She had ideas that children could be brought up without the knowledge of sin, and it was with a bitter shock that she found out that every soul born into the world is of the "fallen Adam." The awakening came when I was two years old. My nurse had been told not to take the children to any house, but she did so, and told me "not to tell." On being asked, I upheld the nurse, and told the lie that we had not been there! By some means the truth was discovered, and my mother fled to my grandfather with bitter tears to tell him that her angel child had told a lie!

I walked when nine months old without any teaching—simply got up and walked across the room and always walked afterwards. The doctor bade my mother not to teach me anything, as he said my enemy was my active brain, which must not be roused. But in spite of this I learned the alphabet myself, from papers, and made my father and others tell me the words as I spelled out the letters, so that I read my Bible *freely* at four years old, having never been taught to read. At four years, also, I used to take up a story book and could describe afterwards every character. From all this it was evident that my education had to be checked until my eighth year, after which I was sent for about three months at a time to a boarding school, the other months having to be spent at farmhouses in the mountains, where I could run wild and live a country life, and where there was no temptation to read. My home was a library of books, my father being a great reader and buyer of all classical works and standard books.

When I was about nine years old, my father leased the old museum at Neath, where his offices had already been for some years. Now he turned it into a dwelling house for his increasing family. The front building consisted of three immense rooms. Retaining the first floor as public and private offices, the others were divided into rooms. Adjoining the front building was a tower five floors high, the walls three feet thick at the bottom, and the top forming a room without a roof—the old observatory, from which place could be seen the surrounding country for many miles. The tower itself was covered with ivy and was the home of thousands of birds. Here in this old home many happy years were spent—an attic with gable windows was our playroom, and our great delight was *books*. As children we sat on the floor in the midst of books and magazines of all sorts, reading, reading, reading!

Four brothers followed me in steady succession until I was ten, so my play-fellows were boys. In the garden we played cricket and climbed trees and had our own little "reading nests" in various corners—sometimes behind the chimney of an outhouse, where ivy nooks could be found—and we even read up in the branches of the trees.

My father was devoted to his children, and I remember well the time when he could walk with six, two-and-two to chapel, and so proudly answer back remarks as to his "quiver full" with joy. He was a delightful companion to us. How I remember the walks with him as a tiny child, when he would describe to me the geological strata of the rocks, and together we would hunt, on the seashore we used to visit, for fossils and remarkable stones. My father, too, had high ideals of honor that have left their stamp upon us all through our lives. He was very careful to teach his children the value of truth, not allowing careless promises to be made to them by the servants or others, but insisting on truth in every word and tone.

At ten years of age I was sent for longer periods to a boarding school at Swansea, facing the sea, more for my health than for the training; but six months was the longest time I could bear even this mild regime of school life, although I well remember always being taken to church in a carriage and sleeping in the bedroom of the proprietress of the school where I could be under her eye. Here I began to realize a little the restrictions of my body, for I distinctly remember a bout of tears in the boot-cupboard, after watching the other children being sent out to play whilst I had to stay indoors as there was "an east wind."

Even this kind care and small measure of discipline did not suit me, and I had to be home again under my mother's eye. And there, when nearly twelve years of age, my first bit of service began.

My mother was an ardent temperance worker, and at that time the Good Templar movement began in Neath. My mother was one of the first to join, and I was keenly eager to be a Templar also, but alas the adult lodge could not admit any one under the age of twelve! But the very first lodge night after my twelfth birthday saw me initiated into the coveted circle, and I began my first crusade as a co-worker with my mother. Great was my delight and earnest desire to prove a good soldier in the temperance cause. A minor lodge was commenced, and it was not long before I found myself chief presiding officer of the juveniles—the lodge consisting of forty or fifty children. Meanwhile a Quaker lady opened a school to which my two brothers and I were sent as day scholars—for myself, the need of frequent changes of air still breaking the continuity of my school life and making the lessons in French and German with my German tutor of very little avail. When about thirteen years old, I began to attend the Sunday school of St. David's Church, the Ven. Archdeacon Griffiths being rector of Neath. My parents were still members of the Calvinistic Methodist Connection, but the services were in Welsh, and the younger generation were more and more making English their language. My parents were large-hearted and true Christians and on very cordial terms with the rector, so that they decided to allow me to attend the church Sunday school, and I afterwards joined the church choir.

In spite of broken school life and great delicacy, I continued to take a keen interest in the temperance cause. So much so that, at fourteen years, I was proposed as hon. secretary to the adult lodge. A Quaker gentleman, who took for private tuition twelve boys (of whom three were my brothers) undertook to train me in the secretarial work, and with so much success that I was re-elected quarter after quarter to my much-enjoyed post until compelled to give it up when I was sixteen, through a great sorrow that befell our happy home. My father had been ill for two years with blood-poisoning caused by sewer gas, with which he had come in contact in his professional work. On April 24th 1877, he died. How well I remember the terrible day, and the funeral three days after, when from a window I watched the sad procession, with two uncles behind the coffin and two fatherless lads on either hand.

My mother was left with eight children, two sisters having followed the four boys, and then a boy who was three months old at this sore time. I was the eldest, being sixteen years old. My father had been a successful man in his profession, but he was not a good businessman. He disliked the handling of money; he dreaded making a will or sending out accounts. At the time of his death he was consulting engineer to most of the great colliery companies of south Wales, and was from every point of view in the prime of life and at the height of his profession. But heavy bills outstanding, and lawyers' costs for administration, arbitration over large accounts, etc., soon spent our all, and my mother found herself compelled to start in business to maintain and educate her children.

The old museum was rapidly transformed into business premises, and here she made an income by her skillful efforts, sufficient to give one of her boys his course at Oxford, the eldest his training as civil engineer, and the third as surveyor. And thus she continued until all were on their feet.

At the age of nineteen I married—a genuine love match. But I loved my husband for his *character*. Girl as I was, I reasoned that a man who never broke his word and never failed in an appointment was a safe one to whom to trust my life! I was still very delicate, indeed so frail was my health that my father's brother thought it his duty to see my fiancé and tell him that he was practically undertaking an *invalid for life!* He stood the test. We married and went to live at Brighton where he was auditor's clerk for the County of Sussex.

As it often is with children brought up in the midst of religious surroundings, the true inward change of heart did not come until I had married and moved away from the old home. At the time of our marriage, my husband was attending the Church of the Annunciation at Brighton. The vicar was an extreme high church man, but he never succeeded in persuading us to go to confession nor in any way to become really earnest in his strong Anglo-Catholic views.

After I had been married some eighteen months, I began to feel very ill at ease about the Lord's return. I knew that I was not prepared to meet him, and I began really to seek the Lord. My conversion occurred without the aid of any human instrument, but the day—New Year's Day 1882—and the hour are imprinted on my mind.

Only a deep inward desire to know that I was a child of God; a taking of my (too-little-read) Bible from the shelf; a turning over the leaves, and the eye falling on the words, "the Lord hath laid upon him the iniquity of us all"; again a casual turn of the sacred pages, and the words, "he that believeth hath eternal life." A quick facing out whether I *did* believe that God had laid my sins upon the Lamb of God on the cross; a pause of wonderment that it really said that I had eternal life if I simply believed God's Word; a quick cry of, "Lord, I *do* believe"—and one more soul had passed from death unto life, a trophy of the grace of God and the love of him who died. The Spirit of God instantly bore witness with my spirit that I was a child of God, and deep peace filled my soul.

The new life bore fruit in that I sought to conquer my besetting sins, whereas hitherto I had found myself at their mercy as I feebly attempted to restrain them. But my attempts still ended in abject failure, and the succeeding few months were a record of bitter repentance and many tears over sins I could not conquer.

* * *

Thus ends the story of her life as commenced by Mrs. Penn-Lewis for the autobiography she hoped to write. (The last two paragraphs have been added from the little booklet *The Leading of the Lord*.) From this point onward it will be our endeavor, by the help of God, to give the spiritual record of this remarkable life as much as possible in her own words, from diaries, letters, articles, and the journals kept during her visits abroad.

* * *

In August 1883, her husband having been appointed Borough Accountant of Richmond (Surrey), Mr. and Mrs. Penn-Lewis left Brighton and settled at Richmond, where they found their way to Holy Trinity Church and came under the deep spiritual teaching of the Rev. Evan H. Hopkins, whose very first sermon was "an opening of heaven" to this intense and hungry soul. She heard for the first time of victory over the bondage of besetting sins through the blood of Christ, of the joy of full surrender, and the possibilities of a Spirit-filled life. Calling upon Mrs. Hopkins one day, she was lovingly asked if she were "a Christian," and her glad answer "yes" was her first open confession of Christ, an answer followed by some heart-searching as she said to herself, "now I have *said* it, I shall have to keep to it!" Mrs. Hopkins also asked her if she had "victory over sin," but she was obliged to confess that she had "never heard of it."

The tiny pocket diaries kept during the early years at Richmond tell in the briefest notes of the deep, deep longing for the uttermost that God could do for her, and the brave and constant struggle for "victory"; while scarcely a week went by without some little reference to her physical condition, showing that the early weakness was in no way conquered and was a handicap she could not shake off.

A half-sheet of notepaper dated 8 a.m., Feb. 28th 1884, gives a glimpse into the entire surrender and consecration of this young Christian. It reads:

> Lord Jesus, on this my 23rd birthday I do again yield my whole self unto thee, soul and spirit, life, time, hands, feet, eyes, lips, voice, money, intellect, will, heart, love, health, thoughts and desires. All that I have, all that I am, all that I may be is thine, wholly, absolutely and unreservedly. And I do believe that thou dost take me, and that thou wilt work in me to *will* and to *do* thy good pleasure. Lord, use

me in whatever way it seemeth good to thee, keep my eyes fixed on thee, ready to obey even thy glance. Thou art my King, my Savior, and my Guide. Take not thy holy presence from me, but day by day draw me nearer until that glorious time when I shall see thee face to face and faith be lost in sight. Amen.

That God took her utterly and entirely at her word, thousands of his people in all lands can testify, to the glory of him who *chooses* the weak things to confound the mighty, and the "things that are not, to bring to nought the things that are; that no flesh should glory in his presence."

An entry after a watch-night service at the beginning of 1886 runs, "Thank God, I commence the year 'right with him,' but I long intensely to be more single-eyed to his glory, my will more lost in his."

Another shortly after, "A day of constant temptation and battle against a discontented, grumbling spirit. Was enabled to hold on all through in spite of darkness: fear I gave way many times, but was kept near to the precious blood..." Again—"Gave way once or twice to hasty speaking. Oh, how I want even the tone of my voice to be gentle. Am more at peace and trusting, but still not very bright, but I mean to keep on trusting..." "Very tired all day, felt ruffled again this morning. When shall I learn peace and the love that endureth all things and is not easily provoked! Difficult to believe afterwards that the Lord *does* forgive at once, so depression instead of fullness of joy fills one's soul. One wants to *feel* forgiven—how much training one needs, and how patient the Lord is!"

But there were also times of deep conscious fellowship with the Lord she was growing to know more closely, and entries read: "Happy day, no cloud, but conscious presence and smile of the Lord—oh, why do I not trust him more utterly in times of temptation?" "Happy day again, the Lord so near and so precious. Such a sweet sense of 'nothing between.'"

About this time, to her great joy, and in answer to much prayer, her husband definitely came out on the Lord's side, and together they sought to serve God and win others to him. Busy days these were, filled on her part with home duties and housekeeping, and in every bit of spare time with seeking individual souls, in quiet talks by the wayside, in her own home, and at meetings in connection with Trinity Church. Mr. Penn-Lewis quickly became a fluent and powerful speaker in the open air, and many notes in the diaries tell with gratitude to God of his earnestness in this work. A mission was the occasion of great opportunities for individual work in March 1886. "Led two children to Jesus," the entry runs, "and had a long talk with young B—. He yielded so far as to promise me to go home and pray God to give him the desire." The next day, "At Hammond's meeting, although poorly all day. Young B— there. I watched for him … after a long time, thank God, he decided … I was led to claim him this afternoon." "Spoke to Walter D—, but no good—Lord have mercy on him." "At College Hall this afternoon—led four boys to decision." And through it all there runs a little refrain of the young wife's practical daily round and common task—"Very busy all day—making marmalade, ironing, etc.," and so on. "Young B—" appears to have been very really "born again," for later on we find him speaking at a meeting, followed by the note, "Thank God, he is coming on well!"

On October 14th, 1886, the Y.W.C.A. Institute at Richmond, which was afterwards to play so large a part in the story, was opened. Mrs. Evan Hopkins was the means, under God, of the establishment of this work, the nucleus being a Bible class for business girls carried on for some years by the late Mrs. Albert Head at her own home.

Mrs. Penn-Lewis undertook the work of librarian in addition to her Sunday afternoon Bible class at a rescue home for girls, and both of these were fresh openings for earnest personal work in dealing with souls and bringing many to repentance and faith in Christ. She was also on the committee of the rescue home, with Mrs. Albert Head and others. She flung herself into the work of the rescue home with characteristic intensity. One of the girls she took into her own home as maid, but after much anxiety and trouble, the girl "ran away with a soldier." The diary tells of strainful days and weary journeys in search of this "lost sheep," returning to Richmond on one occasion at midnight "dead beat" after a fruitless three days' search, in company with the matron of the home, through Chatham, Sandgate, Maidstone, and other places where soldiers were stationed.

The year 1889 was marked out specially as "a year of illness," and the diary entries are one long story of pain and weakness from the pleurisy and lung trouble which seemed to be rapidly developing. Under the constant care now of Dr. Cook, she was weighed from time to time, and the result was usually 91–95 pounds, and never more than the latter. Nevertheless there was no slackening in the work of the Lord. Long committees in connection with the rescue home, prayer meetings, and Bible classes were kept up whenever possible, in spite of the resulting physical exhaustion. In addition, there were now almost daily interviews with girls seeking spiritual help, and these were constantly the subject of prayer and thought, each name being noted in the diary. The Lord was leading his child deeper and ever deeper, down into fellowship with himself in quiet, steady, unseen preparation for his future pathway. During the previous year she had greatly missed a very dear friend in a long absence from Richmond, and this also was part of God's training process for his child.

On the last night of the old year (1888), a longer note than usual tells how both recognized his schooling at this time:

Such a sweet talk with X— over the lesson our souls had learned in our separation. She found she had learned more of Christ, and I knew the same. I discovered that I had been longing for human companionship in the pressing on, and I saw that I must be content to be *alone* in soul if I would press on to the heights. I remembered the picture of "The Broad and Narrow Way" and the number of people just beyond the cross, and the *ones and twos* pressing on to the heights beyond. I remembered even Jesus was lonely in soul, and I saw that if I would press on, I must be content to be lonely too, as far as other people go—content to press on with Jesus alone as my companion. As soon as I saw this, I saw what had, in a manner, kept me lingering about. Now I will not linger any longer but follow Jesus right ahead.

A few days later she speaks of deep heart-searching and prayer over one in her home whom she is passionately desirous of leading to "know Christ," and writes: "I feel so unfit for it, indeed how to do it I do not know. I must be more in prayer. I do not pray half enough. I feel there are depths and heights that I know nothing of, but *I know that my face is 'set as a flint' to press on to fullest blessing.*" And there follows, as on most days, a list of four or five names of those who have come with needs and difficulties, for personal talks and prayer, although on this day she was kept in one room with her chest "wheezy" and painful. The slightest breath of east wind brought her down to extreme weakness and compelled her to keep her room.

It is very striking to see from these early diaries that, as she was at the end, so she was from the beginning of her service for God; always with the severest physical handicap, but always carried above it in victory when opportunity was given for helping others—"A.M. came at 7.15, almost too tired to talk to her... Miss B. came for five minutes, then D. for an hour... she prayed afterwards; it was sweet."

* * *

The most important step in her spiritual life at this time, leading as it did to the recognition of the utter inability of "the natural man" to serve God acceptably and the need of a special endowment of power from on high, was the reading of *The Spirit of Christ* by Dr. Andrew Murray, who was then becoming well known as a teacher of the deep things of God. A snowy Sunday in February, she writes, was spent "reading Murray's *Spirit of Christ* all day. It seems so deep and almost beyond comprehension, but I do long to know more of it. I seem to know so little—may he teach me!" Ten days later it is recorded with joy that fresh light and conviction on this matter is breaking in.

Quoting from the book, she writes: "I came on the words 'To others it comes as a deep, quiet, but clearer insight into the fullness of the Spirit of Christ as being theirs, and a faith that feels confident that his sufficiency is equal to every emergency.' These words fairly 'lit up' to me, and I saw that this had been my experience lately—I have *never* seen his power as I see it now ... Has not Jesus been teaching me knowledge, love, and obedience these last years, and have not I been entering into the fellowship of his death this winter as never before? Have I not been seeing the utter hopelessness of the flesh and feeling keenly its utter insufficiency?"

Of the great change that now took place in her own life and service, Mrs. Penn-Lewis wrote years afterwards in a booklet describing the still greater "fullness of the spirit" which the child of God may receive to equip him for a bold witness to his Lord:

> The distinction between these two aspects of the fullness of the Spirit has been clear in my personal experience ... I was reading Andrew Murray's *Spirit of Christ*, and as I read, I saw that I should know the Holy Spirit as a person. So I took him as the gift of Christ, as simply as I first took the Lord Jesus as my Savior. I well remember the deep peace, the fellowship with God, the communion of the Holy Ghost, and the fruit of the Spirit in love, joy, peace, which followed. But I could not understand why it made so little difference in my service. It did not deliver me from shrinking inability to speak boldly for Christ nor give me power for aggressive service. In these respects I was just the same as before, until, some three years later, I saw there was a baptism of the spirit *for service*, which meant deliverance from the fear of man and power of effective utterance in witness for Christ.

Those who knew this servant of God in later years were often amazed to hear her speak of the agony of fear with which she used to go forth to speak, even at the smallest meeting, and the hours of hard and painful preparation that preceded such a service. That this wonderful new filling of the Spirit of Christ did not deliver her from this is clear from her diaries, for only two days later she made this note: "Meeting at night ... in an agony of dread. Went and cried to the Lord, threw myself on him and asked for calmness and quiet ... as soon as the meeting began

I was quiet, and we had a lovely time—perfect liberty—it was glorious … I was overwhelmed with all this answer to prayer."

Truly the Lord did not fail on his part, giving "seed to the sower" and liberty in the sowing, but with no personal sense of the boundless liberty of the Spirit of God pouring out through a human spirit "released from its imprisonment in the vessel of the soul, and lifted to a position of dominance over soul and body." Neither was there, even yet, any steady victory over her "besetting sins," chiefly the hasty spirit which was an integral part of her Welsh temperament, multiplied—who can tell how keenly?—by the intense physical weakness and exhaustion of her suffering body. But this was never allowed to minimize a fault in her own eyes. After nearly a week of "spring cleaning," with workmen in the house, and long hours of household sewing, during which the constant interviews, meetings, and other service for her master were not neglected, the diary reports: "So worn out at night. Some bitter falls through physical exhaustion—*YET inexcusable!*"

During this spring (1889) a serious cough developed, shaking the weak frame and accompanied by high temperature at night. On April 27th she went down to Brighton to stay with friends, and a week later went on to Eastbourne to the House of Rest, where she remained until the middle of May, too ill to do much more than lie about in the sun or go for short drives, though even here there were constant "interviews." At this time she lost weight rapidly, as much as three pounds in one week, and for the first time coughed up a little blood. It seemed as if her frail life were ebbing away.

On her return to Richmond, the rescue home committee meetings, Bible class, and Y.W.C.A. Institute were again taken up, but November and December found her once more on the south coast. God was still dealing with his servant, deepening the sense of insufficiency for his service, and need of some greater power than she yet possessed to overcome the power of the flesh and its shrinking fear. Many were the efforts made to find some way of deliverance, and on a Sunday in December, at Longstone Hall, Eastbourne, she writes that she "went out (to the penitent form) for deliverance from self-consciousness"; but the degree of liberty experienced after this does not appear to have been great or lasting. A visit to Mr. and Mrs. Albert Head at Hastings was a time of great spiritual uplift and refreshing, when the evening hours after dinner were spent in long talks over the open Bible.

The winter that followed this year of increasing physical weakness was used of God to teach his child what it meant to take his life and strength for her body when needed for his service. "Healing" was not given, the consumptive symptoms continued to develop, but on a cold day in February (1890) with snow and east wind, she wrote in her diary:

"In all day, then claimed of the Lord strength and physical keeping, and *went to my Bible class* (at the rescue home)... came home tired, but happy and thankful."

But the gift she asked and took was for *service*, not for herself, and on the following day, the wind being still easterly, the entry runs, "Stayed in all day... am no worse for last night, but felt I could not ask God to keep me if I went out today needlessly. So against my inclination, I stayed in ..."

In March 1890 came the call to undertake the honorary secretaryship of the Richmond Y.W.C.A., and with (humanly speaking) only a few months to live, Mrs. Penn-Lewis ventured to accept it, pleading with her doctor that if she had but a brief span of life before her, he would allow her to "die doing something for God," for her whole heart was drawn out in service for her Lord.

In spite of ill-health and suffering, she worked and organized and labored incessantly, with Miss Freda Hanbury as hon. assistant secretary. Musical drill, singing classes, shorthand classes, and other activities were initiated with the object of attracting the young girls of the town, in addition to the Bible classes and other meetings at the Institute. Of this period Mrs. Penn-Lewis wrote in after years:

> After a time I became conscious that the spiritual results were not equivalent to the labor of the work. I began to question whether I knew the *fullness* of the Holy Spirit. Without doubt I had received

him and had 'entered into rest' as concerned my own life and fellowship with God. But when I compared the small results of my service with the fruit given to the apostles at Pentecost, I could not but own that I did not know the Holy Spirit in the fullness of his power. My weekly Bible class was a great trouble to me, for I had no power of utterance. Organizing work was much easier, but meetings were a sore trial. Self-consciousness almost paralyzed me, and no practice ever made speaking less difficult. Others might have the gift of speech, but it was clearly not given to me, I said. So all the people I could discover who were filled with the Spirit, I invited to Richmond. Everyone I heard of who knew anything about the Holy Spirit, I asked to come and speak to my girls—I was so anxious that they should get this blessing. I settled it in my mind that I was not the channel. I was not the one to speak. Until one day the Lord turned on me and said: *"Why not yourself?"* These people have quite enough to do without coming to do your work! Why not you the channel?" But, I said, I cannot speak! It takes me a whole day to prepare for my class. What can *I* do? It is impossible!

Blessing there was which might well have contented a less intense spirit, for souls were led to Christ, and in many a private talk God's children were brought to the point of laying their all upon the altar. It was a most successful piece of work outwardly, but the heart of the worker knew its own lack of power; and God was watching for the "fullness" of his own time. "He waited," she wrote afterwards, "until I came to an end of my own energy and strength. *How* I taught the girls in my Bible class! How *full* my Bible was of notes, and how carefully I prepared a dish of spiritual food for them! 'Food' all obtained second-hand from other books ... But they did not change much in their lives! I thought it was the fault of the girls, until the Lord spoke to me and said, 'It is yourself!' 'But, Lord, I am *consecrated!* What can it be in me? I give time every morning to read and pray. I have put everything right in my life as far as I know.' But the Lord still said, 'It is YOU.' And then he began to break me, and there came to me the terrible revelation that every bit of this activity, this energy, this indomitable perseverance, was *myself* after all, though it was hidden under the name of 'consecration.'"

"The soul must always have a 'heavenly vision' to draw it out of itself and away from the things of earth. The 'eyes' of the heart must be 'illuminated' to know the hope of its calling. The clearer the vision, the more entire the abandonment to the Holy Spirit for its fulfillment, and the more intense the thirst after God—a 'furnace of intense desire' which must be created by the Eternal Spirit himself, and which is the supreme condition of knowing God."[1]

---

1   The extracts facing each new chapter are taken from the book *Thy Hidden Ones*, by Mrs. Penn-Lewis.

Chapter 2

Power for Service

1892–1895

The unveiling of the self-life—The Lord's coming in power and its seven-fold result—The outflow of the living waters—The first visit to Keswick—The Y.W.C.A. Institute at Richmond, and "waters to swim in"

This first unveiling of the self-life led, early in 1892, to the little band of workers connected with the Y.W.C.A. Institute at Richmond meeting weekly to wait upon God definitely for an endowment of power and an outpouring of the Holy Spirit upon the work; and as they prayed they were clearly shown that there was a work of God to be done *in themselves* before the outpouring could come upon the Institute. Mrs. Penn-Lewis tells, in the booklet, *Power for Service,* how she read book after book upon the subject of the work of the Holy Spirit, searching out as to whether God did actually promise his children as full an indwelling and outworking of the Spirit as in the days of Pentecost, only to find herself more and more confused by the differing teaching of the various schools of thought. Finally, she writes:

> I said, I will go straight to God and ask him to *prove* to me whether there is *for me* an endowment for service that will liberate me in utterance as it did Peter at Pentecost. I will put it to the proof for myself! Away went the books, and away went the various views and theories. In desperation I said, I WILL GO TO GOD. From this time I never admitted another question, but set myself with steady determination to prove for myself if there was anything in it. Then slowly, as I held on to God, there grew within me a deepening purpose that

at all costs I would obtain this endowment for service—until at last there came such a cry to God for it, as the supreme thing I wanted, that I could say he might take away all things from me if he would only answer this cry. It was a long time before it got to that, but it brought about such an absolute surrender of my will to God that I have never had to fight a battle of surrender of will from that time. I could say he should do absolutely what he liked with my life if he would only give me that liberation of the Holy Spirit that Peter knew at Pentecost.

Peter was the pattern I put before the Lord. I saw that Peter was not nervous that day, and I intensely felt my great need was to be delivered from an overpowering nervousness and a kind of paralysis in speech that fairly mastered me. I cried, "I want the deliverance that Peter got at Pentecost. I do not care what the Christians call it. If the baptism of the Spirit is not the right term, give me the right words to use. I do not care about the words, but *I want the thing*.

In this way I held on to God with an intensity which caused "people" to fall away from my mind, with all they said about this great liberation for service which I was seeking. Then a deep rest came into me that God would do what I had asked, and I could wait his way and time.

Thus I learned the true meaning of "waiting" for "the promise of the Father." I had reached a quiet attitude of dependence upon God that he would answer my cry in his own time. Then I went on with my usual work, not in indifference, but with a steady hold of faith that some time the endowment would come. But I was sorely tested. My experience after that was deeper, and deeper, and deeper sense of failure. Everything seemed to be worse and worse, instead of better and better as I had thought it would be after such a tremendous transaction with God. I appeared to lose all I already had. I grew worse and worse in nervousness and horror in speaking to my Bible class and everything seemed failure.[1]

One outcome of this keen searching of heart and intense desire to know more of the Holy Spirit's power was a ten days' Mission held at the Institute in February 1892 by Miss H. E. Soltau of the China Inland Mission. Bible readings for ladies were held in the afternoons, and meetings for members of the

---

1 *Power for Service and Warfare*, p. 25.

Y.W.C.A. and others in the evenings, including two Sundays. It was something of a shock to the hon. secretary when, after the first evening meeting, Miss Soltau said to her: "I must send to London for someone to come here to pray, for this place is like a *wall!* There is no break—there is not enough prayer to move it." "A wall!" And the secretary and organizer had been so proud of her "consecrated branch!" "I thought there was no branch in the country like it," she said, in speaking years afterwards of this time. "I had talked to the members of consecration, and we *had* consecrated ourselves. It shows how easy it is to get things into our heads and not have them in our lives! 'No break?' I could not understand what she meant. But she said a 'break' was needed, so I stood back and watched—until at last I saw the souls broken down through that broken messenger, and many coming to Christ. By the end of the week *there was 'a break'*—souls were being saved at every meeting and I said, 'Is this what you call a break?' It was an education to me!"

From this point the meetings increased in power and interest, until at the praise meeting which closed the mission, the rooms at the Institute were crowded out, and nearly forty testimonies to definite blessing were sent in, together with thank-offerings of money and jewelry.

After this practical illustration of what "the endowment of power from on high" might mean, the "furnace of intense desire" for such an endowment increased. "Do for me what you did for Peter at Pentecost," she prayed again, as she felt more and more keenly her lack of "utterance" and the bondage of self-consciousness. Then the Spirit of God began to question her and to bring to light the "thoughts and intents" of her heart. We cannot do better than give the story in her own words:

> Then two or three searching questions were put to me by the Spirit of God. The first was: "If I answer your cry, are you willing to be unpopular?" UNPOPULAR! Be rejected? Well yes, I am willing. I have never faced it before, but I am willing.
>
> *Why did I desire the fullness of the Spirit?* Was it for success in service, and that I should be considered a much-used worker? Would

I desire the same fullness of the Spirit if it meant apparent failure and becoming the off-scouring of all things in the eyes of others? This had not occurred to me before, and I quickly agreed to any conditions the Lord should please to set before me.

Again came the question: *Would I be willing to have no great experience,* but agree to live and walk entirely by faith in the Word of God? But, I said, I thought people who had a baptism of the Spirit always had an experience! Did not Finney and Asa Mahan? How am I to know I have had it if I do not get an experience? Are you willing to walk in bare faith on my Word and never have any wonderful experience? Yes! These were the questions put to me by God, and then the matter dropped.

Then came the climax, when one morning I awoke, and lo, I beheld before me a hand holding up in terrible light a handful of filthy rags, whilst a gentle voice said: "*This* is the outcome of all your past service for God." But Lord, I have been surrendered and consecrated to thee all these years; it was consecrated work! "Yes, my child, but all your service has been *consecrated self*—the outcome of your *own energy,* your *own plans* for winning souls, your *own devotion.* All for me, I grant you, but *yourself* all the same."

The unveiling was truly a horror to me and brought me in deep abasement to the blood of Christ for cleansing. Then came the still, small voice once more, and this time it was the one little word—CRUCIFIED!

Crucified—What did it mean? I had not asked to be *crucified* but to be *filled.* But now Romans 6:6–11 became a power to me, and I knew the meaning of "our old man was crucified with him …" and what Paul meant in his words, "crucified with Christ" (Gal. 2:20).

As a little child, I rested on the word thus given, and then it "pleased the Lord to reveal his Son in me that I might preach him"—*I knew the risen Lord.*

This revelation of the risen Lord—the first drops of the "showers" which were to become a very river of "waters to swim in"—came suddenly and unexpectedly, not in an hour of "waiting" upon God, nor in a meeting with others seeking the same blessing—but at the breakfast table in her own home one morning in March, the glory of the Lord was revealed in her spirit as to Paul on his way to Damascus, with such blinding power that she fled to her own room to fall upon her knees in worship and speechless adoration. The seven-fold result is given in *Power for Service* thus:

(1) It was sudden, and when I was not specially thinking about the matter. (2) I knew in my spirit that he had come. (3) My Bible became like a living thing and was flooded with light. (4) Christ suddenly became to me a real person: I could not explain how I knew, but he became real to me. (5) When I went to my Bible class, I found myself able to speak with liberty of utterance, with the conviction of the Spirit at the back of it, until souls were convicted of sin on every side. (6) Power in prayer, so that it seemed I only needed to ask and have. (7) My spirit took its way to God, freed from every fetter that held to anything on earth.

"The cross leads to the Spirit, the Spirit leads back to the cross." After the unveiling of the self-life came the ready acceptance of God's verdict upon it, that even *"consecrated self"* is still "SELF" and must be reckoned "crucified" if the life of Jesus is to be manifested through the human vessel. Then followed the revelation of the risen Lord, whose own Spirit was to come in and fill the emptied vessel—with the result that God worked very quickly to give his child the endowment of power to serve him acceptably, for which she had so long pleaded. For the Spirit of God baptizes into the death of Christ (Rom. 6:3), and thus the human spirit, set free from the domination of the "flesh" and the "soulish" life of nature, becomes an habitation of God through the Spirit, and a clear channel for the outflow of the life of God to others. "Calvary *precedes* Pentecost. Death with Christ precedes the fullness of the Holy Spirit. *Power!* Yes, God's children need power, but God does not give power to the old creation, nor to the uncrucified soul. Some may have a measure of power, but not what God wants to give. Satan will give power to the 'old Adam,' but God will not."

In the evening of that day, on her way home from a meeting, her "spirit was released from every bond, and seemed to break through into the heavens as from some inward prison, finding its place in the heart of God." This experience, so sacred between herself and her Lord, it would be impossible for another to describe, but we are able to give it in her own words, prepared as a foreword to the autobiography she had hoped to write. Written long after the experience, she was able to look back upon it with the deeper knowledge of the ways of God gained through many years of close and intimate walking with him, and, seeing it from his viewpoint, to interpret its meaning and purpose as but the prelude to the "rivers of living water" which were to flow out to others from a life wholly "handed over to death for Jesus' sake."

On March 18th, 1892, traveling alone in a railway carriage from Wimbledon to Richmond, it seemed as if suddenly my spirit broke through into the spiritual world and I was caught up into the bosom of the Father! For days afterwards I felt that I was as a babe lying in the Father's bosom with all the world below lying in darkness whilst I was in light, clear as crystal and so pure that every speck of sin stood out in blackness. The people walking the streets looked to me as in another world. The morning following the Lord stood by me and I clasped his very feet. That night when I went to the prayer meeting, all who were present—young women—were sobbing before the Lord. When I went to my Bible class, the room seemed filled with glory, and from this time there broke out upon the work a very river of life from God, which ever since has been flowing on to the ends of the earth. It was my baptism with the Holy Ghost. For months I had been seeking it with intensity and crying to the Lord for "just what the Holy Spirit did for Peter." God answered definitely what I had definitely asked, and liberty of utterance was suddenly given, as to Peter on the day of Pentecost.

For three months after this sudden breaking through into the supernatural world, I lived in a very heaven of joy and light and gladness, and the very name of Jesus was so sweet that the sound of it caused me to melt into tears and to be filled with exquisite joy. Then came the gradual cessation of this heavenly experience, and—the time of danger. I began to dread the loss of my experience, and to *seek* now the "experience" that seemed to be slipping from me. At this point, I was shown, by the mercy of God, the path of the cross, and the wisdom of God in withdrawing the gifts of God, for the soul to rest entirely in him, and not in joy or ecstatic communion, which made me spiritually self-absorbed and apt to pity others not on my plane of spiritual life. I only wanted to be left alone to retire within for communion with my beloved. The physical being was not in the least involved, and the ecstasy of delight was purely in the spirit, keeping me away in spirit in a realm far above the earth, so that I moved among others and did my daily duties as one in a dream—a spirit in the world of men.

But when I saw that the loss of this spiritual delight and ecstasy meant fruit, through death and a life *in God himself* above his gifts, I gladly chose the path of the cross and consented to walk in the night of faith to that goal where God would be All in All. And through depth after depth of fellowship with the Christ in his death did the Lord himself lead me in succeeding years, until my vision cleared and cleared, to see that the cross of Calvary was the very pivot of all things and was the one great supply to the need of the child of God in every aspect of his spiritual life. And I saw that after all, the baptism of the Spirit, which I had thought was *the goal* of the Christian life, was really meant by the Lord to be but the beginning of a path which should lead the believer into the fellowship of the cross, and through the death of the cross into union with the ascended Lord in the bosom of the Father. I saw that on that night, when my spirit broke through the veil and was taken up to God, I was given a foretaste of the life which God called every child of his to know, and that it could only become a permanent experience as I was led, through death, to part with all things to live "with Christ in God."

Immediately, the living waters broke out in a flood-tide of blessing to others. The diary notes, though brief, throb with the life of God that was poured out upon the Institute. The entry on the day following the experience recorded above is touching in its simplicity. "The joy pouring into my soul. Christ a vision of glory and sweetness! ... 'Turn away thine eyes, for they have overcome me' (Cant. 6:6). I have had to weep for joy today, and at his feet no words can come, only *'Master!'* Most blessed prayer meeting—God's presence overwhelming." In private talks and in

classes and meetings, the presence and power of God were such
that scarcely any soul went away untouched by him. Many passed
from death unto life, some being convicted of sin without even
being spoken to; and numbers of God's own children were led
to fuller surrender of heart and life and realized "the exceeding
greatness of his power" to save to the uttermost. To come over
the threshold of the Institute was to come into the felt presence
of God, and thus many stepped down into the "river" of blessing
quite apart from any human instrument. The prayer meetings,
always the pulse of the work, were now times of great liberty
and rejoicing in free access to the throne of grace, though in the
past they had often been so lacking in liberty that the honorary
secretary, in her earnest longing that her girls should learn to
pray aloud, would sometimes put slips of paper with little prayers
written upon them on the chairs of those she felt ought to join in
audible prayer! No need now to toil to arouse missionary interest,
for in this atmosphere of the Spirit of God, hearts were enlarged
to receive the passion of Christ for the salvation of the world,
and prayer was made that the living waters flowing amongst
them might reach to the ends of the earth. These prayers were
abundantly answered later on by the Lord scattering many of the
members as missionaries to various parts of the world. One such
wrote from India early in 1893:

> God is doing great things for *me!* I could hardly believe that the
> things you told me could really be true, but indeed God is working as
> great miracles here! All day long and nearly every day, I am dealing
> in some way or another with souls. I can see God is speaking to the
> hearts of the headmistresses in some of the chief schools. God has
> filled my own heart with such joy, people are astonished, and I really
> think it is the joy that attracts them.

So the upper room at the Richmond Institute became a sanc-
tuary from whence the rivers flowed north, south, east, and west;
and calls poured in upon Mrs. Penn-Lewis to carry the message of "life more abundant" to other places in Great Britain. A
Ready Band was formed among the girls, "ready for any manner

of service;" and the Sunday night gospel meeting, commenced during Miss Soltau's mission, and held after the usual evening service in the churches, became the opportunity for members to engage in the aggressive work of seeking to reach the young girls who thronged the streets of Richmond on Sunday evenings—"fishing," it was called. Many of these were brought in, and souls were led to Christ week after week who, in their turn, became "fishers of men."

It touched the financial side of the work also, and God's servant learned there a lesson which molded her attitude toward finance for the entire period of her life of service. She was always certain that if God wanted a thing carried through, he would provide the necessary means; and in years to come, when her work had developed into a worldwide one with many diverse sections and interests, she always kept the funds for each section separate, and closely watched to see the Lord's hand providing for this or that, ready to drop anything, however fruitful it had been, should he show, by withholding his hand, that the thing was "finished" in his plan and purpose.

In connection with the Institute, as hon. secretary, she had been in the habit of collecting subscriptions for the work; but now she had to tell the committee that she could no longer use this method. God must move his people to give, and supply the needs of his own work. So, as needs arose, they were laid before the heavenly Father by his trusting children; and many were the romances of answered prayer. On one occasion the Institute stock of coals had run out—barely sufficient was left for a fire that day! The resident worker had not mentioned it, for she knew there were "no funds" in hand; but she and another knelt in the empty coal house and cried to the Lord that he would send the needed supply. That day an anonymous letter was dropped into the letter box. Enclosed was a slip of card with a golden sovereign fastened in and the words, "COALS, Y.W.C.A." What rejoicing there was and what strengthening of their faith to ask and expect that all their needs would be met in due course. At other times the money poured in so fast that it was difficult to keep a record of the items; but whether "straitened" or "abounding," there was an influx of the Holy Spirit into the work that lifted it into another plane altogether—into the realm of the Spirit, where God made himself responsible for its needs, both temporal and spiritual, "according to his riches in glory by Christ Jesus" (Phil. 4:19).

And what of the spiritual liberty and power of utterance asked for? The diary tells of "blessed freedom," of power with others never known before, of messages given "on the moment" without a tremor of the self-conscious misery of the past. "Testing" there was, but the reality of her experience stood the test as she went on with the Lord, step by step, in the work he had already given her. The first test came, naturally, the week following her blessed liberation, as Thursday drew near, and with it the Bible class at the rescue home which had often caused her so much suffering and such intense strain. The entry in the diary for this day (March 24th, 1892) reads: "My testing day! Trusted for message, and used no help! Mrs. —— was there, but I was kept in perfect peace." And of the same evening at the Institute, she wrote: "Still victory! I went to class fully trusting. Between fifty and sixty there, and intense power, full liberty and full joy—it was glorious!" And from this particular meeting there was "fruit" unto life eternal, as during the next few days one and another came for "talks"—two hard backsliders brought back, sobbing, to the Savior's feet; a fellow-worker seeking "the anointing," and another rejoicing in full surrender, "the last link snapped." So, one by one, her fellow-workers came into the "tide" with joy.

"I rejoice with you," wrote Mrs. Evan Hopkins on March 25th:

...that you are fully in the stream and the stream in you. Glorious indeed is this anointing! Where will it end? "Waters to swim in"—no little trickling rivulet—"ye have an unction." This is the positive part of the blessing. Cleansing and keeping are only the preparation... the anointing abideth and continueth ever more and more if we do not hinder; then we may expect a continuous inflow and outflow. We have plunged in; we are no longer standing on the brink; and now comes the willing, joyous giving out to others, and "everything shall live whither the river cometh..." No more "I can't"—What a change! He can, *he can,* HE CAN! May the Lord bring many more to hunger! He only makes them hunger to satisfy and fill. Blessed, blessed it is to know this. It is worth going through the hunger and the "death" in order to get such a blessing.

Referring to this experience in another place, Mrs. Penn-Lewis gives us a further glimpse into the significance of the "gradual cessation" of the manifest "glory" in her own spirit:

I remember once I was utterly sick with the joy of being used by him to win one soul. The joy was so great that I said, "Oh Lord, I really cannot bear it!" He said so softly in reply, "How could you bear to be used to win five hundred?" And then he said, "Will you part with all that keen joy that exhausts you, and just let me have you and use you to others, with nothing for yourself?" I saw the wisdom of this and said, "Yes, Lord," and then found that I could go through marvelous scenes of blessing to others which once would have overwhelmed me with joy, without any exhaustion to my fragile frame!

The secret of a fruitful life is, in brief, to pour out to others and *want nothing for yourself*—to leave yourself utterly in the hands of God and not care what happens to you.

I also owe a great deal to the books of Madame Guyon and the way she showed me the path to the life in God. The first time I read her *Life* it deeply moved me. I was at the Vicarage at Richmond, in Mrs. Evan Hopkins' room ... I had never heard of Madame Guyon, but in that room I picked up her *Life* and asked if I might read it.

I was just at the height of a glorious experience of the baptism of the Holy Spirit. The glory of the Lord's conscious presence with me was so unspeakably sweet that it was most difficult to bring my mind to the ordinary affairs of life. But as I read the book, I clearly saw the way of the cross and all that it would mean. At first I flung the book away and said, "No, I will not go that path; I shall lose all my 'glory' experience." But the next day I picked it up again, and the Lord whispered so gently, "If you want deep life and unbroken communion with God, this is the way." I thought, Shall I? No! And again I put the book away. The third day I again picked it up. Once more the Lord spoke: "If you want fruit, this is the path. I will not take the conscious joy-life from you; you may keep it if you like, but it is either that for yourself or this and fruit—Which will you have?"

And then, by his grace, I said, "I choose the path for fruitfulness," and every bit of conscious experience closed. I walked for a time in such complete darkness—what Guyon describes as "the darkness of faith"—that it seemed almost as if God did not exist. And again, by his grace, I said, "Yes, I have only got what I agreed to," and on I went.

I did not know what the outcome of this would be until I went to take some meetings, and then I saw the "fruit." It was just as if the people had been soaked in a life tide from heaven! It was not a case of individual blessing—the people were *all* submerged in a flood-tide of life from God which quickened them, released them, and brought them out into a new life. I did not need to speak personally to them; there seemed nothing to do but to give the message as God gave it to me, and the Holy Ghost did the rest. From that hour I understood and knew intelligently that it was *"dying"* not *"doing"* that produced spiritual fruit . . .

The Keswick Convention of 1892 was one of the most remarkable of those early, wonderful conventions, for there were giants in those days! The Revs. Evan H. Hopkins, C. G. Moore, C. A. Fox, F. B. Meyer, Dr. Elder Cumming, Messrs. George Grubb and W. K. Campbell just back from their time of mighty blessing in Australia, Mr. Samuel Wilkinson and Dwight L. Moody were among the speakers this year, and fresh from the out-poured tide of life at Richmond, Mrs. Penn-Lewis plunged into the stream of life at Keswick and found herself in one spirit with them all. She speaks, in her diary notes, of the marvelous "half nights of prayer," when prayer followed prayer "in a rush that could not be stopped"—an unforgettable experience. Her intimate friendship with Mr. and Mrs. Hopkins brought her in touch with many of the speakers, and the convention proved to be a time of blessed and wonderful fellowship and of rich "feasts" upon the Word of God. The outstanding formative experience of the convention was hearing "the Australian party" tell of the mighty outpouring of the Spirit of God upon the Geelong Convention:

This convention, so largely attended and so gloriously owned of God, had its beginning about three years before in the souls of a few ministers of the gospel who felt that they, in common with hundreds of their brethren, were working with impotency instead of power. They accordingly banded themselves together to plead for the "promise of the Father." They met at different times, and one by one seem to have entered upon some measure of their great inheritance in God the Holy Ghost. The convention took place on September 15–17, 1891. The whole trend of the Spirit's mind seemed to be in one direction, the discovery and the removal of hindrances, the getting to the point of full surrender, uninterrupted communion, and divine fullness. The speakers were somewhat limited in number and were not all men of prominence. Preachers of much greater mark sat still in their seats and were neither asked to speak nor pray, for the inflexible rule was that none should attempt to instruct others about the anointing of the Holy Ghost who had not themselves received that anointing.[1]

The convention was marked by clean-cut surrender to God for all his will to be done at all costs, and by an overflowing joy which followed in hundreds of hearts, so that, as Mr. George Soltau wrote: "Literally 'our mouths were filled with laughter and our tongues with singing'… It was impossible to restrain one's heart, the Lord giving us such a foretaste of heaven. Talk of 'fleshly excitement,' I wish to bear my testimony that it was nothing less than the fullness of the Spirit. We were verily drunk with the joy of the Lord and with the vistas of the possibilities of faith opening up to the fully surrendered life of the believer. But it was equally manifest to us all that this joy and blessing is only to be received and retained and increased by the death *to* self and *of* self and the most painful crucifixion of self."[2]

The outpouring of the Spirit of God is given for service to God in the bringing of salvation to others more than for the believer's own personal life and blessing, and therefore wherever a pure experience of this outpouring is given, the result is seen

1 Report in the Melbourne *Missionary*, October, 1891.
2 Gal. v, 24.

in souls saved and believers quickened and brought into a closer relationship with God. So it was in Australia, and so it was in the work of God at Richmond, of which we have endeavored to give a brief outline. Pages might be filled with the marvelous workings of God, not alone through the Bible classes and meetings at the Institute, but through the faithful witnessing of the members themselves as they moved among their work-fellows; and in the shops and workrooms of the town, many girls and women were brought to the knowledge of full salvation. The yearly attendances at the various classes increased from 6,900 to nearly 13,000 during the three years following the outpouring of the Spirit of God upon the work; and at every meeting held, definite blessing was manifested. Week after week souls were brought "out of darkness into light," while numbers of God's own children entered into an experience of the in-filling of the Holy Spirit never known before, resulting in a closer walk with God and a keener desire to watch for and win souls, as those who must give account.

As the "sound of abundance of rain" went forth, strangers and Christian workers from other places came to Richmond seeking to know the secret of this tide of blessing and went away praising God for a similar anointing of the Holy Spirit, so that in many other parts of the country there was spiritual revival and blessing by means of these God-possessed workers. Visitors dropping in to the Institute for one evening only, met with the Lord and were set at liberty from many a yoke of bondage; and thus the living water flowed out from that hidden and insignificant center to the ends of the earth. And this blessing was *wholly* from the presence of God in the midst, for the work did not center around the workers but around Jesus Christ. A worker said that as she opened the door to enter, she "fell back with the *intense sense of God.*" It was indeed "holy ground." The Lord himself was the leader, and the workers learned to stand aside and watch him deal with the souls, as they were cast upon him and taught to consult him over all their difficulties, relying upon his unfailing response and guidance.

The outcome of this influx of the life of God was necessarily a deepened desire to be "spent out" for others, and as every "member" became a "worker" it became the work of the leaders to provide outlet for these young souls full of love to their Savior. They were grouped into bands for various branches of service, including a register of classes in the various Sunday schools of the town needing temporary teachers; and nearly one hundred of these classes were supplied by volunteers from the Y.W.C.A.

Among the young women who received blessing at this time at the Institute was one Mary Tugwell, cook to a wealthy family in Richmond, who, in obedience to the call of God, gave up her worldly position and prospects to become general factotum in the little house in Halford Road. Her commission from God to "tarry by the stuff" was as clear as that of her mistress to "go down to the battle," and thus she was able to set God's frail servant free from household cares for the spiritual ministry he was laying upon her. In after years, when she had become the beloved house-keeper, nurse, and friend, Mrs. Penn-Lewis loved to tell how all her public ministry and strenuous editorial labors were made possible by the faithful co-operation in the background of "my dear old Mary," not only in the daily ministries of the home, but in a deep and understanding fellowship in prayer.

"What has the Y.W.C.A. done for you?" was the question asked of the members at the end of 1893, and we give the following from the many glowing replies sent in:

> What has the Y.W.C.A. done for me? It has changed my whole life and given me:
> In the place of doubt—Assurance.
> In the place of heaviness—Joy.
> Instead of grudging service—willing obedience.
> I thought of God as my Judge—I found him my Friend.
> I thought of Christ as a mystic ideal—I found him a blissful reality.
> I worshiped him afar off in cold dreariness—Now I know and love him as the chief among ten thousand.

I believed in the hereafter I should see and know a Christ who dwells in heaven—I found that Christ would dwell and reign in the heart of the believer, and I know it to be true.

I had a dissatisfied, aching void, a longing for something, I knew not what. At the Institute, Christ spoke to me. His words filled up the silence of my heart and made the whole world musical. Incarnate love took hold of me and claimed me for its own. I followed in his sunlight, holding fast his mantle.

"Awake O north wind; and come, thou south; blow upon my garden, that the spices thereof may flow out."

—*Song of Songs, 4:16*

"The soul is already a temple of the Holy Ghost. It was the eternal Spirit who imparted to her the gift of life from above, at the very beginning (John 3:15). It was he who cleansed her heart (Acts 15:9), took possession of its throne for Christ the King, and caused her to receive him as a living person. He testified to her of the crucified, risen, and glorified Lord (John 15:26); he guided her into all truth concerning her death with him on Calvary's cross, and her union with him in his resurrection and ascension: he brought her out of the sphere of the earth-life into the heavenly atmosphere on the resurrection side of the cross. Abiding in that atmosphere, clearly beholding as well as indwelt by the risen Lord, the soul is now ready for the breath of God to move upon her and to use her as never before."

Chapter 3

The Pathway to Life in God

1893–1895

The story of the "child branch" at Neath—Dr. Andrew Murray—
The first message in print—Working for Time or Eternity?

Through an unexpected visit by Mrs. Penn-Lewis to her
native town and the leading of God through "natural happenings" which fill a life lived in the power of the Holy Spirit
with romance, there came into being in Neath an offshoot of the
Richmond Y.W.C.A., "a tiny twig of the Lord's planting" that
steadily grew into a sturdy tree. "No tongue nor pen can ever
describe it," wrote one, a year and a half later, to *Our Onward
Way*, the prayer union magazine of the Association. "Numbers
of workers have been blessed here, and the working of God has
been far beyond the limits of the Y.W.C.A.... The rivers of God
cannot be held in a Y.W.C.A. room, but it *can* be the point from
which they may flow." And in the same magazine (February
1895) the story is briefly told by Mrs. Penn-Lewis herself in a
letter written from Neath as follows:

Neath, S. Wales, Nov. 30, 1894

"O Lord our God, we will praise thee, for thou hast done marvelous
things," is the language of our hearts as my co-worker and I look
back upon our month's visit to S. Wales. We think it will stir other
branches if I try to tell the tale of what God hath wrought and of
the blessed outpouring of the Holy Ghost which has been given us.

This Neath branch is but one year old, but the record of its first
year's work bears the impress of the hand of God which has been

51

upon it in a very marked way from the beginning. We rejoice to look upon it as an offshoot from Richmond, where it has been watched and borne up with ceaseless prayer; for this Neath branch had its beginning in a tiny Bible class which I was led to commence among business girls when on a visit here in May 1893. Sixteen came that first evening and eight of them found the Lord—a blessed seal upon the work which, in a short eighteen months, has grown into a vigorous tree.

In November 1893, being again on a visit to Neath, a Y.W.C.A. branch was formally started with a roll of forty members and thirty honorary and working associates. Numbers were won for Christ during the opening meetings, forming a nucleus of definitely Christian members; and the committee from the commencement determined to work wholly upon spiritual lines, seeking first and foremost the salvation of souls. A furnished room was opened in January 1894, when God touched the hearts of his stewards, and every need was supplied. Space will not permit of further details of the year's work, but it closed with a roll of 78 members and 50 honorary and working associates, whilst the balance sheet showed £4 in hand. The first special mission to young women ever held in the town was arranged for November 1894, and again I had the privilege of coming to our "child branch," my co-worker, Miss Florence Jackson, with me. We left Richmond on November 2nd and commenced on the following Sunday with meetings in a large mission hall in the town. The hall for the evening service was crowded, even in aisles and doorways, and souls were led to Christ. A meeting was held at the Y.W.C.A. room afterwards, and again souls were led to Jesus.

On Tuesday November 6th a drawing-room meeting for ladies was held in the afternoon, and the public annual meeting in the Town Hall at night. The people filled the hall ere the gas was lit; every bit of standing room was occupied; the entrance stairs were thronged to the foot, and numbers were turned away—a marvelous meeting for a Y.W.C.A. The power of God was evidently upon this public meeting, and we heard afterwards of souls saved that night.

The mission proper commenced in the Y.W.C.A. room the next night, and never shall we forget the week that followed: night after night the girls thronged in and souls were *swept* into the kingdom! The presence of God was so manifest that every barrier was broken down, numbers broke into prayer in the meetings, and when asked to go into another room to be dealt with, without hesitation they would stream in, and before each other, kneel and yield to Christ. It has been our joy personally to deal with over one hundred souls, the majority of whom have since given clear witness to their Savior. There has been no hesitation in boldly confessing Christ in their homes and business houses. Five business girls in one shop are rejoicing together; another young Christian from last year now rejoices over two sisters gathered in. It was blessed to see the converts of the night before bringing their friends to be led to Christ, and taking them to the prayer-room.

But pen cannot describe the scenes we beheld night after night, and I must pass on to tell of the anniversary tea which closed the week's mission. In a large hall lent us for the occasion, over 200 sat down to tea, and then we had a three hours' meeting for praise and testimony, when numbers rose to their feet to confess their new-found Savior—not only the young converts, but numbers of God's own children, to whom God had revealed the glorious secret of *Christ in you*, the only power for life and service. When all were asked to rise who had received definite blessing, about 180 rose, and we sang, "What a wonderful Savior is Jesus, my Jesus!" As we closed this blessed anniversary and praise meeting, all the unsaved who desired to seek Christ were asked to go into the vestry, when numbers instantly arose and pressed in. As I closed the large meeting and went to assist Miss Jackson, what a scene met my eyes! The vestry was packed, and in the middle of the crowd Miss Jackson was kneeling, leading weeping souls to their Savior, quite oblivious to those around. It was a glorious ingathering that night. In addition, forty new members were enrolled.

We then felt it was necessary to give these young souls something to do for their Savior, and the following Monday a meeting was arranged to organize bands for work. The Y.W.C.A. room was crowded, sixty to seventy being present. Eighteen girls were grouped into a tract band for the weekly visiting of some poor districts, money being collected there and then to purchase the tracts! Eighteen others were grouped into a cottage mission band for weekly services in different cottages. Ten others formed a visiting band to look up all the Y.W.C.A. members and assist the committee in keeping in touch with each one. Thirty others were grouped into a singing band to sing for Jesus at different meetings. Smaller groups were arranged for street fishing and helping in the Sunday (after-service) gospel meeting; each of these bands being in charge of a different worker.

A junior branch was also formed, starting with twenty members, many of whom found Jesus on the first evening. Some of the new converts are already leading this. A missionary evening has also been arranged, and a missionary fund is to be started in the faith that God will choose out one to be our own missionary.

I have not mentioned that this year-old branch has also its "twig"—a Bible class in an adjoining village numbering about 27 members. One meeting was held here, arranged by the girls themselves. Another feature of the mission has been special meetings for young ladies of leisure; the blessing on these has been most marked. Several have come out boldly for Christ, and some of the usual dancing sets have been broken up.

Our farewell meeting was indescribable. Barriers of reserve had been swept away, and members and workers were rejoicing and testifying to what God had wrought, one young lady saying she was longing to bring down her trunk of ball-dresses for the doll-dressing for India!

Outside the Y.W.C.A. we have had public meetings on power for service; numbers of Christian workers have been dealt with by God, and some leaders in different places have clearly received the anointing.

It has truly been God working upon the town. Open doors have been given us in every direction. We have held forty-five meetings in the twenty-eight days! The living waters have swept in most unlikely places and touched most unlikely people. We have no space to tell of our three days' visit to the Swansea Y.W.C.A., where again we had full meetings and God worked his wonders—a matron and nine girls with her seeking Christ at one meeting, whilst many of the workers were blessed.

Truly it has been *all of God*. This record is but a faint glimpse of all his wonders wrought by himself alone. "Not unto us, not unto us, but to thy name give glory" is the language of our hearts; nothing in the broken earthen vessels but the fulfillment of John 7:38–39, "rivers of living water."

I write to provoke (Heb. 10:24) the workers of all Y.W.C.A. branches to cry unto God for an outpouring of the Holy Ghost upon their branches; then they too will know how "everything shall live whither the river cometh" (Ezek. 47:9). "Launch out into the deep." "At *thy* word I will." "And *when* they had this done ... a great multitude of fishes" (Luke 5:4-6).

* * *

"Each year in some way has its own characteristics," wrote Mrs. Penn-Lewis in the ninth annual report of the Richmond Y.W.C.A., dated 1894–1895:

> ...and this last year will be known as one of scattering, after three special years of ceaseless reaping, through the manifested presence of the eternal Spirit in our midst. Early in 1895 we were led to pray definitely that God would "scatter" his children whom he saw to be ripe for his use in other places, and he quickly took us at our word. Week after week numbers of old members were removed to other parts of the country, some to their usual sphere of work—yet again to be transferred to other Y.W.C.A. branches and there to be used of God; others were sent abroad; yet others into training for mission work; some into immediate service for Christ; whilst one has herself become a Y.W.C.A. secretary in a large town in the north of England. From all these it is our joy to hear of God's seal upon the training in Richmond through his hand upon them as vessels meet for his use.
>
> So the "scattering" went on; and as one after the other was removed, we wondered who would be the next! Then he asked us to surrender to him our beloved resident worker (Miss M. Lower) who on September 5th, with one of the members, went forth to mission work in South Africa. With joy we recognized the answer to our prayers, and gave her gladly to minister to the needs of young women in that dark continent, whence we hope ere long to hear of another offshoot from the Richmond Institute ...
>
> As we thus utter the memory of his great goodness in the past, we look forward to the future with renewed hope and confidence of blessing through the clear way in which our God has called and given to us our new worker, Miss Butterwick from Eastbourne, who has been associated with the Y.W.C.A. work there for fifteen years. Miss Butterwick visited us for some six weeks in January 1895. When it was known throughout the Institute that God had called Miss Lower to Africa, "Oh that he would send us Miss Butterwick,"

was the unspoken thought of many hearts. God *did* give us Miss Butterwick. The committee so clearly recognized his hand in all the details of his call and guidance to her that they could only say, "it is the Lord's doing," and thankfully accept his provision for the need.

In the year 1895, at the invitation of Mr. Robert Wilson (for the Keswick Convention), Mr. Paynter (for Guildford), and Colonel Morton (for Mildmay), the Rev. Andrew Murray spent the summer in England, accompanied by Mrs. Murray, finding a happy home while in London at Corrie Lodge, Wimbledon, with Mr. and Mrs. Albert Head, whose dearest wish was to bring these greatly used servants of God into contact with as many as possible of the Lord's people. "We were quite amazed at the dear old man," wrote Mrs. Head. "He is so thin and worn looking … We feel indeed he has come to this land as God's messenger, and he is so simple, depending utterly on the Lord to use him simply as his channel of blessing to his people …"

A few days after their arrival in England, a great welcome breakfast was given by Mr. and Mrs. Head at Exeter Hall, a most remarkable gathering of about 120 leading Christians of all denominations, including such well-known servants of God as Revs. C. A. Fox, F. B. Meyer, Lord Kinnaird, Lady Hope, Mr. Denny, and Amanda Smith. Mr. and Mrs. Penn-Lewis were also among the guests, the latter having the privilege of a long talk with Mr. Murray—the first contact of a fellowship in God which deepened into a bond in the Spirit between two souls who knew God "face to face." "You are very rich," he told her, "richer than Cecil Rhodes!"

To the pages of an old copy of *Our Onward Way* (August 1895) we are again indebted for a backward look upon the movement of God in those days, and have, in an article by Mrs. Penn-Lewis, a glimpse into God's message through Andrew Murray, so closely in line with all he had been teaching her in the past three years.

The occasion was the annual summer outing for the members of the Richmond Institute and their friends, in July, when Mr. and Mrs. Albert Head kindly invited them to Corrie Lodge to meet their honored guests. After tea on the lawn, a sharp shower drove the party, numbering about one hundred, into the drawing-room for the closing word from Mr. Murray. Mrs. Penn-Lewis's notes of the meeting are as follows:

Mr. Head led the meeting, and after Mrs. Murray had told us of Y.W.C.A. work in Cape Town and pleaded for intercessory prayer on behalf of the young women in South Africa, Rev. Andrew Murray rose to speak to us. We truly felt the presence of God as he talked quite simply of *"The Heavenly Treasure in the Earthen Vessel"* (2 Cor. 4:7) somewhat thus:

First, the Treasure. In heaven there is a treasure that fills the heavens, and here am I, just a common little jar that may be as full as it can hold of the heavenly treasure.

God has only one treasure—his beloved Son. He calls him "my treasure," and God has put *all* his riches and all his treasures into Jesus. In him are hidden all the treasures (Col. 2:3).

God delights in his Son, and as God delights in him, so may you. You may have a share and become unspeakably rich in Jesus, as he will pour himself into you.

"God, who commanded the light to shine out of darkness, hath shined in our hearts, to give the light of the knowledge of the glory of God in the face of Jesus Christ" (2 Cor. 4:6).

The light of God
The glory of God
The face of Jesus,

all these are heavenly things.

The face of Jesus is the treasure. Many believers do not know that they have such a treasure. Some years ago a field in South Africa containing £40,000 worth of diamonds might have been bought for £1,000, all because they did not know the value of the diamonds. If we do not know we have this heavenly treasure, we are very poor. Do learn to say, I am *so rich!* I have such a treasure! I am rich beyond all thought—so rich to give away!

But how does God give this treasure? Not as we give. We give perhaps a shilling to a beggar, and he goes away and we see no more of him. But not so God. This is a blessing like the sunshine—it cannot be received and taken away. You cannot have sunlight a minute longer than it shines into you—it must be got from the sun moment by moment. So this heavenly treasure keeps me waiting upon God all the day that it may shine into me.

The heavenly treasure is love. The moment love seeks itself it is dead. It is just the love of Jesus shining out and seeking those in darkness. Sunshine cannot keep itself to itself. It is the mysterious nature of this heavenly sunshine that directly we begin to grasp it to ourselves it seems to die away. We cannot have sunshine and keep it to ourselves. See the sun shining on that tree? If the tree should say, "Nobody must see me," can it be hidden before the darkness comes on? Whilst the light is on it, it *must* be seen. We are earthen vessels made to hold the heavenly treasure, and nothing else—made to let the life, and love, and riches, and treasures of Jesus shine out.

Now let us look at the earthen vessel. On a table one day I saw a silver jug with *milk* in it, and a little brown earthenware jug with *cream* in it. But nobody refused the cream because it was in an earthen jar. We like the silver jugs, but God loves to put his richest treasures in the earthen jars. This is a very important lesson. Christians think so much of their weakness—"I am so stupid, so weak, so foolish; somebody else is gifted, and she can do better!"—we forget God wants the earthen jars!

In South Africa there was an infidel, and no one could deal with him; and one day the minister sent the elder of the church, a clever and pious man, to see him. He argued with him, but he could not be convinced; it was of no use. But there was an old farmer who had prayed for years for the infidel (he was a blacksmith). Early one morning he took his horse and rode to see this man, who greeted him with, "Well, what brings you here at this hour?" The old farmer stammered badly, and when he was greeted like this he could not get a word out. The infidel laughed. This made it worse. At last the old man burst into tears, and stammered out, "I am so anxious about your soul," and hurried away. This led to the conversion of the infidel. Ah, see the heavenly treasure in the earthen vessel.

This teaches us courage, but humility. I have nothing in myself. "He that humbleth himself shall be exalted;" he that confesses that he is but an earthen vessel shall be filled with the heavenly treasure. Oh the curse of pride and self. We want God to give us something that *we may be something,* but God wants us *"nothing."* A heavenly treasure in an earthen vessel. Paul had been in danger of forgetting this. He had preached with the demonstration of the Spirit and power. He had been caught up to the third heaven and heard things impossible to utter. Then God allowed "a messenger of Satan" to humble him. Paul prayed about it three times, but Jesus said, "No, Paul. I have taken you into the third heaven, and you have been in danger of thinking you were a heavenly vessel. I have sent this to humble you, and my strength is made perfect in weakness." So Paul said, "Praise God, I shall rejoice now in all the troubles that come."

Then Paul says afterwards, "Though I have labored more than all, *I am nothing*. I never dream that I am doing it. I am not a whit behind the chief apostles, yet it is not I." Now, after talking about the heavenly treasure and the earthen vessel, *what about the application?* Who among you desires to be an earthen vessel filled with the treasure? Ah, the need of it! Four millions in London who never go to a place of worship. How awful in a Christian land. Ought we not to call it a heathen land? And among the one million who *do* go, how much formality, and what a small number really *know* Christ and the heavenly treasure. If everyone here gave up her life to God to be a vessel filled with the treasure, it would not be too many. Nay, if we were a thousand here, it would not be too many. Now to go back to our illustration. Before the cream was put in that earthen jar, I am sure *it must have been clean*. So God must cleanse pride and selfishness from the earthen vessels.

Then that jar must not only have been clean *but empty*. No vinegar nor wine nor milk left in to mix with the cream. So many of the earthen vessels are full, not of sin but of other things—lawful things, good things. Yes, the *good* must go out as well as the sin—the things that nobody can say are wicked—or else there is not room for the heavenly treasure. The love of father, mother, sister, brother must be laid down for God to fill with the love of Christ.

Then the vessel must be very low. The lower down, the easier to fill. Some vessels may be clean and empty but not low enough. They do not hide themselves in the dust, therefore God cannot fill them. Oh, let us pray, "Lower down, lower down, lower down, Lord; nothing, nothing, *nothing*, that God alone may be exalted!"

This address was listened to with rapt attention, and the time that followed was very precious as one and another led in prayer, seeking to be earthen vessels—clean, empty, *low*—for the heavenly treasure to be manifested in them. Quietly we then broke up and made our way to the vehicles which awaited us, Mr. Murray giving a little word to the few who were near him.

After giving our farewell thanks to our kind host and hostess, with glad and praising hearts we started on our moonlight drive to Richmond, the rain being over and gone. The snatches of hymns, "Oh, the peace my Savior gives," etc., that occasionally broke on the still night air from the occupants of the different brakes told of the gladness filling many hearts as they rejoiced over the heavenly treasure which they had seen exalted in the earthen vessel that had brought them the message that night. "And they glorified God in (him)"—(Gal. 1:24).

> Oh to be but emptier, lowlier,
>   Mean, unnoticed, and unknown,
> And to God a vessel holier,
>   Filled with Christ and Christ alone!

* * *

The first little booklet sent forth by Mrs. Penn-Lewis had its birth in as unpremeditated and spontaneous a way as the steps of a little child with its hand in that of its father; and throughout nearly forty years of ceaseless and fruitful toil for the master, this principle was always "the pattern in the mount" to her. She initiated nothing, built up nothing, "pushed" nothing. With her eyes steadfastly towards God in "face to face" communion and fellowship, she knew with a deep inward consciousness that *of herself* she could "do nothing"—but whatsoever she saw "the Father doing" (John 5:19) she followed in humble but determined obedience to the "heavenly vision." And in this we trace to its source that quiet, underground stream which, like Ezekiel's river, has quickened with the life of God everything "whithersoever it goeth," and which has penetrated to the farthest corners of the earth, wherever God's children are to be found, without any of the ordinary machinery of human "propaganda." In her last years there were those who thought she should retire to some quiet spot and devote her remaining strength to literary work. "They do not understand," she said, "that I am *not a literary woman*. I cannot write one sentence unless I receive it from God." And the spiritual needs of the people of God were the channel of her inspiration as she moved among them in her conference work or touched their lives through her vast and worldwide correspondence.

From the time when, as a young Christian worker, she received the fullness of the Holy Spirit in liberty of utterance and power for service, *"Christian workers"* were her burden before the Lord. She saw that the word "crucified," with which God had liberated her, was the key to liberate others for his service. "I saw clearly," she wrote in the booklet before quoted,[1] "the principle of death with Christ as the basis for the full working of God through the believer. It was as great a revelation to me as when I first saw my 'iniquity laid upon him' on the tree ... 'Crucified with Christ,' there is *room for him to fill us;* and we have only to consent to be *out of his way* on the cross and to yield implicit obedience to his workings. How simple the plan, yet how deep, for it gives no place for the creature to glory before God!"

She therefore realized that every Christian worker thus liberated would mean "fruit an hundredfold" for God, as they in their turn took the message of deliverance to their own spheres of work; and from that time on, more and more the guiding hand of her Father led her among the "leaders" of his people, with a special ministry to all who were called of God to minister to others the Word of life.

In the spring of 1895 Mrs. Penn-Lewis was invited by Miss Soltau, head of the Missionary Training Home of the China Inland Mission, to give the message at the Good Friday devotional meetings at Mildmay—the commencement of a blessed ministry extending over seven years of Good Friday services. On this occasion there was given in briefest summary, from the Word of God, the subjective teaching of the "death with Christ" in the Holy Spirit's dealings with the believer, which had become to her own soul a very "pathway" into a life "within the veil," "hid with Christ *in God,*" "in the bosom of the Father."

1   *The Leading of the Lord*

Not a glimpse, the veil uplifted,
But within the veil to dwell,
Gazing on his face for ever,
Hearing words unspeakable.

—Gerhard Tersteegen

An outline of this message was taken down in longhand and sent out as a circular to missionaries in China and to workers at home; and so deeply did the message meet the need of those who received it in this form, that a friend asked permission to have it printed as a booklet. Mrs. Penn-Lewis was thus led to fill in the outline and issue it in booklet form under the title *The Pathway to Life in God*—the first small beginning of the Overcomer Literature.

The first edition of this booklet was sold out within one month and the proceeds used to print another edition, with some slight alterations and additions explained in a footnote thus:

> Aided by the helpful criticism on the first edition, the writer has been enabled to make clear many points that were obscure; and for want of space much that was not essential has been struck out. It will be seen that the booklet has been written mainly to faintly interpret the death with Christ on the subjective side of the Holy Spirit's dealings. It has been written from experience, and confirmed by numbers of letters in the writer's possession, as well as by the witness of God to many another soul. There is no desire to dogmatize or systematize or to insist upon one point more than another, only to show *in the main,* the *experimental* pathway. The Holy Spirit is not bound and will lead souls along this road in a thousand different ways ... The writer earnestly prays all to whom the booklet is not of present use, to put it aside until God in his own time and way becomes his own interpreter.

The second edition was also rapidly bought up, and the issue of the booklet within its first five years reached the high figure of thirty-two thousand! It was welcomed by many Christian teachers of the day for its pressing of the positive aspect of the believer's "death with Christ" (Rom. 6:11; Gal. 2:20). A writer in *The*

Life of Faith pointed this out, saying: "The very valuable part of her teaching is as to the detailed individual working of the Holy Ghost in the soul of the surrendered believer, holding it firm, guiding it in thought, feeling, and action, reaching down into its secret sources—'All my springs are in thee.' This is an important side of sanctification which is rarely dealt with ..."

As the little booklet, and others which followed, found their way to those in many lands to whom the message was sent of God, a flood of letters of thanks and testimony poured in upon the writer, from which we cull a few interesting and suggestive points. The Rev. W. D. Moffat, of Edinburgh, who from the first encouraged, nay pleaded with, Mrs. Penn-Lewis that she would expend the liberty and power given her of God to preach nothing else but *"Jesus Christ and him crucified,"* watched with keen interest the working of God through this first written message, and on one occasion wrote as follows:

> Last night we had down to tea a missionary and his wife from Madras, and to our great delight he told us that, at a regular united meeting of all the missionaries in Madras, your *Pathway* had been the theme of study, conference, and prayer, page by page and meeting by meeting ...

A letter from Mrs. Moffat, written shortly after, tells how she "met a minister who taught his congregation on the blackboard from *The Pathway."* He told her there had been a wonderful conversion of an old man, his beadle, who watched him day by day preparing the lesson on the board. He boldly came out on the Lord's side, and the minister said there was hardly a dry eye in the congregation over this old man.

Mr. J. H. Smeeton, an accountant in one of the great London banks, who afterwards, at the age of 62 years, went out to Algiers to work for God among the blind beggars of that city, wrote:

> Though, as I told you, I had a sight of the death to "self" and the life of the risen one, and was able by faith to realize that I had a share in both, yet my experience is still on p. 7 ["The breaking of the vessel

already 'filled with the Spirit' and the melting by the fire of God."[1]] only more so ... I have been utterly powerless to speak to souls even when they looked to me for a word, and my life appears nothing but humbling and breaking down. Your *Pathway* has given me the key to it, and my prayer is, and has been, "Lower, Lord, lower still." But seeing that from the helplessness of the grave it must be that God raises from the dead, I find I have been waiting for a resurrection experience, which does not come by waiting but by FAITH ...

This last sentence contains a truth vital to all who would know in their own lives what it means not only to be "crucified with Christ" but the other half of the experience, *"risen with him"*— "twin parts of one fact" (Mabie). How many have found that the *"experience"* of the risen life for which they watched and waited has not been manifested to their spiritual eyes—until at last they have cast themselves upon God in utter self-despair, willing, if it be his will, not to "see wind nor rain" nor any visible fruit. Then the channel has become clear and the life of God has flowed into and out through the human life, often unseen and unrecognized by the "channel," and only manifested in "life" to others—"that no flesh should glory in his presence."

> Is it strange that from the golden chamber
>   From the secret place,
> Come they forth with everlasting radiance
>   Of his glorious face?
> Telling mysteries that to babes are simple,
>   Hidden from the wise,
> Fragrant with the odors of the lilies
>   Of God's paradise.
>
> —Gerhard Tersteegen

Before we pass on from the story of the "rising tide" of blessing to the wider service which was in the purpose of God for this servant of his, let us gather up some of the basic lessons with which God laid the foundations of the worldwide ministry which grew out of it. The following "testimony" from the pen of

1   that is, in first edition.

Mrs. Penn-Lewis appeared in the little organ of the Y.W.C.A. for secretaries and workers, called *Go Forward* (April 1896) and gives a glimpse into some of these lessons:

> The conviction has been growing upon me for some time that if our Association is to maintain its power and retain its hold upon our young women it must be by the force of its *God-possession.* It must be a weapon in the hand of God, and consequently "terrible as an army with banners" to sin and worldliness, or be an utter failure from God's standpoint... Are we to descend to carnal means and be a worldly "success," or shall we launch out upon God—determine that nothing among us shall grieve our God—be a living object-lesson, in this worldly age, of faithfulness to God, and a channel for the living waters to flow out to thirsty souls all over the world?
>
> Shall *we* be among the few who have not "defiled their garments" and who esteem the reproach of Christ greater joy than the "success" in Egypt? In short, the question comes to us: "Shall we work and live for *time* or for *eternity?*"
>
> We cannot wield the sword of the Spirit *and* carnal weapons any more than souls can gain Christ *and* gain the world. There is no middle course. An awful "paralysis" in truth will steal over the branches whose workers attempt this...
>
> But this again is negative! If we sweep out all that is doubtful, what is to take its place? Bible classes and prayer meetings are most unattractive unless we have in them the positive attraction of the Holy Ghost. It is possible, as I have found, to have a "consecrated" branch, with everything swept out that trenches on the world, yet with no attractive power.
>
> The negative is to *"sweep out"*; the positive is to *"sweep* in"! "Come, O breath, and breathe upon these slain that they may live... and they stood upon their feet, an exceeding great army" (Ezek. 37:9–10, R.V.). A mighty in-sweeping of the breath of God ("a rushing, mighty breath," Acts 2:2, Dr. Elder Cumming) would sweep out all doubtful things by the expulsive power of his glorious presence...
>
> I cannot forbear giving my personal testimony in this matter. I have proved the presence of God to be more attractive to our girls than the old attempt at mild entertainments. Our attendances rose from 6,900 to 11,447 in less than two years after the mighty breath of God swept upon us. The truth is that *we cannot compete with the*

world. We must win by the force of something far above competition, and this is the presence and power of the Holy Spirit.

Then as to funds! I have found that when God is ungrieved and in unhindered possession of the work, Phil. 4:19 is absolutely true. If we go down to Egypt for help, he *must* let us prove Egypt a broken reed. And how we scrape, and what mean things are done in our God's name, he only knows! But if we knew how to draw upon our resources in God, even in silver and gold, we should act in all the business matters connected with his work as daughters of a King, and be seen to be children of our Father, who giveth to all men bountifully and upbraideth not. Difficulties about funds most often mean *something wrong in work or workers,* and unless we are prepared to let God search us and put aside the "accursed thing" it is useless to expect him to respond to our needs...

Speaking at a conference for Christian workers many years afterwards, Mrs. Penn-Lewis emphasized this note again. Urging the renunciation demanded by the call of Christ to entire consecration, she pleaded the necessity of giving something real and tangible in exchange for the unrealities and pleasurable excitement which the world calls "life."

The subject under consideration in open conference[1] was "The Christian's Attitude to Amusements," and many of the ministers present had expressed their deep perplexity as to how the modern cry for perpetual "amusement" should be dealt with. "Years ago," said Mrs. Penn-Lewis,

...we had just the same battle in the Y.W.C.A. It is literally true, and we have to face it, that if the young people are crying out for something, there is some spiritual need not being met. We are none of us emporiums of divine truth, and it simply means that there is some spiritual supply required; and we must ask God to meet the need. In our Y.W.C.A. we had all kinds of social activities, but when God came in, no one wanted them; and girls who had said they would never come to the Institute, came! What is needed is the *positive influx* of the Spirit of God to fill the churches, and that God shall do such a deep work *in us* that there shall be a stronger

1   The Swanwick Conference, 1920.

force of life flowing out *to others*. I think that if a person goes to the theater, there is within a craving for something they lack, but it is misdirected. It is natural to want *life,* and all these things point to unsatisfied souls crying out for "life." I do not think we can condemn them—they must get "life" somewhere—but can we not give them LIFE? There is a vacant place, an inward necessity, in every one that nothing but the cross of Christ will meet; and if you recognize that, you will be able to give your witness without condemning others. We need to recognize that deep down in every human being there is a capacity for God, and these souls will never find rest until they find their rest in God.

I am intensely sympathetic with young folk when they see the old folk jog-trotting to prayer meeting! Have you no sympathy? Would *you* have gone? That is what drew me into work among young girls—I had such sympathy with them. They want life, and if we do not give them the right kind of "life," they will get the wrong kind. We need *life* in our churches, *life* in the prayer meetings, *life* everywhere! "How shall we get the young people into the churches?" Give them life—life from God. In our Y.W.C.A. Institute, we used to have souls saved even at our sale of work! I went down to Neath and helped to start a Y.W.C.A. branch there, and God moved in the town. I remember at that first meeting we got together all the Neath ladies we could, and we gave a tea—my little mother and I. We gathered about seventy girls out of the shops and the ladies played games with them!

At eight o'clock I said, "Girls, *we are going to pray.*" In an instant there was quiet, and we led many of those girls to Christ that night. The Spirit of the Lord fell upon that meeting—I am sure I took six of them at a time and led them to the Lord. But you will never help young people if you do not love them. I do so long that God's people will be more *human,* have more heart—cleansed heart, with Christ in it—you can do anything with people you love and who love you. This is not *natural* love, because it loves the ugly and the unpleasant. It is the "love of God shed abroad in our hearts" that is needed. We are too occupied with our own spiritual growth and progress. Oh God, let us die to ourselves! Lord, come thou and live in us, so that thy life can flow out to others through us!

"Come my beloved, let us go forth to the field."
—*Song of Songs 7:11*

"The world lies before her in the light of God. No longer can our little corner of the vineyard be more important than the rest. 'My church, MY mission, MY cause' has given place to the great field of the world. She has heard her beloved say, 'Other sheep I have, which are not of this fold: them also must I bring, and they shall hear my voice' (John 10:16), and she enters into fellowship with his great heart of love. She knows his 'must' in this is as imperative as the 'must' that led him to Calvary (John 3:14; Matt. 16:21).

Intense yearnings possess her soul; she begins to strive in prayer for those whose faces she has never seen, longing that their 'hearts might be comforted,' as hers has been, and that they may know the mystery of God—even Christ (Col. 2:1–2)."

Chapter 4

The Regions Beyond

1896

The pillar of cloud moves to Leicester—The first journey to other lands—The Scandinavian Conference of the Y.W.C.A.—"Everything shall live..." (Ezek. 47:9)

The stream moved on in Richmond for four blessed years after the outpouring of the Holy Spirit in 1892, varied with fruitful service in other places through unsought open doors in all parts of the United Kingdom. The "six months" which medical opinion had allowed the Lord's messenger became six years. With tubercles in the lungs healed by God at the time of the fullness of the Spirit, but leaving large cavities that were only kept from active disease in after years by the mighty power of Jehovah Ropheka, this frail servant of the Lord was physically enabled to endure and to accomplish labors in his kingdom beyond all natural power and resources. Then came the call to wider service, which from the human and natural standpoint appeared utterly impossible. "But by this time," she wrote, "the knowledge of my resources in God had grown, and I was able to cast myself in utter abandonment upon him and find all sufficiency for all my need, at all times and in all circumstances."

In March 1896, Mr. Penn-Lewis having received the appointment of Treasurer to the Corporation of Leicester, the "pillar of cloud" moved on to that busy manufacturing city in the center of England. At first the thought of leaving Richmond came as a shock, not only to all connected with the work there, but to Mrs.

Penn-Lewis herself, for the tide of blessing was at its high water mark. But God was setting his servant free from organizing work that he might open up the way to the regions beyond, and within one month of the removal to Leicester there came the first call to another land. Raised by the hand of God from the verge of death, her husband felt, with her, that her life was a trust from God to be used only for him. With one heart and mind, together they yielded that life afresh to him who had given it back to them. A letter written in 1897 to a relative, who apparently had suggested an easier path to these devoted "fellow-heirs of the grace of God," shows how entirely and wholeheartedly the husband shared with the wife the sacrificial spirit of this wider call to service, and how both recognized the constant separation entailed as a joyful sharing in the pathway of the Lamb, who "loved the church and gave himself for it":

My dear X—,

What revolutions God can work in lives! How little I thought, even five years ago, that he would give me the world for my parish and send me hither and thither as he sent Paul, with the "woe is me if I preach not ... yea, necessity is laid upon me ..." How little I thought, when on the edge of the grave, that he would raise me up to be his witness and place upon me—less than the least of all saints—the "mighty ordination of his pierced hands." How little did I think that he would knit with me in blessed oneness of heart and fellowship my beloved husband, and give him to see me as a trust given back by God from the grave when, humanly speaking, I should have been "with Christ, which is very far better." Raised up as a miracle of God's wondrous grace, how can either of us "rob God" and appropriate for our own selfish use the trust given for his own special purpose?

My life is not my own. I can do nothing else but be obedient to the heavenly vision—since God has chosen the foolish things to confound the wise. Here am I, raised from the grave to be his instrument! Here am I to be spent, every breath, for the God who gives me breath. Our home is not our own, it is God's. We have nothing. We glory in being the slaves of Jesus Christ, my dear one and I. How we bless God for his grace to the chief of sinners! What glory it is to suffer all things lest we should hinder the gospel of Christ!

Oh! X—, what selfish lives God's children are living—making use of the merits of Calvary for their own salvation only, and living for themselves. Sacrifice is counted a foolish thing by the followers of the crucified Christ! In the day of eternity, how few will bear the marks of the Lamb! How short the time to suffer and to sacrifice in the service of souls; how paltry will things look at the judgment seat of Christ! How *mean* we shall feel when we see in the light of the eyes of fire how little we have given our lives in the service of a world lying in the evil one.

How we bless God, my husband and I, for the opportunity, in the little while, of counting all loss for Christ. We feel how little it is—how brief the time! We covet that our God may do the most with us in our short lives—and then we shall be together to rejoice over the glorious harvest for all eternity. Think you that we shall regret any sacrifice then? When we look in our beloved master's face, shall we regret giving our home and our lives for him? Oh the joy now! What will it be then?

I return you the books you sent me. I have nothing to say about them. I have determined to know nothing among men but "Jesus Christ and him crucified." I am not concerned about "systems"... I very much fear they spend their time, like the Athenians, over "some new thing," but I have no time for it. Hungry souls are thronging me, pouring upon me their letters from all quarters of the globe. People in soul-need telegraph for interviews—I have no time for "systems"; the Christ is enough for me, and I find him enough for all the deep heart-need of souls ...

In obedience, therefore, to the heavenly vision and the clear call of God, in June 1896 Mrs. Penn-Lewis crossed the North Sea to Stockholm to attend the first Scandinavian Conference of the Y.W.C.A. and to give the word of the Lord at the devotional meetings. Delegates from Norway, Sweden, Finland, and Denmark gathered for four days of conference, some of the gatherings being private and others open to all. The story of these wonderful days is briefly and simply told in journals kept from day to day during the visit and sent home as fuel for prayer to the home-circle, and a group of others who were upholding her at the throne of grace.

The First Visit to Other Lands

Journal: Gothenburg, 1ˢᵗ June, 1896

I left Tilbury on Friday, May 29th, on board the Swedish vessel *Thorsten*. It did not seem like going alone, for there is no loneliness when Christ is all in all. It was only a great privilege and joy to be sent forth by him. We sailed out of the Thames at 2 p.m. and it was past ten when I left watching the sunset and turned in. We were going along smoothly and all was well. I awoke early on Saturday morning, thinking to go on deck, but soon found that the wind had risen, and the boat was rolling too much to make anything possible but our berths that day. It was a very rough passage. I do not know how the hours passed, only that I had one anchor—"my Father is at the helm."

On the Sunday afternoon, steering in between bare rocks and little islands, we steamed into Gothenburg, four hours late. When I reached the shore, to my surprise and joy I was greeted by an English clergyman and his wife, who said, "You are to stay with us." So away they took me to their home. I found he was the English chaplain here, his wife a Russian lady. They were longing for Christian fellowship … It did not take long to find out their eager souls—the little wife saying with tears in her eyes, "I am *so* hungry, Oh so hungry!" I found them reckoning *The Life of Faith* and *The Christian* every week their greatest treasures, but with no spiritual fellowship here—few English—no parish—little work—yet longing to be used of God. We plunged into spiritual things at once. I told them of the Lord's leading of me, and then we took the Sixth of Romans and read it together, God revealing and doing his own work. The Lord had said to me on board ship,

> "In the beginning—God"

and here I found it verified at once. An English home and welcome instead of a Swedish hotel!

Tuesday, June 2nd

Yesterday, after a quiet morning, we went out to dinner with some Swedish Christians who knew English. Then we were driven, at

8:30, to the Gothenburg Y.W.C.A. for a meeting. Such beautiful rooms, but no carpets, only spotless boards About sixty or more girls came, though it had only been given out on the Sunday night that I could hold the meeting. First they sang a hymn in Swedish and the Y.W.C.A. president led in prayer, afterwards turning to me to begin my talk. She was to interpret for me. I felt at a loss for a moment, and then I began. At first it seemed impossible, but as I got used to it, it became easier; so I just simply told the girls what Jesus could be to us, and then a little about the work in England. Tears were in many eyes, and all seemed so grateful for the word. When we closed, I went to the door to shake hands, and they each made such a funny little curtsy as they went out. We could only talk with our eyes. It seemed so strange to see a Y.W.C.A. Institute so like the home one but in another country and with another language. When we drove to our place of abode, at 10 p.m., it was quite daylight!

Wednesday, June 3rd

I left Gothenburg at 7:50 this morning and started on my long railway journey to Stockholm. The country is very beautiful, with pine forests. The houses are wooden, and painted red, with occasional peeps of lakes here and there as we go along. I am much struck with the politeness of the people. Even the men lift their hats to one another.

Thursday, June 4th

After writing in the train yesterday, I heard some singing of Swedish hymns in the third-class carriage. I went out into the corridor and opened the door between. I saw a large number of men with their hymn-books open, singing away. Some of the passengers in our carriage followed me, and one young man said something to me. I touched my lips and shook my head. Then he fetched out a Bible. I went for mine and showed it to him. Finally it occurred to me that we might talk in that way. I took his Bible and found Galatians 2:20, and he read it, looking at me so brightly. Then I turned to Romans 6:11, "Reckon ye yourselves to be dead indeed unto sin..." He replied "Ja! Ja!" I turned on to Acts 19, "Have ye received the Holy Ghost since ye believed?" Then to Acts 1:8, "Ye shall receive power..." and Acts 2:39, "The promise is unto *you!*" He followed intelligently, then looked upward and said "Ja!" Someone else rubbed up a little English and took my Bible, saying, "You—a—believer?" It was so good, this fellowship through the medium of the Word of life.

I reached Stockholm at 9:50 p.m., after fourteen hours in the train, but no more tired than after a much shorter journey at home. The Lord had carried all the way. Truly he is "El Shaddai"—the "God that is enough."

> "When I sent you ... lacked ye anything?
> And they said nothing" (Luke 22:35).

Stockholm, June 4th (continued)

Today I have had two meetings. The first was in a private draw-ing-room with about forty Christians present. It was with much "fear and trembling" (1 Cor. 2:3) that I went. The adversary kept telling me that it was impossible to "grip" the meeting by interpreta-tion. Waiting upon the Lord to be shown *how* to speak through the interpreter, the light dawned upon me. I saw that at Gothenburg I could not forget my interpreter. I spoke *to her* and she had to pass it on. Now I saw that I was to do exactly as I would in England, with my interpreter as a kind of "echo" by my side. I was to ignore him and speak directly to the people.

It was amusing to see the usual characteristic of our English meetings, for the people sat away in the corners just as at home! Of course my first request was that they would kindly come close together. Then my interpreter gave out a hymn and prayed. As I rose to speak, with the first word I knew that God was there. It was per-fect liberty, and as easy as if I had been speaking in English. I soon forgot my "echo," and so did everyone else. God took hold of every heart. After silent prayer, I rose that we might separate, but nobody moved. There seemed a deep hush and the awe of God's presence upon all. I asked if they had any questions, and answered those that were asked. Then I asked all who meant to have God's best to answer Yes, and a "Ja!" came. Still no one moved. Then we went to prayer again, and souls poured out their hearts to God in their own language. Then—after a two-hour meeting—we broke up. This, for a first gathering, showed prepared ground. God is evidently going to move among us. The relief to my own soul that interpretation, in

God's hand, was not going to prove a "fetter" was immense.

In the evening we had another meeting—a public one in a public hall. It was again a time of great liberty. At the close we had tea, but again they did not seem inclined to break up. So we gathered for prayer and took up the petition for an outpouring of the Holy Spirit upon all the countries represented. I said we needed a spirit of utterance and liberty. There is a great deal of dumbness and stiff conventionality to be broken down here—their very politeness has become a barrier. But God has broken through already. I told them how God dealt with me and that the Holy Spirit would set them free. Then there was a ceaseless stream of prayer. Afterwards my interpreter said, "You have had here tonight Swedes, Norwegians, Finns, Russians, and English." I replied, "How like Pentecost—God grant the same outpouring!"

Friday, June 5th

Today at 1 o'clock I went to the training home for nurses to speak to them and dine with them. We had a good room full, with other friends present… God touched many hearts again. One lady present was a Russian princess. She and her husband had to leave Russia because they were converted and would not have their children baptized into the Greek Church. She asked me for a private meeting in her own house, when she could also ask a few gentlemen, and this was arranged for Monday.

In the evening came the first conference meeting, the reception of the delegates by the president. This is the first Scandinavian conference of the Y.W.C.A., and about 70 delegates have come from Norway, Finland and Sweden. After the president's address of welcome, I gave the message the Lord had clearly given me, upon "God's army of women who publish the tidings." I did not know then that our sisters were yet in the battle of strong prejudice against the "handmaidens" prophesying—strong prejudice based upon misunderstanding of Paul's word of rebuke to the chatterers of his day, the women who would persist in asking questions at the wrong time and in the wrong place; while in the same letter he gives instructions to the women who *did* prophesy and preach, how they should dress when so engaged. Neither did I know, when God gave me this message, that it was one of the subjects to be discussed at the conference because many were not certain of the mind of God in the matter.

It was just like him to meet their need and strengthen their hands by taking my mouth to give them the Scripture and show them how, when God gives the word, the "women who publish" must needs be a "numerous host." We saw how Psalm 68:11–12 (see R.V.) must surely have been a prophecy of these days in which we live. How it was repeated and confirmed by Joel: "I will pour out my spirit ... and your daughters shall prophesy." How it was partially fulfilled on the day of Pentecost, when Peter actually quoted these words to explain and give Scriptural authority for all that the inhabitants of Jerusalem saw! In what a matter-of-fact way it is recorded that Philip had four daughters who "prophesied" (Acts 21:9). How delightful it is to read 1 Cor. 1:27–29 as the list of the ranks in God's army of women. Yes, thank God, *"foolish"* enough to depend upon God for their wisdom; *"weak"* enough for the "endynamiting" with God's strength; *"base"* enough to have no "honor" but God's honor; *"despised"* enough to be kept in the dust at his feet, and better than all, "NOT"—*"nothing"* enough for God to be everything!

Saturday, June 6th

Today I am not needed at the conference as the delegates have all their discussions. I have had, however, an English meeting in the drawing room of Baroness ——. It was a very unusual meeting, about twenty or thirty people of rank, including the Russian princess. I only felt they were "souls," and how solemn an opportunity it was. God kept me in his hand, perfectly at ease—I knew he would give liberty. They all understood English. I had to speak to them of *sin* and of being *sinners* in the sight of God. As I spoke of peace through the blood of the cross and the heart satisfaction that Jesus could give, as well as the blessed life of Jesus manifested in an earthen vessel, the hush of God again stole upon us. Heads were bowed as tears flowed, and Jesus himself drew near.

This afternoon I went for a drive and then was admitted to the conference to hear the discussion on "How to help young believers." The discussion was in Swedish, but I gathered the gist of every speaker's remarks through little words given to me by my neighbor. God is very manifestly in control of the conference. It has had its birth in prayer and absolute dependence upon God. There is as little "machinery" as possible. The simplicity and freedom is very delightful, while the subjects discussed are of vital moment in spiritual work. The praying souls are looking on almost wondering at their God and praising his "exceeding abundantly."

Monday, June 8th

Yesterday I only had one meeting, at 1:30. It was very, very hot, and the place full, about four hundred people. The audience consisted of factory girls, conference delegates, military men, fashionable ladies, Christian workers of all kinds, some pastors, and the Prince and Princess Bernadotte of Sweden. God very manifestly moved in great power as I spoke on the work of the Holy Spirit in conversion, sanctification, and service. There was a marked "hush" of the Holy Ghost as we closed with silent prayer. At the door afterwards numbers thanked God for the message by the English "thank you" or by tears and a pressure of the hand ... I then had a chat with the secretary of the Young Men's Christian Association who told of real conversion work in the Stockholm branch.

Today I had another English meeting, in the drawing room of the Russian princess. Princess Bernadotte was there, and the Baroness Palmstierna, with whom I am staying; the husband of the princess, and many others. The Lord's presence was just melting. I saw many eyes wet with tears as God gave fullest liberty on Philippians 3. "I count all things but loss that I may win Christ ... " Paul's surrender of the earthly for the heavenly; what Paul had suffered the loss of, and how he could say through all, "I count it but refuse." How Paul saw "the heavenly vision," and then for ever moved among the things of earth to count them but refuse in comparison with Christ.

Truly it was an hour with God. One soul there had been summoned by telegram from the country by the princess when I promised the meeting. She was one led to Christ some months before by her—one who had been an unbeliever, an infidel, I think. It is beautiful to see women like this leading souls to Christ and then caring for them afterwards in this way.

After this meeting I stepped into a carriage and was driven to the chief Stockholm hospital, a very large place, to speak to the nurses. Many are true Christians. It was a blessed time. In the evening, at the foreign missions meeting of the conference, I gave the closing word on, "How shall they preach except they be *sent?*" At the close, a lady, passing out, put a gold chain in a worker's hand "for China."

Tuesday, June 9th

This morning the whole conference took the Communion together in a Finnish church. It was a very solemn service and fitly closed the actual days of conference.

My special work now really begins with these two days of waiting upon God, following the conference. All these meetings were "open to all," and many of the brethren made good use of their opportunity.

About 300 were present at the first morning meeting, and God began the breaking work at once. My message was on the "Fire of the Holy Ghost," and truly "the fire of the Lord fell." It is blessed to see the hush of his presence, but still more blessed when he works so mightily that souls are utterly broken down, and so it was this morning—numbers were too broken to hide it. After we quietly broke up, I had occasion to go into a side room. There was one weeping alone. She knew a little English and said, "Oh he never had one so hard as me. I am an utter failure, he will have to do it all himself." A few words, and she entered into rest. I turned to another room, and there was another weeping on a couch. We could not talk; I could only give her a loving touch and leave her to God. So God worked in a way none of us will ever forget.

At the afternoon meeting I had to go on with the message of the "Fire"—this time the blessed results of it in the life of the "new creation," born out of the "midst of the fire" (Ezek. 1:5). God was with us again in mighty power, and it was with hearts full of joy and thankfulness that we drove home for 5 o'clock dinner. Truly he is doing exceeding abundantly above all we thought.

The brother of my hostess was here to dinner. He is an officer in the army, and has come to Stockholm on purpose for the meetings—such a bright Christian, converted through Lord Radstock sixteen years ago ... How beautiful to see the whole family, after dinner, kneeling together, and hear each one pray, in broken English because of me—it was very touching.

"To him be glory in the church. Amen."

On board the Thule, homeward bound. Thursday, June 11th

The last days were too full to add a word to my journal—and how shall I describe the last meetings! On Tuesday night the hall was crowded, seats being added again and again. At first it looked such a mixed audience, "mixed" in a spiritual sense, that my heart failed me when I looked at it. It seemed impossible, by interpretation, to handle such an audience. I noticed Prince and Princess Oscar there again, with several pastors and other gentlemen.

God had given the message about the "carnal" or "self-life"— such a difficult one to put clearly by interpretation, it seemed to me. I could only throw myself on God, and truly he was "El Shaddai." He simply "held" the audience, and gave the greatest liberty and simplicity. Speaking through an interpreter, and pausing after every sentence, one did not dare to add to the brokenness of the thread by turning much to one's Bible, but the Lord brought passage after passage to one's memory so clearly that it seemed like a tender father handing the message to his little one, bit by bit. The line of thought was never broken, and the words never came too rapidly. It was a proving of God to my own soul that I can never cease to thank him for.

The Tuesday (three meetings) had indeed been a glorious day, but Wednesday was indescribable. I began at 10 a.m. with a soul needing help, then went to the 11 o'clock meeting. The hall was full, and again some pastors and other gentlemen among the delegates and workers. Evidently God was working deeply. Never did Romans 6 seem so simple and so clear. Every word seemed to come direct from God. How impossible, otherwise, it would be to speak of the deep things of God and make them *clear* through the medium of another voice. Yet so it was. *God* did it—and it really seemed easier to speak than to an English audience, for these people had hungry hearts and had never had the privileges of English conventions—so the truth passed right "home" in the power of God. *Light* is an awful thing if not obeyed! How this meeting *drank in* the story of "deliverance through death." Melted by the "fire," convicted of the "carnal" life, they were ready for the message of the cross.

After speaking for an hour, an opportunity was given for any to leave who wished, but very few moved. Questions had been sent in the night before, so I dealt with them now. The people were too eager, the time too precious, to stop before we were obliged to. We might never meet again, and numbers were going back to places where there would be no human help. Those who knew no English got friends to translate their questions, and we had a blessed time dealing with them.

When the first meeting closed at 12:30, there was an interval for lunch, during which I dealt with soul after soul in a continuous stream (in broken English and by interpretation) right up to two o'clock, the time of the next meeting—with the exception of ten minutes for a cup of coffee. Truly "no leisure, so much as to eat," but I could understand how the Lord forgot his food in the joy of dealing with the Samaritan woman. He had "meat to *eat*" that many of us "know not of." How absolutely *God is enough* for spirit, soul and body in these blessed days. Truly, the life-streams flowing quicken one's whole being in their outflow. "Waters to swim in," in truth!

> "Believe ye that (HE is) able to do this?"
> "Yea, Lord!" "According to your faith be it unto you."

On the last day (Wednesday) in the afternoon, I spoke again on the NEW LIFE in Christ, dealing yet further with practical difficulties discovered in the personal dealing in the interval for lunch. At the close we asked any to leave who wished to do so, as we were going to spend a little time in waiting upon God, specially with the thought of the "endowment of power." I confess, I only expected a few to stay, but only five or six went out, and there were about 300 people purposed to wait upon God without hurry. It seemed incredible, but upon our knees we went! I may add here that in Sweden it is not the custom to kneel, but to sit and bow the head. That day, however, they instinctively turned to their knees.

I said that anyone might pray if they would be brief and definite, as we were short of time. A few led in prayer, but so softly that not many could hear, and the noise of the traffic outside made it more difficult. I then rose and said that no one need attempt to listen. The impossibility of hearing one another tended all the more to our isolation with God. It did not matter if several prayed together; let everyone ideal with God direct, as if they were really alone.

A moment's pause, and then—almost the whole meeting broke out in audible prayer, each dealing with God for their own personal needs. For about ten minutes the murmur of ˉprayer rose and fell, like the rippling of a brook; a hush, and then prayer again and again, from all parts of the hall. Men's voices, and women's, then a pastor. I stood and looked on amazed. There was no jar, only beautiful harmony, yet everyone praying in his own language, in complete oblivion of the presence of others. I could only think of that wondrous day when "all began to speak as the Spirit save them utterance."

We rose from our knees, many with streaming eyes, and the holy awe upon us as we sat awhile in instinctive silence told of the immediate presence of God. Then we stood *en masse* to unitedly cry to God for an outpouring of the Holy Spirit upon Scandinavia.

We closed the meeting at 3:30, but souls were waiting again. One little card put into my hand touchingly read: "Cannot speak English, but I ask you—give me a word from our Father for *my only* part!" It was nearly five when at last we got away and drove to the home of the kind friends who entertained me. Souls were there again, waiting, and we prayed and praised together with overflowing hearts.

The "family tie" between the children of God is no nominal thing in Stockholm. To be "converted" in Sweden means a clean cut with the world and a drawing together of God's people, irrespective of position, more like the record in the Acts of the Apostles than anything I have seen,

"and all that believed were together..."

At 7:00 p.m. we left for my train. At the station one after another came with flowers and a loving "God bless you." So I moved out of Stockholm, after fourteen meetings in seven days, and dealing with individual souls in an almost ceaseless stream. I was not in the least tired, for the Lord had simply carried me "on an eagle's wings." I enjoyed watching the lovely scenery, and such a gorgeous sunset, until 9:20 when we stopped at Guesta for supper. The night was too hot to sleep well, and I awoke at 2:00 a.m., and the sun was shining. I slept again, and at five o'clock was out in the corridor of the train watching the morning light on the lakes, learning the secret of reflecting the face of Jesus Christ by the utter *stillness* of the water, stilled like a polished mirror, until every fleecy cloud in the sky was perfectly reflected. The lovely forest scenery we passed through added to the enjoyment of the journey.

I reached Gothenburg at 7:10 a.m. and drove to the house of the English chaplain for breakfast; and now we are "homeward bound" on a calm sea, in lovely sunshine. It all seems like a dream, to have traveled so far in one brief fortnight, to have had such blessed fellowship with those I had never seen, and to watch our God work so gloriously in such a short time.

"Oh magnify the Lord with me, and let us
exalt his name together!"

"Blessed be the Lord, who only doeth wondrous things!"
"And again they said, *Hallelujah!*"

"Let us lodge in the villages…"
—*Song of Songs 7:12*

"She is now so free in spirit and heart that she can move about quickly as he pleases. A lodging will do, for her home is in him. She has many times said, 'whither thou goest, I will go: and where thou lodgest I will lodge' (Ruth 1:16). Now he must lead her forth and fulfill his promise, 'Every place whereon the sole of your foot shall tread shall be yours' (Deut. 11:24). The lands must be claimed for him: for they will yet become the kingdoms of our Lord and of his Christ. Like Abraham, she is content to be a pilgrim and a stranger, to sojourn in tents in the 'land of promise' which she will afterward receive as an inheritance when she will reign with him. 'The meek shall inherit the land, and shall delight themselves in abundance of peace' (Ps. 37:11)."

Chapter 5

Russia

1897

Berlin, Warsaw and St. Petersburg—A visit to Moscow—
Russian friends, and some letters

The visit to Sweden, which God so greatly blessed, led still further to the "regions beyond." In the fall of 1896, a Russian lady visiting London invited Mrs. Penn-Lewis to Russia. This was a still greater test of faith for one so frail in body. But the leading of God was so clear as to be unmistakable, and launching out in faith that he who *sent* was able to *keep* his sent ones, January 1897 found her en route for St. Petersburg. The journals of this first visit to Russia tell the story of how the little spiritual church of God in that land eagerly learned the two-fold message of the cross. Others have since built upon this foundation, but then the message was new to the precious and beloved saints in St. Petersburg. This journal is given here just as it was written to friends at home. As all evangelical work was at that time under severe restrictions, little reference could be made to the deep and far-reaching work done by the Spirit of God in this visit. But the journal serves to lift the veil and show something of the way the Lord is able to care for his messengers when they go forth at his command, and also to show the response of his people in St. Petersburg to the opening of his Word and their gratitude for all spiritual help given.

Journal: Thursday, Jan. 14th

I left Leicester at 12:30 a.m. and on reaching London drove to meet a little group of the Lord's praying ones for prayer and committal to him ere going to Victoria to join my traveling companions.

For days the Lord had been ringing in my heart the words

"Not disobedient to the heavenly vision"—

so I knew he was leading me forth. Many were the gracious promises given to the little group as we waited before him in prayer.

Joining my traveling escort at Victoria, we started off at 8:30, reaching Queenborough at 10:05, and going direct on board. I had a deck cabin alone and soon went to sleep, conscious of nothing more until the stewardess called me at 3:30 a.m., when I dressed and joined the group of passengers on deck. It had been a splendid passage. Our small goods were taken to the customs house; and then, after a time of waiting in the quaint, foreign-looking waiting rooms, we joined our train, leaving Flushing at 5:30. We first made tea in our carriage, and after breakfast settled down to doze until we reached Oberhaussen, when telegrams were sent to our loved ones. The long day wore away with nothing specially to note excepting that we found we were gradually getting into colder regions, for at Hanover it was hard frost—icicles hanging on to the roofs of the houses. We reached Berlin at 8:30 on the Friday night, not a bit overtired. It was cold and frosty at Berlin, with snow on the ground.

From Berlin to Warsaw

Our train left Berlin at 10:50, and here we parted from the friend who had brought us thus far and would now return to England. My traveling companion and I were safely installed in our sleeping coupe, and then he left us! It was strange for a moment to be left alone with the next thing the Russian frontier; but here Mlle. P— would meet us, so now we had only to settle to sleep and wake up on the borders of Russia. Russia began to be more real when our conductor came along, a big burly man, speaking much Russian and little English. After some twisting and turning we began to get settled. I climbed to the top berth and managed to get myself and my hand luggage on a shelf—then sleep—and next the frontier!

At 6:00 a.m. came the call, and coffee—one hour to the frontier! How to dress and re-pack was the next problem. We got it done just in time, when the conductor said "four minutes more"—how we scrambled—then came Mlle. P—, with such a loving welcome, and two great porters seizing our baggage.

On Russian ground we stood, snow all round, numbers of gendarmes and officials about. Mlle. P— led us off and up some grand staircase into a beautiful suite of rooms where breakfast was awaiting us. I thought it was an hotel, but it turned out to be a suite of apartments at the frontier reserved for the emperor's use! There is no hotel, only a customs house and a waiting room for passengers, whilst their luggage is being overhauled. We should have had to wait in this waiting-room, but the Countess S— had arranged this for us, her father being the governor general of Poland. So it was reported among the officials that we were relatives of the governor! "The ladies belonging to Count S—" was said by one official to the other as they examined our luggage, so it was done very slightly and was soon over.

Meanwhile I was wandering about the suite of rooms, admiring the parquet flooring and oak furniture. When we had finished our breakfast, the train was announced as ready to start, so we descended the staircase and were escorted to our first-class carriage by the chief of the gendarmes and his staff. This was crossing the frontier royally. Just like the Lord! How I enjoyed *Daily Light* that morning, "All things were created by him"—thrones, principalities, powers, all by him and FOR HIM. How he knows the way to go before his "sent ones."

At Warsaw the Countess S— met us, and again we were taken into reception rooms reserved for the emperor, whilst her groom saw to sending off our telegrams and attended to our luggage. Then the governor general's carriage and two cabs took us to our hotel, where we are comfortably resting for two days. The rooms are very comfortable.

Saturday, January 16th

I felt so well and so rested after dinner that I thought I would call on Rev. C. H. Titterton, our old Richmond curate, who is working here as a missionary among the Jews. It was so nice to see him. It was with great interest I heard about his work and saw the room attached to his suite of apartments fitted up for church service. After a chat we returned to the hotel and I was glad to get to bed.

Sunday, January 17th.

A quiet day of rest. In the evening Mr. Titterton came and we had another long chat over the Lord's work here. God is giving him encouragement, and he tells me there is great awakening among the Jews.

Monday, January 18th.

At 12:00 Mr. Titterton called for me, and we took a conveyance outside the hotel—with a very skinny pair of horses. We were driven at tearing speed over pebbly roads, among crowds of people, to a place where there was a little Bible depot. Here I had a conversation with the Jewess in charge (Mr. Titterton translating into German), then we drove to his place for dinner.

Today is a Russian holy day, and opposite my hotel window is a public garden—a frozen lake covered with skaters, a band, crowds of people, some dressed as in England. Numbers of military about and thronged with Jews. It is a large place—about 500,000 people.

Warsaw to St. Petersburg

Tuesday, January 19th.

We left Warsaw last night about 8 o'clock. We failed to get sleeping cars, so made the best of a first-class carriage. I could not sleep for some time, it was so hot! At 12 o'clock we roused up and made some cocoa, then succeeded in sleeping. Outside it was snow—snow everywhere. We were traveling due north. In the morning, on reaching a station, Mlle. — went out and got us some breakfast. Russian tea in glasses, etc., etc. Now, hour after hour, we are making our way through vast tracts of snow—rarely passing a place that might be called a town, but more often groups of peasants' houses, so poor, so rough, so few.

At one station I saw peasants in their skin coats, simply undyed sheepskin with the fur turned inside.

The journey takes 24 hours from Warsaw to St. Petersburg and nothing much to be seen but snow.

St. Petersburg, January 20th.

We reached here at 7:30 last night. Somehow I do not feel the hours in the train long; they pass so quickly. On arrival, our luggage was seized by men chattering away in a most unpronounceable language; we were then packed into a cab, and driven to our destination.

The scene was so new and picturesque. Snow everywhere, and sledges flashing about, the drivers in quaint garb and fur caps.

I arose this morning refreshed and rested, and soon went out in a sledge, wrapped up in furs and shawls. We drove as far as the great River Neva, to see it all frozen, with the traffic upon it. All the trees covered with frozen snow made everything look so beautiful. They say it is quite "warm" for Petersburg; 12 or 14 degrees of frost.

The houses are so beautifully warmed (double windows, wadded, that no drafts can come) that indoors you do not feel the cold, whilst out-of-door clothing is so sensible that you quite enjoy it.

Although I only arrived on Tuesday night, it had been arranged that I should speak on Wednesday night in the schoolroom attached to the British-American chapel.

Rev. A. Francis, the minister in charge, gave me a hearty welcome and full freedom in the meeting, speaking so nicely in his introduction, that they had been praying for revival, and now God had sent a messenger who had not been "disobedient" to the "heavenly vision" calling her to a distant land. This was so wonderful, for I had not told him of the Lord's message to me the week before I left England.

The schoolroom was quite full as I spoke on the "Heavenly Vision" that came to Paul. At the close the people thronged around me. Two Scotchmen—members of the Faith Mission—gave me a hearty greeting. A brother from Finland, with the stamp of Christ in his face, said in English, "I knew the voice of the *Lord* tonight."

Then the Bible Society workers spoke to me of the work in their charge. I was soon booked up for days of work, and Mr. Francis announced further English meetings next week. The Lord's presence in *glory* had been manifested this first evening, and it was a blessed token of all he was going to do for us.

Thursday, January 21st.

At 11:30 this morning Madame K— and I started out on a shopping expedition—rolled up in furs, snow boots on, and shawl round my head. We took a sledge, and then for an hour and a half scampered about St. Petersburg, in and out, shop after shop, English-looking and yet so foreign, turning aside to look at the Winter Palace, noting this and that cathedral. We came in to lunch covered with fine snow.

In the afternoon we had a little gathering of girls, to whom I spoke. Then in the evening, drove to the house of Princess Lieven for a meeting. A large room, packed with people, gentlemen and ladies, "of chief women not a few," and many of the poorer classes.

Mlle. P— interpreted, and God gave me a clear message on "All things New." How they listened, and many wept under the dealing of the Spirit.

After the meeting a little group of us stayed to talk, and I was deeply interested to meet a young lady (Baroness Wrede) from Finland who spends all her life in visiting the Finnish prisons—she began at 19. She is the only one given liberty to do this. She has a cell in the various large prisons and stays two months at a time seeing every prisoner alone. Her face was a picture and an inspiration.

We drove home in a sledge about 11 o'clock. One can hardly describe the scene; the broad road called Nevsky Prospekt (the Regent Street of Petersburg) with electric light down the middle, the snow around, the numbers of military, the strange dresses, the large buildings, the numberless sledges dashing by, horses scampering along, etc., etc. It is all of ceaseless interest to me; sometimes it seems more like a dream than real.

One said to me today, "I have waited many years for you." At the close of the meeting tonight I asked all whom God had convicted to say so aloud, and a large number broke out. Then to the decision that all "old things" might go, came a hearty cry of "Da, Lord." The meeting seemed deeply moved.

It seems they are "dumb" here as elsewhere, and that this is unusual—but *God* knows how to open lips and melt hearts.

Friday, January 22nd.

The days are beginning to fill up. Rev. A. Francis called this morning to arrange about further meetings in the British-American church.

Then one came, and we had dealings over salvation. Then another called to see what help he could give in writing, etc., and we soon got into a talk over the endowment of power. He described to me very clearly the death-pathway God had led him along last year—"spiritual consumption" he called it. He said he saw his soul "dying," and he could not help it! Here is God's work without any teaching. He was very clear about the new life in Christ which had since come, but it was quite a revelation to him to hear of so much beyond. In the afternoon came a little group of ladies to talk and pray over what could be done for girls, and we had a helpful time.

At 8 o'clock I was driven to a meeting of Germans, Finns, and Swedes—Baron Nicolay translating. God was mightily present and there was a very great response.

Saturday, January 23rd.

At 10:45 I drove in a sledge to see an institute for Protestant girls, Germans and others, working under government statute, very much like our Y.W.C.A. Then in the afternoon I was driven in a private sledge to the house of Mdme. K— where I had a very special little meeting. In an adjoining room, where they could hear, sat a little group of ladies of the Court—one an old lady of 75 who never goes to anything of the kind. The Lord gave a clear gospel word on Calvary.

In the entrance hall afterwards were men-servants in great furs, drawing on their ladies' fur shoes and wrapping them in beautiful fur cloaks. After this meeting we came home for rest and then went again to the house of Princess Lieven, where we had another large meeting, to which I spoke by translation. It was not easy to deal with "self" second-hand, but God made it first-hand, for several spoke of the way God had met them. One man said it was a photograph of himself; and a lady said, "You are like soap and water to our hearts!"

Several came to ask for interviews, and then I turned back and found a group in a corner talking. I joined them, and we threshed out personal matters.

Sunday, January 24th.

Indoors resting all the morning, then a private sledge was sent for me at 4 o'clock to take me to the Institute for girls that I have referred to. A very large number there, and although I spoke by translation, God completely broke the girls down. Numbers were weeping as they gathered round me afterwards, kissing my hands in the Russian fashion. God evidently brought many to his feet that afternoon.

Mrs. Penn-Lewis in Russia

I then went to Princess Lieven's, where I dined; then I was driven in their private sledge, under magnificent furs, behind a pair of beautiful black horses, to another house, where we had a very large meeting in the dining room. Mlle. P— translated; and then, when the people had gone, Mdme. Tchertkoff and I had a quiet talk and prayer.

I slept there, and next morning took prayers, and went to see the school in my hostess' grounds, speaking to the assembled children.

Monday, January 25th.

After tea I had an interview with a lady by translation. It was difficult to help her, poor thing, with her mind full of reasonings and not knowing her language.

After an hour we came to a point for prayer—then I hurriedly had supper and started off for a meeting in the English church. A most blessed time and very great liberty. The place full of the same people as before. Home at 10:00 and up till 12:00 with a soul made a very full day.

Tuesday, January 26th.

One degree above freezing point today, which means a thaw and tiredness! Roads in swamps of water and slush. At 10 o'clock I had an interview, then another—afterwards an hour's sledging before lunch. At 3:30 I had another most difficult interview, succeeded by two ladies who were most refreshing. Two definitely, intelligently seeking the baptism of the Spirit—translation was no difficulty—God made all clear to them and they went away rejoicing.

Afterwards I went with Mdme. K— to dinner and then drove to another part of St. Petersburg, to another meeting. We were just *crowded*—the people were simply mopping off the perspiration! They were oh so eager. Broken words was all I could give them, but how God worked. Sheep without a shepherd—poor souls. I spoke in the simplest way—then they broke down, men weeping and praying.

I was simply *pressed* upon afterwards for interviews, but I had no time—so much could not be touched at all. Pray for all the Christians here. God only knows their need. Would to God the people were as eager in England. What a privilege to be sent here to feed his sheep. "I myself... will gather" is our comfort.

Wednesday, January 27th

All the morning out with Mdme. K—. Went over a large cathedral. It was sad to see the poor people prostrating themselves on the ground and kissing the pictures of various saints. We then saw the church where the emperors are buried, saw the tomb of the late czar and the mass of silver wreaths sent for his funeral from all nations—so many that the pillars and walls of the whole church were simply covered with them.

We drove along by the side of the frozen Neva—roads are made across it, marked out by fir trees and gas lamps put in when freezing. Here and there they were cutting out blocks of ice for ice cellars. It was such a lovely day. The sun was shining and the roads were frozen glass after the thaw of yesterday.

After lunch I had two interviews, and then at night a meeting in the British-American chapel. I dined first with Rev. A. Francis, the chaplain, and the meeting afterwards was *crowded*. In the front seat there sat a lady of very high position. Her face was a picture; her eyes seemed almost starting out of her head with eagerness; she was drinking every word and seemed afraid to lose a sentence. Her face is printed on my memory.

At the close of the meeting I saw a gentleman in military dress whom Mr. Francis introduced to me. Afterwards he came and said he was upstairs and would like to see me. So I went! And this gentleman began to question me. What did it all mean? He could not understand it! If *this* was the Christian life, *who* were Christians? Could it be lived every day? Did it not mean being shut off from everything—how would the world go on? He was thoroughly roused—he had had a sight of the Christian life as God meant it, that fairly staggered him. It was a most interesting conversation, showing the *effect* of the real Christian life upon a worldly man. I could say much more, but enough—like Felix, he "trembled"—to *yield to God* is another thing. Oh that all worldly people might see in God's people a life so "other-worldly" that they must confess it is of God. I learned afterwards that my interviewer was a gentleman of the court who had charge of the emperor's private estates. He had with him an Englishman who seemed to be a tutor—at any rate the Russian turned to him again and again when at a loss for an English word. "I will come and see you again," said my questioner; but as I looked at the Englishman's face I said to myself, "No, you will not, if your companion can help it," for I saw a deep antagonism to the theme of the interview in his eyes.

Thursday, January 28th.

This morning Baron Nicolay called to take me out in a sledge and see the Bible depot, where Rev. Wm. Keen told me about the work.

After lunch two ladies called, one from Finland—she and her husband had been missionaries in Bulgaria—she had only been to one meeting, where God met her and revealed himself. She said she saw herself now as having died with Christ, and Christ all in all in an "empty vessel." The other lady said God had answered every question she had, in last night's meeting—her only desire now was to be wholly God possessed.

After one more interview came a young student—a Jew, Israel V— by name. A lady sat by me and translated our conversation. He did not waste any time. He said last year he had been given a New Testament and on reading it, God showed him Jesus Christ as the Messiah; and now he knew God was working in him—he knew he could *see* the kingdom—but what did it mean to *enter* the kingdom—and he read the two verses in John 3—had he to *hear* a voice? I said the Holy Spirit came sometimes like a soft and gentle wind, and you *heard* nothing—he had come thus to him. He continued that he was conscious of inward battle, and how sometimes "Israel V— had his way." But he wanted to know God, so that others might know that he knew him, for so few people seemed really to know him; and he wanted to be used by God the very most that was possible. God made everything clear to him and gave me answers from the Bible. He was so intelligent and so receptive. He got assurance that he was in the kingdom that night.

Afterwards we went to another meeting, at Princess Lieven's, where the large ex-ballroom was packed full of people—out in the hall, people standing—it was a crowd. I spoke on Pentecost. Oh, the hungry faces—the meeting was so moved that it would take little to break it down, but I felt it better to close it early and ask all to go quietly home and wait alone upon God. Quietly they then dispersed, and I had several important talks with different ones afterwards.

Friday, January 29th.

I was so tired this morning that I rested until noon, when I went out for an hour. and then in the afternoon had a drawing-room meeting—a most blessed time. There were not seats enough for the people, it was so full. It is blessed to watch the same ones coming time after time.

In the evening I had a very large meeting of Germans at the house of Baroness Nicolay (mother of Baron Nicolay)—Sunday school teachers, deaconesses, and many men. I had to be very clear in speaking of *conversion,* and of the work of the Holy Spirit, as they are very dim over all that. God gave me great liberty and power. I reached my abode at midnight—quite ordinary hours to keep in Russia.

Saturday, January 30th.

I spent the whole morning out of doors. Mdme. K— and I drove to the outskirts of St. Petersburg to a part called the Islands—where the wealthy residents have houses in the summer, and you can look out to sea, for the Neva runs in and around numbers of islands which are connected by bridges. Now all is solid ice and snow. It was snowing all the time, but so warmly clad are we that we do not feel it.

In the afternoon I rested; and then in the evening I went to Princess Lieven's to meet a group of thirty, knowing English, for a talk about the Holy Spirit. We sat over our Bibles from 8:30 to 11:00, and the discussion was very vigorous. Objections and difficulties were threshed out, and I pinned them all to Dr. Andrew Murray's "seven steps to blessing." All—although *leaders*—said openly there was a fullness of the Spirit they had *not* got! And then we stuck awhile at the point, "I believe it is for *me*"—but finally got to the end, and broke up at 11:30, after prayer from most present. A most important meeting, and some dated their dealing with God for the fullness of the Spirit from that night.

Sunday, January 31st

At 10:00 this morning I started for a meeting in the palace of Princess Lieven, where God gave me much liberty on "the corn of wheat." I then lunched with the Princess, and in the afternoon at four went to another place for a packed meeting of girls. Then in the evening Mr. Francis took me to a little mission room amongst the English population. Oh the indifference—the English indifference—in a foreign land! It was like being transported to the north of England, among the working men who have heard so much that they can hear no more. I could have wept with shame, and wielded the sword of the Spirit with its keenest edge. There was much convicting power I knew.

Monday, February 1st

I was very tired this morning. The dear friends are begging me to let my return ticket go, and stay another week; but I hardly know how to say "Yes" without some break between. I have been at continuous work ever since my arrival, and the indoor life is very enervating. Scarcely a breath of air seems to get to you—double windows with wadding between, and warm air from heated stoves—made it almost impossible even to sleep.

At 11:30 a private sledge was sent by Baroness Nicolay to fetch me to lunch for a definite talk over spiritual things with the group in the house. As soon as I arrived, out came the Bibles and into Romans 6 we plunged—it was most definite and to the purpose.

I returned home in the afternoon to meet again a group of thirteen ladies, and for two and a half hours we discussed the question of how to work among girls in spite of the restrictions for Christian work in Russia. Then at night I had another meeting in the schoolroom of the British-American chapel—very full and very blessed. The people are so receptive.

After the meeting Mr. Francis came to me and said "Mrs. Penn-Lewis, you are tired and you must stop work." "I will escort you to Moscow," said an American gentleman standing by. "The very thing," said Mr. Francis—"I have friends there. Change of air—rest and see Moscow!"

I felt it was of the Lord. I knew my work was not finished, but I also knew I needed a break, so I agreed to let Mr. Francis settle things for me. This American gentleman was going on business, so he could be my escort. I agreed to rest after the Tuesday meetings.

This last fortnight's work has been very heavy. Ceaseless interviews and group meetings in various places—after a meeting people would press upon me to know if I received at my apartment. I should have been overwhelmed if I had said I did.

Anyhow, the days were so full—although I always got a drive each morning—that by Sunday night I wondered how I should hold out; and although I saw the tremendous need, I hardly dared commit myself to say I would stay after Friday of this week. I began to find myself flagging and needing a break, for the atmosphere, spiritually, exhausts you much more than the free air of England. It is awful to live under the *feeling* of restraint. I had talked so much that, on Friday, my voice began to go!

Tuesday, February 2nd

This morning I rested until Mr. Francis called to tell me how he was arranging matters. Then at 2 o'clock came three ladies for a most important interview. Indeed, the deepest work with the deepest results—I am not free to tell until the day of eternity. This interview means the most far-reaching consequences. God has worked mightily amongst "chief women, not a few." At 4:00 I drove to Mdme. K's where I had another meeting. I had to tell them there would be a cessation of meetings for a few days whilst I went to Moscow.

Afterwards I stayed to dinner, and then a carriage was sent for me to go to Baroness Nicolay's, where we had another very large meeting of Germans. A marked advance over the first, for now they simply drank every word and God *poured* it through me, so that I could hardly bear it. The faces told how God was revealing and dealing. It was glorious!

How *marvelously* God is working. Many are thanking God for the answered prayer of years. But the work must of necessity be spread out. We cannot go on in the same place—there are "many adversaries." If it could be public and free, there would be a wondrous reaping of souls; but alas, it cannot be. To meet the needs here it takes much longer than a few days in England.

I cannot tell you how kind all have been. God overwhelms me with wonder when I see him make strangers do so much for me. God has touched souls in all directions in a most wonderful way. The dear things are so "hungry"—so utterly different to the stolid indifference in England.

Wednesday, February 3rd

My voice is much better with today's rest, but such consternation among the friends. I have had to fight for my liberty—they would like no air to blow on me! These dear people's hearts are very large.

God's purposes are marvelous in this visit. This is the history of a lifetime rolled into a brief few weeks.

Moscow, February 4th.

We arrived here this morning. On Wednesday, in St. Petersburg, I rested all day and did not go out. I seemed to have a cold; my voice was weak and I was a little feverish. Several called through the day—one lady came with a large Orenburg shawl, like a very fine Shetland—and then in the evening friends came to arrange about Moscow. It was arranged to send me in charge of a young lady who would look after me, and knew Russian and English well. So on Thursday night I was settled in a sleeping coupe en route for Moscow. I slept all the way and was quite rested when we reached here at 10:00 a.m.

There is certainly a marked difference in the air. When we arrived there was a brilliant blue sky and a strong sun shining upon the snow, making it so dazzling that your eyes could hardly bear it. The brass domes of Moscow churches also added to the glare. They say there are forty times forty churches in the place, and numbers of them have four or five minaret domes in burnished brass with huge crosses at the top. Painted pictures in niches and outside the churches abound.

We drove and engaged rooms at Hotel Slavansky Bazar and then had a proper breakfast. Afterwards we took a sledge to drive round. The sun on the snow was so dazzling that I could hardly open my eyes for a while. The air is so clear and so crisp—the snow crackles under the sledge as we go along. It is about five degrees colder than Petersburg. The beards of the sledge drivers are white with frost, little icicles hanging to the hairs. The coats of the horses are white likewise, with long icicles to their mouths. Fifteen degrees of frost here. I so much enjoy it. It is most exhilarating.

We drove about the Kremlin and the streets of Moscow and then called on Mr. Francis' friends, but they were so far out of the town that we shall stay in the hotel. The brother of Mr. S— called today, but we were out.

Saturday, February 5th

Last night I developed a cold in my head, which became very severe. Mr. S— called in the evening and seemed much alarmed about it. He evidently thought I was going to have influenza—so I agreed to stay in today. It certainly got bad very quickly. My eyes were running like a tap, and my face became raw with the water.

Mr. S— came again on the Saturday afternoon, and I seemed very little better. A cough was coming, and I saw that the Lord would have to work for me or I should be laid up. Mr. S— began to talk about a doctor, so I thought he considered me pretty well gripped by the cold.

My companion went out with him to get some things, and I took the chance to talk to the Lord about it. I saw the Lord's dealings with me. In the heart of Russia—practically alone—with a bad cold getting a grip of me—with no single soul to ask to pray with me—and in a hotel far away from even the friends I had in Russia. A telegram to Petersburg would take half a day at least, for things move slowly here. It was a blessed test. No shade of fear or question. I was not alone! It was all the same in the heart of Russia as in England. How lovely to be put into fresh places to prove his power! I just knelt and told the Lord that the work had to be finished in Petersburg, and I must be well, and that he could not let the friends there be disappointed. Then I opened my Bible on "Jesus, knowing the power proceeding from him had gone forth, said… thou art healed of thy plague." And it was done!

The running water of eyes and nose stopped instantly. My companion came in—she looked at me—"you are better?" "Yes," I said, "the Lord has done it." I then was fresh and bright for writing, and had a good night.

On Sunday afternoon Mr. S— came for me and was very astonished.

I went out with him to see his aged parents for a quiet talk, and then stayed indoors all the evening.

Monday, February 7th.

Such a lovely day. I rose quite bright and well. No trace of cold or cough! Brilliant sunshine. Today the Lord gave me liberty to see Moscow. Mr. S— came for us at 11:30 and we started out—first to the Kremlin, and inside the fort to the Coronation Church. Very gorgeous. The pillars, walls, and roof all one mass of pictures, and any amount of gilt relics, and all sorts of things. Some of the pictures had movable glass frames; inside in the halos were jewels, etc. In a side chapel there was an open coffin with a mummy—just an inch of the breast exposed, with a bit of glass over it, and people were stooping to kiss the spot. I could not stand much of it. My companion was relieved, I doubt not, when I said I did not want to see more churches. "This kind of thing is nearly played out," he said. What must an unconverted man think of all this travesty of the real thing?

We next went into the Treasury, answering to our British Museum. I hurried through rooms of curios until we paused before an immense glass case containing the gorgeous cloth of gold panoply, under which the royal party walked at the coronation. In it were the cloth of gold and ermine robes of the czar and czarina, the white silk dress the czarina wore, and the coat of the emperor, the robes of the empress dowager—all very interesting, as one had read in England of the grand affair.

We then went over the palace, which was very grand and beautiful. Afterwards we drove round the walls of the Kremlin, which is a large fort on a hill in the center of Moscow, and in it are four or five churches, the palace, and the Treasury.

After lunch at the hotel, we got a sledge with a good fresh horse and went an hour's drive out of Moscow to some hills, from which we got a lovely view of the city and district. It was the very spot where Napoleon stood and gazed at the city. Each side of the main roads the snow was piled up some feet; but when we turned off the main road to go to the hills, the dips in the snow made it something like an American switchback. We saw some birds with brilliant red breasts and blue wings.

After returning to the hotel, we had dinner and then left by the night train. These are so comfortable. Twelve hours journey is nothing when you can go to bed and wake up at your destination.

The Last Week

St. Petersburg, February 8th

Reaching here at 10:00 this morning, I found quite a handful of letters waiting me; and I was at once seized upon for details of arrangements.

After sketching out plans, I rested; and then at 2 o'clock Miss Wolkoff sent her carriage for me to use for the afternoon. This dear lady and her sister said the Lord had said to them at one meeting,

"Lend me your carriage and horses"; and so next day they sent to ask if I would use them for his service. Every day afterwards, in the morning, came the servant, "What time do you want the sledge—or the carriage—today?"

I first drove this afternoon to Mr. Francis, and then he took me to call at the American embassy. Afterwards to one or two other places where I had to go. Returning home I found Madame Tchertkoff had come to tell me of God's work in a prayer meeting whilst I was away. It had been very dead and dumb, but the leader had opened her heart and broken down the meeting; also many of her girls were blessed.

When she had gone, Princess G— came for a chat, and God brought her to a definite point to see her union with Christ. After this I went to Princess Lieven's to dinner, and here met a blessed group of believers, gathered definitely to wait on God for the fullness of the Spirit. I was told of one lady who had come to only one meeting and went away exclaiming "I have found him—I have found him—I want no more theaters—he is mine." Another, just going to be married, had been told not to come because they thought her mind would be too full of other things to be interested, but she had come, and God was speaking to her so that she would not miss a meeting.

We had a blessed two hours of talk and prayer, and this group banded themselves together to wait on God every week for an outpouring of the Spirit on the Russian Christians. One said to me: "Twenty years have we waited for you! God sent a messenger twenty years ago to tell us of 'Christ for us,' and one or two others come now with the same message—but *now* God has sent another revelation—Christ IN you. Twenty years have we been babes, but now it shall be no more 'I'—we are *so* happy—*so* happy!"

Wednesday, February 9th

We were out, Mdme. K— and I, by 10:30 this morning, shopping. Then we lunched and I went with Mlle. P— to call on a lady in loneliness and unable to get to the meetings. Then we called on Mr. and Mrs. S— to tell them about Moscow, and at night I had a meeting in the British-American chapel schoolroom. The American ambassador and his wife were both there, and numbers of the usual friends, with continually new ones, who were only just hearing of the meetings.

Out in the morning, then at lunch met a Mrs. K—, with whom I had a private talk and clearing up of personal difficulties. Then at 2:30 came a little group of German workers to talk over their work and the need of the Spirit-power. These five agreed with me that they would ceaselessly unite in waiting upon God for the outpouring of the Spirit on the German community—the need and the possibility of this has never come to these dear Christians. So this is the second group banded for this. To rouse them to see the need and the result of this crying to God is no little gained for God's kingdom.

Before this group had gone, came the ladies of another group—the same who have met before to discuss what could be done for young women. For another two and a half hours we faced this again, and they too banded to pray that God would show them clearly what to do, and equip them with the Spirit. Then I slipped to another room with one lady, and she told me of the witness of the Spirit given to her in Col. 3:3—her face was lit with joy.

In the evening I had another meeting in the British-American schoolroom, and heard of much blessing—thank God!

It is wonderful to see God touching every section of the Christians here, and picking out the souls that will most touch each group—the movement of the Spirit is like a wave of life. To him be glory!

I slept at Mdme. K—'s last night, and at 10:00 this morning came a lady to tell me how God had blessed her. He had said to her before I arrived, "Tarry until ye be endowed"—(I found several God had thus spoken to! And they had had no teaching to put it before them—it was entirely the preparation of the Spirit!).

Afterwards Mdme. K— and I went out and called at several places. I met a lady at lunch again, and then drove to the chapel for an afternoon meeting. A most lovely time on 1 Cor. 13. The presence of the Lord was *melting*—they told me afterwards how they felt they could do nothing but weep at his feet.

I then went to dinner at Baron Nicolay's, where I had again in the evening a crowded German meeting. I spoke upon the work of the Holy Spirit, and a lady said it was the first time she had ever heard that God had given the *Spirit* to work in them. Another said what "glad tidings" it truly meant to hear that *God* came to *us*—*God* longed for us—*God* drew us—and that it was not we who had to struggle to get, and do our utmost to attain. In every direction it is indeed a new revelation of God.

Saturday, February 12th

At 10:00 again, I had Mrs. K— to see me: a dear young Christian, with her husband bitterly resenting her becoming a Christian, and she seeking to know how she was to win him for Christ. It was a blessed time we had together.

Afterwards Miss Wolkoff and I went for a sledge drive (snowing). We passed Peter the Great's house, and I got out to see it. Such a tiny house, and one part of it used as a chapel. Service was going on—a blaze of candles before a picture—a priest with a cross holding it for the people to kiss—people on the ground prostrating themselves and others kissing the picture. We then called at the Bible depot and went over the premises.

In the afternoon I had another meeting at 4:30 in the chapel (British-American). A full room. Then to the house of Baron Nicolay for dinner and an interview with Miss —, governess to the daughter of a grand duchess. A beautiful true child of God.

In the evening, I met by special request a group of men—the leaders among the Christians. We had to talk by translation. They desired to know about the anointing—and we went into the matter personally and collectively until 11 o'clock, when Baron Nicolay drove me home. Then this group also agreed to wait upon God for the outpouring of the Spirit. This had been another full day and was the preparation for a very crowded Sunday.

I am overflowing with his life since that time at Moscow, and these last days need supernatural life to carry me through, for these dear people are making the most of their opportunity.

At 9:30 I began by going to the British-American chapel and speaking to their little fellowship meeting at 10:00, conducted by a Scotchman. Just a little group they were, but some were weeping. God spoke, and they agreed to form another little group of prayer.

I then went to a private house for a meeting at 11:00, and we had a most blessed time. I spoke on "the end … is love," and there was deep impression. When we went on our knees, numbers prayed—several at the same time, oblivious of the others—many in deep brokenness of spirit, and we could not close the meeting. I rose to go, and yet prayer after prayer kept coming; it seemed impossible to stop.

I lunched here, and then had a private talk with young Prince Lieven, who is in the navy, truly given to God and seeking the fullness of the Spirit. I then went home and lay down for just half an hour, when I had to start again for the large Bible class of young women at the German Institute.

I went in and found an eager roomful waiting for me, and I had rapt attention as I spoke to them (translation) on "Vessels." Afterwards the head worker said the girls wished to know if I would carry to England a thank-offering to our Richmond missionary—all of their own accord—and some began thrusting paper money into my hands. But I could not stay. I had another engagement, so I asked Baroness Nicolay to bring it all to me next day. I said goodbye to this dear class of girls, and went to dine with Mr. Francis, then went downstairs with him to his evening service in the church. He had announced that I would give the address! He had on his black gown, and I followed him to the rostrum and sat on a chair by his side.

The church, which was such a nice one, holding about 400 I should say, was quite full. It was my last meeting and was a fitting close. All the people had gathered, and the American ambassador was in the embassy pew, Princess G—, Prince G—, and also to my joy, young Prince Paul Lieven, and a number of English.

The first part of the service was so simple and nice, and then the Lord gave me a message of great liberty on the fire of God. It simply poured through, and the fire did fall. God seemed overshadowing us in manifested glory. Mr. Francis then closed with prayer so beautifully. Afterwards I was simply besieged, the people pressed upon me—praising God for blessing. Cards of names, requests for interviews from some I had not seen. I had kept the Monday to do my packing, but no use—it was slipping away with special interviews—people I had to see—melted souls. It took me nearly an hour to clear the entrance hall. God indeed had worked.

I reached home tired but so thankful for the power that had carried me since 9:30 a.m., through four services and many interviews. El Shaddai.

Monday, Feb. 14th and Tuesday, Feb. 15th

At last I have got away! I began to wonder when I should leave. Four weeks today I reached Petersburg, and what a wondrous time it has been. God has broken forth like the breaking forth of waters. What a privilege to have been sent with the fresh message of the revelation of the risen Christ within the heart. "If Christ *for* you" has meant such deep work in the Russian Christians, what will "Christ *in* you" mean?

The last days were very full, and the tidal wave of the Spirit seemed to grow higher and higher every day after Moscow, until it culminated in that wonderful fire of God that seemed to fall in the church on the last night.

After such a full Sunday I had to be up very early on the Monday morning to do my packing—much had to be rearranged for the return journey.

At 11 o'clock Mdme. K— called in a private sledge for me to go and finish some shopping. Then we returned to her place to lunch and found Princess G— there for a talk. She was praising God for all he had revealed to her. At 3:00 I had to call somewhere else on a most important interview, a lady who had melted down at the last and now desired to see me. We plunged at once into personal talk. She said how God had answered all their prayers and how she had the clear assurance in her own soul that he would give her the fullness in his own time.

I then returned home and had an interview (translation) with another lady full of joy. Another came at 6 o'clock to tell me, with tears, how she and others had been led out in prayer and all had been answered. She had it on her heart to gather another group for prayer.

At 6:30 I drove to the American embassy to dinner, and for a last time of fellowship and prayer. At 8 o'clock I drove back again to Liteinaia, where I had said I would be after 8 o'clock to see friends and say goodbye. Such a group of dear Christians, each praising and blessing God for all he had done. One and the other called me aside to tell me how God had blessed them. It was very blessed to kneel all together and thank our faithful God; for, as I told them, it was all so absolutely the work of God himself that it seemed that I had NO PART in it at all. All they said passed over me to him, for "I am not." I had proved it was safe to obey God and to follow him "not knowing," and they had proved how fully he met the longings he himself had created.

Then I told them a little of how God had asked me to go, and told me nothing of what it would be—that I had obeyed his call "not knowing" in truth, the consequences of the climate to my fragile body (and found he was a wall of fire); "not knowing" how I should stand the traveling (and found I was not even tired); "not knowing" whom I was coming to (and found hearts as warm as their country was cold)—truly a God worth trusting.

One dear lady said, "I thank you—I thank you—I thank you— that you were 'not disobedient'..."

We broke up about 11:00, and it was past 12:00 when I got to rest. Up again early on Tuesday morning to complete my packing. Well I did, for at 9:30 an English lady and her daughter came, both with tears of gratitude, to say goodbye. At 10:45 we left the house, and as our train moved out at 12 o'clock, I left a happy group on the platform. The last words were: "Praise God—Praise God."

Yes, "unto him be glory in the church for ever," for his grace to redeemed sinners.

The Journey to England

Wednesday, February 17th

I must not omit to tell you of the journey home, for the Lord does not leave us half way. If he takes us out he brings us safely home again.

I have a Russian lady traveling with me all the way to England. She only knows a few English sentences, and she has to do all the business, but with a dictionary and signs we are getting along alright. There are not many passengers, so we have two sleeping coupes thrown into one. The Lord gave me this morning: "Ye shall not go out with haste, nor by flight, for the Lord will go before you, and the God of Israel shall be your rereward" (Isa. 52:12). *Why the last part* I don't know yet, but I gather that I am to go out as calmly and quietly as I came in, and not as if I was escaping the country! No "beating a hasty retreat!" He said he would be unto me a "wall of *fire*" and I have never felt the cold uncomfortable once.

I was told ere I left today that two seeking ones had already received the fullness of the Spirit. Another said she had had ten girls at her new group on Sunday, and a fourth said the Lord had *specially* given her Isa. 4:3–6 that morning for the Christians.

Thursday, February 17th

I must add to the story. The Lord's promise was true! He is wonderful! We reached Warsaw, after 25 hours in the train, at 1:30 on the Wednesday. At the station was a private carriage and a groom to meet us. He could only speak Russian—my companion and he talked. I heard the word "hotel"; and then I gathered there were no rooms at the hotel we were expecting to go to, but at another. So after some little difficulty we reached Hotel de France about 2:00. When we were settled and having some lunch, the English clergyman came—the one referred to in our journey to St. Petersburg.

After a while Mdme. A—, my traveling companion, went out with letters to post. Then came the hotel waiter for the passports. In a little while he came back to say mine was out of order!

This is a serious matter in Russia; your passport is everything. It seems it should have been stamped by the officials before I left St. Petersburg—and the friends there either had forgotten it or did not know it should be done. Mr. Titterton had to talk German to the waiter over this. In the Lord's gracious providence, I was expecting a lady of very high position in Warsaw—the daughter of the governor of Poland—to see me. I said it had better wait until she came. At 5 o'clock she arrived; I told her of the state of affairs, and she at once wrote a note to some official about it, and then we waited and talked. About 7:00 p.m. this very official appeared and presented me with the passport, saying he would telegraph to the frontier about it.

I then drove to the place of the English clergyman and had a small meeting in his drawing-room. At 9:00 the aforesaid lady called for me and we returned to the hotel. Then she came with us to the station and her man attended to our luggage, as we left Warsaw at 11:30. We went to sleep, and at 4 o'clock reached the frontier. I was fast asleep, but we roused up and got our things together, and turned out into private rooms again (the emperor's) where the gendarmes treated us with great politeness. We had some tea and our passports were carried off. At 5 o'clock we were told the German train was ready to take us on. We settled in, and then our passports were returned and we moved off out of Russia.

Thus the Lord got us happily over the frontier. The telegram from Warsaw had done much.

We reached Berlin at 12:00 and found our luggage was behind at the German frontier. Now I knew why the Lord was our "rereward!" They telegraphed for it, and we settled down at Berlin with the friends with whom we were to stay.

I took a meeting that night in Berlin. Our luggage turned up on Friday morning, and we left for England by the 12:00 train. Went on board at Flushing at midnight and had a smooth passage. We were at Victoria by 8:15 a.m., and at 9:30 were in Richmond—where we breakfasted.

"O magnify the Lord with me, and let us exalt his name together."

* * *

In a letter to her husband, written during the brief rest in Moscow, the natural longing of the little human "vessel" for her home and loved one is touchingly revealed:

>...I am thinking out the plan of getting home. I fear I shall reach London too late to get to Leicester that Saturday night. Do you think you could come up to meet me and spend Sunday with me at Richmond? The Hanburys would be delighted—could you manage it?... My difficulty is this, I cannot travel straight on night after night in the train, and Mr. Titterton has begged me to rest at Warsaw. There, he has to get police permission for the tiniest meeting in his drawing room, and the Countess S— has obtained a special permit for him to arrange a little group of English friends—so, *so* dry... I will wire you from Berlin just before I leave, that you may

know the time of arrival. If you possibly can manage it, I should rejoice for us to be together for the Sunday at Richmond—it would be *hard* to be in England and not see you at once... Neither you nor I offer to the Lord that which "costs us nothing," do we?... Do pray that all the Lord has sent me for may be rapidly done in the last few days, so that I can leave without feeling I am leaving *too soon*...

From a circular letter sent after reaching home, to the circle of praying friends:

My dear friends and faithful intercessors,

I herewith send you the journal of my visit to Russia, that you may join with me in praise and thanksgiving to our God for all his wondrous works... All that it has meant you will know only in eternity; until then, the greater part of the work must remain as the Lord's secret. That it has been purely and only God, through a broken vessel, you all know—and that all the glory is his. I did nothing but *watch him work*. I had only to be 'NOT disobedient' to his leadings. May it encourage each of us more fully to 'launch out into the deep'...

I cannot leave the subject of Russia without begging you to bear that great empire on your hearts in continual prayer. Pray that God will, in his own time, give them religious freedom...

Yours in his blessed hand,

Jessie Penn-Lewis

The Lord's "little flock" in St. Petersburg would gladly have kept the messenger for a longer period had not many waiting engagements in England called her home. Her Highness Princess Nathalie Lieven pressed her to stay in her country home for a time of rest before returning, and a letter received by Mrs. Penn-Lewis shortly after her arrival in England is a link with one of God's precious martyr-saints of Russia, well-known for her labors in the gospel and her connection with such servants of God as Dr. Baedeker and Lord Radstock:

Cremon, 23rd February, 1897

Thank you dear Mrs. Penn-Lewis for your kind note ... I am indeed very sorry that you could not come and have a rest here, not taking in consideration the joy we would have had in the fellowship in the presence of our Master. But as it was not our Father's will, so I know it was the right thing for you to return straight to England. The Lord shows us, step by step, that we have to do his will, and indeed consider our *selves* dead. I understand you thoroughly, my dear sister, and can only wish you God's abundant blessing wherever you go and whatever work he gives you to do.

I am thankful for having had the joy of meeting you on earth, before we meet in the presence of our beloved Master ... We shall be *very* happy to see you again if our Father will bring you back to Petersburg one day.

My three girls and Miss K— send you their hearty Christian love. Goodbye, dear sister in the Lord. May the grace of our Lord Jesus Christ be with you.

Yours affectionately in the Risen One,

N. Lieven

Space forbids the quoting of many letters from Russia here, but the following brief extracts serve to show that the work done was not in any sense an evanescent one, dependent upon the presence of the messenger:

St. Petersburg, May, 1897

Thank you ever so much for your letter and the notes of the beautiful London meetings. We are all reading them by turn, and I cannot tell you how blessed they are to us. Indeed, the Lord has been revealing more to us within the last few months than during twenty years past. When the notes come back to us, we shall have them translated for those who do not know English. We have now found a Christian lady who translates well, and we hope to have all your booklets done, little by little, as well as your Bible readings ...

It is wonderful to feel the new links that are forming between the souls the Lord is leading into the deeper knowledge of himself. The work that the Holy Spirit begun through you among God's children here is evidently progressing silently since you left ...

* * *

We cannot pass from this first visit to Russia without some further reference to the two sisters who lent their carriage daily for the use of the Lord's messenger. Ladies of high position, related indeed to the family of the czar (and with a title so long as to be inconvenient for ordinary use), Miss Olga Wolkoff and her sister heard the voice of God calling them into co-service with "the little apostle from England," as many lovingly called her; and from this time onward, God planted these Russian sisters into the roots of her ministry in a way that only Mrs. Penn-Lewis herself could fully tell. In all her future journeyings on the continent of Europe, she was accompanied by the younger sister (often referred to in the journals as "the Courier"), who would travel to London to pick up her frail charge, and carry through all the arrangements and business of the journeys, watching over and caring for her with the thoughtful devotion of a mother, while the elder sister "gave herself" to the ministry of prevailing prayer for both message and messenger.

The month of August (1897) was spent with these beloved friends in Switzerland as a time of rest and recuperation, with practically no meetings, though some translation work was carried through. A few extracts from the record of this real "holiday" will give us a glimpse into the God-given friendship which was to mean so much for the kingdom.

"Let us get up early to the vineyards."

Song of Songs, 7:12

"There is no room for sloth in a life of obedience. There is ceaseless activity in the realm of the King of Kings. 'My Father worketh hitherto, and I work,' said the Lord Jesus when he was on earth in human form. If the angels are given charge over his hidden ones, to 'keep them in all their ways' (Ps. 91:11), they have much to do. There is a 'creaturely activity' that hinders God, and a 'passivity' that is not of God, a passivity that is only another name for sloth. When the Lord is permitted to still the fuss and activity of the creature, and to bring the soul into restful co-operation with him, he is able to work through his instrument MIGHTILY! (Gal. 2:8, A.V.), the soul adding on her part 'all diligence,' even to the getting up early, as the master did, to see to the vineyards—first, O hidden one remember: in intercession WITHIN the veil!"

Chapter 6

In Journeyings Often

1897–1898

A Visit to Switzerland—Some light on the difficulties of work in Russia—Second visit to St. Petersburg—To Finland and Copenhagen

Journal: Paris, 27th July, 1897

I left Victoria at 11:00 a.m., meeting Miss S. Wolkoff and Miss Kruse there ... We had a smooth passage and pleasant crossing. At Calais nothing would suit my kind friends but a first class sleeping salon, so that I could lie down all the way to Paris ... At Paris Miss Olga Wolkoff met us, and we drove to Hotel de Holland. I found a lovely suite of rooms, private salon and bedrooms, all opening one into the other and all on to a balcony, from whence we could look out on Paris and get plenty of air. To my great amusement, I found the dear Wolkoffs had their Russian bedding with them, and on my bed I found four pillows covered with pink silk and fine lawn pillowcases. They looked lovely. On the bed was a yellow pongee silk wadded coverlet—made for my use, I heard. I got to bed after many questions as to what I needed, and at midnight came again an anxious procession of Miss Wolkoff and her maid, bearing a hot water bottle and a nightlight, which they had forgotten! All their kindness and love is very touching.

Paris, July 28th

After tea in my room, we left the hotel for a drive ... In the afternoon I rested, and at 5 o'clock we again drove, ending with a visit to the Louvre Magazin, a very fine shop. Miss Wolkoff wanted to give me some gloves, so she bought a dozen pairs for me and various other things. Their kind hearts seem to wonder what more they can do. My English gloves they did not like—I must needs have French ones.

Interlaken, July 29th

We were to leave for Interlaken at 11:20, and sleeping cars were taken—an extra one paid for that I might be alone... At Spiez came the first sight of the Jungfrau, the snowy queen of the Alps. At 1 o'clock we reached Interlaken and drove to our hotel. We look over the town, and our suite of rooms takes one side of the hotel. A private salon with a beautiful large covered balcony in the center, and on each side of it two bedrooms—mine the end one, also with a balcony, looking toward Lake Brienz and on the left at the Jungfrau... we have a most extensive and all round view...

They are very good to me. I think of Paul's words, "I know how to be abased *and how to abound*"—the latter is my portion just now. I am not sure but that I prefer the first—it is more bracing. Nevertheless, in all things "I have learned the secret," and "none of these things move me." I suppose my Father would not thus have dealt with me if he did not know the "abounding" *would not get inside!* I wonder sometimes what he means by it all—why he should do it—unless it is to prove that the abasing and abounding are all alike in him, and one passes through each in spirit untouched by either...

I forbade another midnight procession last night; and when I was just getting to bed a tap came at the door, and a voice, "We are afraid of the midnight procession—but please will you drink?" (that is, would I have some milk).

Sunday, August 1st

Most lovely weather. The morning I spent in my room alone, then we lunched on our balcony; and after tea we had reading and prayer, spending the evening in the same way. We are too far out of the town to go to any service without driving, and we see nothing of the hotel visitors. This is real rest! No strangers, and we four of one mind for restful, effortless fellowship. God could not have planned better.

August 2nd

At 9:45 we drove to a little station and entered an alpine railway going to the top of a mountain called Schynige Platte. It took an hour and a quarter to go up, and the view as we ascend is most wonderful—one moment, the plateau on which Interlaken is built, and the two glorious lakes at each end of it; then as we curve round the side of the mountain we see the Valley of Lauterbrunnen, and then the Valley of Grindelwald. At the top the air was lovely, and before us was spread a magnificent range of snow mountains...

Monday evening we spent at the translation of one of the *Pathway* leaflets into Russian. They had done it roughly in Russia; but so many expressions could not be translated into Russian that they wanted to go over it with me, so that I could alter, and give them other words to take the place of the peculiarly English expressions.

August 4th

In the morning we drove along the right-hand side of Lake Thun, the road winding through tunnels cut in the rock. It was very beautiful and I enjoyed it so much. In the evening we were at the translation again (*The Glorious Secret*)...

August 6th

Tomorrow we move to our mountain retreat at Abendberg. We can return here later if we wish, but a week of real quiet, where tourists do not go, will be good. There are some Christians there also...

I have not had much quiet for reading or writing. The long daily drives have taken the mornings, and I have been so tired that I have slept in the afternoons; and then the Russian translation, dinner, and early bed have taken the rest of the days. I have had to "let out the tired" these first days, and hope for more quiet reading in our retreat. Several times the Lord has given me Psalm 91, and there I rest...

A letter came from a Mons. B— saying they had heard I was there, and he and his family are staying at Abendberg—could he come for a chat. So he came on Sunday afternoon—a true worker in the Spirit.

Abendberg, August 16th

Yesterday we each had a quiet morning, with a Bible reading after tea, in our private sitting room. Two German ladies joined us at their own request. Now it is wet, and we are finishing letters and re-packing our trunks to return to Interlaken tomorrow. Here we shall stay until Friday, then go on to Vevey to see the Lake of Geneva, starting for England on the 24th, as I want a couple of days in London to see some Russian friends who are there, returning to Leicester on the 28th, and then to Wales on September 2nd...

* * *

The whole party returned to England together at the end of August, and thus the great desire of the Russian friends to meet Mr. Penn-Lewis was fulfilled. Remaining in England during September, they were present at the week of meetings at Langland Bay (S. Wales), and at the Rothesay Convention, in both of which Mrs. Penn-Lewis was taking part. At these gatherings, also, another friend from Russia, Baron Nicolay, was present, and a weekend spent by him in the home of Mr. and Mrs. Penn-Lewis at Leicester resulted in a warm friendship springing up between the two men.

Looking back, in the light of the literature work which grew up in later years, it is striking to see the "vision" which God gave to these spiritually childlike Russian ladies. They declared that they saw, in the purposes of God, a worldwide ministry lying before the one through whom God had so greatly blessed them and their own circle. They therefore spent much time and thought, during their stay in London, in purchasing and sending down to Leicester a quantity of "equipment" for future needs! A room was furnished as a study, with desk, bookcase, nests of filing drawers, a typewriter, and paper and envelopes of every kind, shape and size; (many of these things have been in useful service for God from that day until the present time!). Reference is made to these gifts, and others, in the letters of Mrs. Penn-Lewis to her "Beloved Philippians"—a loving title of which it is not difficult to find the genesis!

* * *

Written after the return of the Russian friends to St. Petersburg:

Leicester, October 24th, 1897

Beloved Philippians,

The Lord pour upon you his fullest blessing for all your loving ministry to the most unworthy little earthen vessel he could have found. Phil. 4 keeps coming to me—"I have all and abound... I am full, having received the things which were sent from you. An odor of a sweet smell, a sacrifice acceptable, well-pleasing to God... My God shall supply all your need according to his riches in glory by Christ Jesus"...

We had good meetings [S.A.G.M. meetings in London], the Lord mightily in the midst. I was given quite a fresh message on 'stewardship' in Luke 16, specially that God was watching to see how we handled the earthly goods handed to our care as "another man's" (that is, *God's*) ere he committed to our stewardship the "true riches." If we failed in being faithful in that which is least—the earthly things—then God saw that we should fail to be faithful in the usage of the heavenly mysteries. How solemn this is! Faithful to God in present opportunity and service, and then given the greater... It was so much to my own heart, and I resolve that God shall get out of my life and surroundings in the future even more than in the past. "Necessity is laid upon me. If I do this of mine own will I have a reward—if not, still a stewardship is entrusted to me" (1 Cor. 9:16, R.V.)...

On Tuesday I go to Coventry Convention... I hear that all the ministers and their wives have been asked to tea by the convention committee, and I am to speak to them, on Thursday from 5 to 7. Please pray much for me...

After a flying visit by the two sisters to England in November 1897, to talk over plans for further ministry in St. Petersburg the following January:

Leicester, November 11th, 1897

Thank you for letting me know of your safe arrival [home]. The Lord prospered you in the path of his blessed will... He has so clearly taken in hand the pattern of your lives, and he will reveal his mind step by step...

But it is strongly on my heart to ask you now to be satisfied concerning my needs—I want you now to be looking to him to show you how we are to be his channel of blessing to others. I thank him again and again for giving you the ministry of intercession for me. Now, beloved ones, enter into fellowship with me, and stand with me in God to look out on the fields white unto harvest, and ask what are his purposes through us, as one heart and soul for others... So do ask our Father if he does not want you to begin at the translation of *The Pathway*. Do not, I pray you, spend the weeks between your arrival home and our January meetings in much preparation for me...

The enclosed copy of a letter which came today from Moscow will encourage you! I felt deeply touched and humbled at the faithfulness of our God! I was in Moscow three days, and felt so sure that God had not given me touch with one soul. Did we think there was one soul in Moscow able to take the message of *The Pathway*? But the Father knew he had one... It has been the greatest joy, for no place I have ever been into has failed to have one touch of God...

Beloved, Russia is on my heart!... You are God's chosen vessels to send these messages into Russia—see your stewardship! There is no need for you to spend much time or thought in further caring for the messenger... the Lord plainly tells me we must now stop thinking of the earthly things and turn our whole attention to the need of souls... You have been his channels in arranging machinery for the work, and he will now take you into fuller purposes than that...

If the Holy Ghost takes hold of you, according to 1 Chron. 28:19, he can inspire you to translate *The Pathway* before I come, so that it will only need a little conversation, and I can bring the MSS away with me. If you will respond, and not say "Who am I... that I should... God will take hold of your mind and your pen. You are only to be a channel... The time is short—let us arise and say, "Thine is the power and the glory—here am I. I will not be disobedient to the heavenly vision"...

Will you think of your time as a stewardship, and ask the Lord not to let it be wasted by any unnecessary talk over all the earthly side of our travels? Pass on the spiritual lessons, but forget the rest. The time is too precious. Ask the Lord to keep all waste out of your lives, to make the uttermost out of every moment, and to reduce all the necessary earthly duties to the least possible amount of waste or time.

I want to tell you how I see God reaching the whole world with these printed messages! The very first use of the cardboard boxes you bought has been to send a very large order to the Rev. H. B. Macartney to take back with him to Australia! He is vicar of a church in Melbourne, and no one could do it so well … He returns next week and is going to send the booklets to Australian conventions and scatter them throughout the colony. Glory be to God!

Next, I send you a letter from America. It touches me when poor people write for the booklets. I shall send this dear soul a small parcel as a gift. I see so clearly my stewardship—I must take every open door to scatter them; and when people cannot afford to buy, I feel God wants me to give, as far as I can … So you see how matters are developing. I could not do these things had you not been faithful to your stewardship; but now I have a trust committed to me, and you are partners in issuing these messages of God in all the world …

Next, I have heard that Miss Soltau goes (to China) on Wednesday week. The will of the Lord be done. The time is short, so short! There must be no waste of the master's vessels or time. In heaven we shall have time for the fellowship—now, necessity is laid upon us. I am ready to be spent out to the uttermost for our Master's glory …

With what joy did the two Russian sisters see their stewardship and embrace it!

"Thank you ever so much for your long and loving letter," Miss Olga Wolkoff replied, a few days later. "We feel deeply touched by it. You are as the voice of God to us, and we do trust the Lord will enable us to be obedient to his call, and through your faithful stewardship fulfil all his purposes concerning Russia and all over the world. It would be a great joy and honor for us to be joined to you in this blessed work. With thankful hearts we say 'Yes' to the Lord, asking him to guide us and be our wisdom and power"…

The departure of Miss Soltau for China was a keen loss, deeply felt, for from the days of the mission at Richmond in 1892, a close tie and deepening fellowship had existed between these two truly "emptied" vessels. But God was pressing upon Mrs. Penn-Lewis, more and more, that "time" itself was a stewardship for which his children would have to give account; and deeper and deeper came the conviction that in the printed message God had an arrow that would wing its way where the spoken word could never reach. By this time there were quite a number of small booklets in print, and several somewhat larger ones, including *Conflict in the Heavenlies,* the substance of addresses given on Good Friday 1897 at the China Inland Mission Hall, which, after running through two editions, eventuated in the much larger and fuller exposition of the same subject, *The Warfare with Satan and the Way of Victory.*

In this brief memoir it is impossible to give any adequate account of the abundant labors of these years and the distances traveled, quite apart from the journeys abroad. After Russia in January, the engagements of Mrs. Penn-Lewis in 1897 included: Norwich, Derby, Manchester, London, Glasgow—five days' meetings at the Christian Institute, with gatherings of some 900 people. Here also she met and had fellowship with Dr. Elder Cumming, who was present in some of the meetings, and with whom she lunched at his home on one of the days. Then to Dunfermline and Edinburgh, and on to Birmingham, as one of the speakers at a three-day convention held in the town hall, where, on the third day, she addressed, in "a mighty hush of God's presence," a gathering of 3,000 souls. A brief period at home, given largely to literary work, then to Doncaster, Brighton, Richmond, and Finsbury. After August spent in Switzerland—Swansea, Langland Bay, Rothesay Convention, Manchester again, four days' meetings in Leicester, the annual meetings of the S. Africa General Mission in London (the valedictory meeting of another dear friend, Miss Bessie Porter); Coventry Convention, another visit to Edinburgh, a full week in Belfast, and in December, meetings at the headquarters of the Church Army in London. All these engagements being interspersed with short but precious times in her own home occupied with writing, a growing correspondence, many interviews and Bible Readings given in Leicester, chiefly in connection with Holy Trinity Church, where Mr. and Mrs. Penn-Lewis had found congenial fellowship and a warm friend in the vicar, the Rev. W. J. Thompson.

In 1898 the stream again moved on to Russia, Finland, and Denmark in the spring, with return visits to Finland and Denmark in June; and one result of these visits was the rendering into Finnish and Swedish of many of the booklets then in print, which had followed the issue of *The Pathway*.

An illuminating sidelight upon the difficulties of all evangelical work in Russia in those days, and the extraordinary secrecy with which any spiritual ministry had to be undertaken, is gained from a letter referring to the proposed second visit of Mrs. Penn-Lewis to St. Petersburg. The chaplain of the British-American church, whose kindness and sympathetic help are referred to in the journal of her first visit, wrote in October 1897:

> I have just heard from a friend that he leaves for Berlin today, and I take advantage of the opportunity of getting a letter posted on the other side of the frontier.
>
> So many 'sectarians,' as they are called, attended your meetings in our hall last year that the attention of the ecclesiastical authorities was drawn to the fact; and I received a hint that some who are not favorably disposed attempted to make trouble.
>
> Personally, I am prepared to run any risk when God's work is to be done; but so many interests are involved, and amongst them that of God's work itself, in the relation which my church and its pastor bears to the authorities here, that I am bound to be very careful not to prevent further usefulness by immediate and temporary efforts.
>
> If, therefore, you can possibly find a center other than our hall for your meetings, will you do so? I will talk over the matter with Baron Nicolay when he comes. But I am so desirous to see you here again, that if the refusal of our hall would block your way, I should probably feel compelled to do my utmost to persuade my council to invite you. All the council members, however, are more cautious than I, and I might fail. On your last visit I did not consult them, but with a clearer view of possible danger, I am morally bound to submit the matter to them.

I write in greatest haste, but believe me, in fullest sympathy and with an earnest desire to do God's will.

With warmest regards, Yours very sincerely,

A. Francis

Fines, confiscations, imprisonments, and exile were remorselessly imposed upon any who dared to differ from the czar's religion…

The enemies of evangelical truth did not hesitate to point even to certain well-known princesses—widowed ladies—whose only offence was that of Daniel, 'concerning the law of their God,' and demanded their banishment. Their over-zeal in this instance, however, met with a stern rebuke from the czar. 'Let my widows alone!' he exclaimed. And thenceforward they entertained their Christian guests and held Bible-readings and prayer-meetings in their drawing-rooms, none daring to make them afraid.[1]

It was in the drawing-rooms of these noble ladies that Mrs. Penn-Lewis gave many of the Bible readings mentioned in her journals. During her second visit, however, as will be seen from the chaplain's letter, the greatest caution was necessary in writing or speaking of the spiritual work accomplished. In after years Mrs. Penn-Lewis would tell, in rare moments of reminiscence, of blessed gatherings held in an upper room of a certain palace, where the princess and her Christian coachman might be seen kneeling together, with others, to partake of the Lord's Supper, the company dispersing afterwards in twos and threes through different exits, that it might not be known that there had been a meeting of the hated "dissenters." Two photographs of a beautiful woman in court dress, signed "Alexandra Josephine," which always occupied a double frame in Mrs. Penn-Lewis' room, were a valued memento of several "command" visits to a grand duchess (aunt to the czar), who hungrily drank in the message of "life out of death," and who remarked on one of the occasions, "I am writing all you tell me to my daughter, the Queen of Greece."

Brighter days were in store for the Christians of Russia, when

---

1   See *Dr. Baedeker and His Apostolic Work in Russia* by R. S. Latimer. (Marshall, Morgan & Scott Ltd.)

some eight years after the time of which we write, the czar gave his subjects freedom in matters of religion. "The greatest event of Russian history" (then), was the edict of liberty of conscience of 1905; and in all parts of the empire, men and women left the Greek Orthodox Church and became evangelical Christians. Surely, in the providence and foreknowledge of God, a season of sowing and reaping, in preparation for the avalanche of suffering and martyrdom which, in the next decade, overwhelmed the vast empire of Russia, sweeping into its maelstrom many true and humble servants of the King of Kings amongst the nobility of the land.

After much correspondence with the friends in St. Petersburg, and much earnest prayer on both sides that their faithful God would hinder all arrangements outside or beyond his perfect will and purpose, on January 18th, 1898, Mrs. Penn-Lewis once more set out for Russia, Miss Sophie Wolkoff coming across to London in order to travel with her.

"I believe our God means me to come," she says in a letter to Miss Wolkoff, written on receipt of Mr. Francis' communication ... if only for the inner circle, to deepen and establish the work begun last year; and *then* will come the hundredfold fruit which no man can quench or hinder ... It seems to me the best way would be to have English drawing-room meetings for the English, German ones for the Germans, and very quiet little groups of Russians *only by invitation,* in your room ... Let us not attempt public work. I believe God is sending me for the few of the inner circle, and my coming had better be kept quite secret ... I believe if we are all careful, and work quietly and faithfully, all can be managed ...

Extracts from Letters

St. Petersburg, January 28th, 1898

I am going to write a letter to you which you will understand to be only about *surface matters.* There is much that is *vital,* and for all eternity, worth the long journey here.

You will have heard that I had quite an exciting start, by crossing the Channel on a foggy night and having a little collision on the way. Our foghorn made a great row all night—who could sleep! When at last there came a crash, I knew what had happened. The other vessel, in backing, carried away a good deal of our bow, etc., and left a big hole in her side above watermark.

All's well that ends well! We got to Berlin twelve hours after our proper time, and I was very tired. One night on the steamer with the foghorn blowing, and then another night (not anticipated) in a first class carriage (but no sleeping berths), hooked on to a slow train which stopped with a bump and shriek at every tiny station, certainly was not what we hoped. However, it was well we were on land, so we thanked God and took courage.

At Berlin it was clear cold air and bright sunshine. We stopped for the day at Hotel Continental. All day I had interviews, and a meeting at 5 o'clock, translated by Count Bernstorff.

We had most comfortable sleeping coupes for the journey to Warsaw. We settled in at Friedrichstrasse station at 10:50 at night. I was so tired I went to bed, and slept as well as if I had been at home. My Russian companion never seemed tired or sleepy. She had the tea basket out and tea ready for me at 6:00 on the Thursday morning. At 7:00 we were turned out at the Russian frontier—Alexandrovna—and I had the amusement of watching the officials peep into my baggage. It all looked so innocent; they only looked in and shut it down again, whilst some people had even their medicine bottles uncorked and had to turn out every corner. We had some tea, and then started again.

At Warsaw a meeting had been arranged for the evening. God wrought gloriously—far beyond last year! We were asked to lunch with Count and Countess P— on Friday... We talked all afternoon, and at 5 o'clock came a telephone call from a lady who had been with them at the meeting—"where was I to be found?" They told her I was there, and she hurried round—broken-hearted. "How could she find the way to God?" She did not even know the A.B.C. (she said) of having faith! I shall not forget, as we knelt and I opened the Bible at Matt. 11, how she placed her finger, in its white kid glove, on the words "I will give you rest," and came to him for peace...

A little adventure came again at the Hotel Bruhl, for all our luggage had gone downstairs when my Russian companion exclaimed "the tickets!" The carriage was waiting and we had not too much time, but she was in such a state of fright that she could not remember when she had them, what they were like, or anything else. I motioned to the waiter to bring back the baggage, and calmly hunted through her bags, etc., but no tickets! At last, just, and only just, in time—a shock-headed Russian peasant put his head in at our door and handed us the tickets! They had been laid down on the Gladstone bag and carefully carried downstairs upon it, until in the street they had slipped off. It was very important, because sleeping coupes are scarce.

We just caught the train and soon went to rest. I was so glad to wake up and see the (now) familiar snow on Saturday morning, and through the snow we plodded all day until we reached St. Petersburg at 7:30.

Miss Olga Wolkoff met us, and a tall footman to take our etceteras. Outside was their closed carriage. The coachman remembered me and smiled. By the way, you know the bigger the coachman is, in Russia, the better the style! They wear a great fur coat and a beefeater's hat, and look about two yards round the waist. If the man is thin, they put cushions all round him to make him look big! One day in the sledge, Miss Wolkoff told me the great big man who was driving us was a very thin man—he didn't look like it!

I feel the air of the indoor life very much. Before I could sleep on Sunday night I had to have the windows open and the room refreshed with cold air. You can hardly imagine what it is like—not one chink where a breath of outside air can come in. I am bound to go out to be able to stand it.

Monday morning we went in the sledge to the islands, just where the Neva sends water into the Gulf of Finland. There are many canals and rivers running out of the great Neva, and all frozen. Last week there was what they call an inundation. The current of the Neva is so strong that it runs down into the Gulf of Finland at a great rate; then a mighty wind came and forced it back until it burst the ice and threw up on the banks great blocks of ice like rocks. These we saw as we drove along. Then, looking out to sea, I saw on the ice a kind of triangular raft on great skates, and sails put up so away they went on the ice just like boats with sails. It must be very pleasant.

Driving back we passed, on the Neva Quay, the Winter Palace. We could see the emperor was in residence, as stationed about all the entrances and round about the palace were special police—fine looking men in light gray coats—on special duty.

On Monday it snowed heavily, and on Tuesday came a keen frost. I drove out to a suburb to lunch with an English clergyman. The air was keen; the sun was shining. The hair on the horses stood out like coconut chips. The beards of the men, and even the eyelashes, were frosted. One dare not breathe one breath *direct,* or one's lungs rasp. Only eyes and nose can be allowed to be seen on days like these. One heavy fur coat is not enough—over that I wear a *shooba,* a long cloak lined with gray Siberian squirrel, and a collar lined with black beaver—high up, until one's head is buried in it—and over my astrakhan hat a thick shawl. Then cloth boots, high, lined with flannel and fur; rugs, hot water bottles to the feet, and over all, the heavy bearskin belonging to the sledge.

It is most interesting to watch the life around: the sledges, the ice, the people, the gendarmes. One poor fellow came too hurriedly round a corner, until his sledge swerved and made his horse dance. The gendarme ran after him and gave him such a bang with his sword—more forcible than polite!

On Wednesday came a thaw and fine rain; three degrees above zero is not pleasant here. We went out in the closed brougham, and had to shut the windows because of the mud flying in. At night it began to freeze again, and on Thursday the streets were like glass.

On Friday morning we went out in the sledge on the sunny side of the Neva, and the horses simply flew on the icy roads, with the sledge slipping along behind. I have been out most mornings. The other parts of the days are taken up with other matters, but Saturday I keep free for a real holiday. They said I should have a drive in a Russian troika this time, so this morning (Saturday) we went by train to Tzarskoe-Seloe, just outside St. Petersburg, where the emperor mostly lives, and there we got a troika—something the shape of a sledge, but for four, and not unlike a cockle-shell on runners. To it they harness three horses, one high one in the middle and a shorter one on each side. The harness is very gay with color and bells. The driver is gaily dressed—and away you dash on the snow. We drove about the park, and went right into the quadrangle of the palace, which is magnificent—all white, with bronze figures and ornaments. We drove for two and a half hours in lovely park roads, between fir trees, down hill and up. How I enjoyed it! When the horses had a clear road before them and were given rein, they flew, the bells jangled, and the driver shouted to anybody likely to get in the way—it suited me exactly—this wild dash on the snow. I do like swift driving, I must confess.

We reached Tzarskoe station for the return train. There was a straight road to it and our driver wanted to do it in style, so he gave rein to the horses and we dashed up to the station with all the sledge drivers waiting and watching to see how he did it. The horses were wet with their work. At St. Petersburg the landau was waiting, and we got home in time for afternoon tea.

Now I must close. As I have said, I have gathered up the surface matters to interest you, but remember it is only surface. God is working and doing great things—eternity will tell that tale.

I go to Helsinki in Finland for a few days on the 7th of February, so as to get a break from here. All is well, and I am quite well.

En route, Helsinki to St. Petersburg, February 11th, 1898

Fourteen hours' journey today gives me the opportunity of writing you another letter, again more or less on surface matters. It is nice to remember various points of interest. I am keeping no journal this time because so much cannot be written of really vital matters.

All last week I was in St. Petersburg, driving in mornings when able, and various other engagements in afternoons and evenings, so that I had hardly time to write at all.

On Saturday morning, Miss Olga Wolkoff and I were out in the sledge, when, as we were driving down the Grand Morskoi, the footman said the empress was coming. We stood a moment, and her closed carriage dashed by with a great Cossack in gorgeous livery behind. Everybody raised their hats; we fell in behind and followed the carriage. Our coachman said in Russian, "She is going to her sister's; we will go too!" So we dashed after her. We had a pair of horses, and the gendarmes began to think we were attached to her suite, as we were following the carriage full speed; so we were saluted as we dashed along. Then at last she drove into the courtyard of her sister-in-law's palace; and we watched a moment as she stepped out, dressed for lunch. We then turned back and had a few salutes as we passed, having much enjoyed our scamper. On Monday afternoon we were out again and she came by, this time in an open sledge with two beautiful horses and the brilliant Cossack behind her. We did not follow this time, as she was near the Winter Palace and evidently returning home.

On Saturday afternoon we again went by train to Tzarskoe—the suburb of St. Petersburg where the emperor mostly resides. Outside the station our sleighman recognized us and rushed up with his sleigh. Then we secured a troika and had again a two hours' drive, all through the lovely park around the Tzarskoe Palace. It was snowing, and was like driving in fairyland. Great pines all white with snow, frozen lakes, indescribably beautiful; the great white palace gleaming in this fairy scene, as here and there we caught sight of it in the trees.

Finland

On Monday night we left for Finland. Not a comfortable journey. They said the sleeping car was broken, so they had put on a first class car, which seemed to me rusty with age. It groaned and creaked and scraped most dreadfully, and hot steam from the stove made us think we should be cooked. Poor Courier had the seat where the steam was coming in, but I did not know of it until next day. We reached Helsinki at 10:30 Tuesday morning...

At night I had a meeting in the Y.W.C.A., and I was just spent out. I could not get to the people through my translator. I was so tired next morning I felt it must be altered.

I had seen a lady who seemed just the right one—she understood what I wanted to say; but she was delicate, and her husband would not let her undertake it. I begged Madame Forselles to telephone to her husband how much I needed her. He consented, and we had a most blessed meeting... a large hall filled with people, and my "channel" was so fully one with me that I was as free as if I had been speaking in English. These meetings were all in Swedish.

Then on Thursday I had another Swedish meeting. The people were deeply moved. These meetings were worth the long journey. Thursday night I had another meeting in the same hall, translated into Finnish by a Finn. He, too, perfectly understood, and I had great liberty. It is deeply moving to meet the Lord's people in different countries and to find all with the same inward life, taught of the same Spirit. And then the hunger to know more of the life of God is very touching. England seems to me in awful responsibility, with all the light and teaching there.

Between the meetings at Helsinki we had some sleigh drives. We found one man who could understand Russian, so he took us about. Helsinki is on the coast, a beautiful watering place in the summer. Esplanades and a lovely bay, with many islands. As far as the eye could see, all was frozen. A great fortified island stood out in the center of the entrance to the bay. We drove to it on the ice, and all in and out of the fortresses, snow and ice everywhere. Then again we turned and went all along the ice on the sea, going inland. No need to say "is it safe?" Our Russian sleigh driver was quite interested. He drove us toward one island and said he had something to show us. We reached a great iron cage in the ice, on the edge of the island, and behold, a great white polar bear! Such a monster, and such a beauty! Snow white, with black nose and paws. Our horse would turn his back to it; he did not like it at all. On the island we went, and saw it was a kind of zoo, all deserted and buried in snow. All about we drove, meeting men on snow shoes; then we went to fresh cages, and lo, a Russian wolf—slim, graceful, like a beautiful gray dog. He danced about and got more and more frantic as our horse stood near. We were glad there were iron bars between.

As we drove back to Helsinki the scene was beautiful. On the land, the town covered with snow. At the quays, vessel after vessel frozen in. Out to sea, the great fortress island, little islands, white snow and dark fir trees in all directions. Ice and snow as far as you could see—driving past buoys that would otherwise be dancing in sea water—skating grounds marked off in squares with fir trees—all most interesting.

In Russia the country is so flat that it is very uninteresting, but Finland is most beautiful. It is not unlike Switzerland (only no mountains hereabouts) with its pine trees. Today the sky is clear blue, like a summer sky, and the sun dazzling and brilliant, making the snow glitter. Everywhere it is snow—forests of pines, and all dressed in white—fields all dazzling white, without a footmark on the pure white covering. It seems as if one would never be tired of gazing out at the beauty of the background of blue sky and the sunlight on the great pines dressed in white.

We reached the frontier at 9:00 tonight, and then I have a full week in Petersburg ere I turn homewards. My courier (Miss S. Wolkoff) is with me, and she is so good and thoughtful. We shall probably return to England by the Nord Express, the week after next.

I am very well and feel the benefit already of this brief change to Helsinki; the air is clearer and more bracing than St. Petersburg.

I have arranged about the translation of the leaflets into Finnish, and given permission for them to be published in a weekly Finnish paper...

* * *

The work in Russia finished, places were taken in the Nord Express and all arranged for a through journey home, with no customs troubles, etc., until reaching London; but the Lord had other plans. A letter arrived from Copenhagen that meetings were being arranged, and there seemed a clear call from God to change the plans and delay the home-going.

"The prospect" [of returning direct], wrote Mrs. Penn-Lewis to her husband,

> ...entirely fitted in with all I would personally have wished—but how could I dare one moment to yield to my personal wishes rather than give direct obedience to God?... How blessed it is that I can be sure of your acquiescence in what seems to be the will of God, and that you strengthen my hands to obey the indications of his guidance... This is the path of obedience, and for his dear sake we can so love the souls he died for, that we can give each other for his service; and the sacrifice of the present time is not worthy to be compared with the glory that shall be revealed in us—we shall come rejoicing, bringing in the sheaves!... I can truly say that all that would be fascinating to the flesh here is utterly naught to me. It does not appeal to one chord in me. Nothing but the yearning over souls and the intense vision of what they are to him through Calvary could uphold me and make it possible to stay on...

A rapid survey of this additional piece of service is given in a circular letter sent out to the prayer helpers on her return. We take up the story where the home letter left it:

> After one more week of deep proving of God in a special way, I left my "land of promise," and turning aside at Berlin (my Russian friend with me) we went across the Baltic Sea to Copenhagen... We arrived on Wednesday night. On Thursday went out to lunch to meet a group of leading Christians, and two hours over our Bibles to see "whether these things were so" followed. On Friday we had a drawing-room meeting at the same house—such a number of *men* present, who keenly followed every word. At 9:30 we broke up for tea! Then back to the drawing-room for an eager group to question me until 11:30 p.m. (practically another meeting!) Saturday this was repeated... On Sunday I had my only meeting by interpretation, a Salvation Army lieutenant being my interpreter, and well she did it. It was a most powerful translation—rapid, brisk, exact, almost to the inflexions of my voice. Her whole soul seemed in every word. The meeting was deeply moved, and there were many also who came to Christ.
>
> When the meeting was over I tried to get away (we had a two-day journey before us), but I was entreated to go upstairs a few minutes. There I found a small room full of workers, and three Lutheran pastors—"Would I tell them more about the Holy Spirit?" So I started again and told them how God had dealt with me as a worker, over the power of the Holy Ghost...
>
> At the station next morning came a little group of thankful hearts, and the last words I heard were these: "It is blessing for Denmark—great things will come out of this." Right along it has been all of God, "a path prepared to walk in." In every place it meant touching the leaders, those who must be God's future channels of blessing in each country. God is now evidently equipping his future instruments. There is little doubt that he is making preparations for some mighty movement that the near future holds, and those of us who are sent quietly and silently to the preparation of the future instruments may thank God and take courage...

"Oh mystery of mysteries, Calvary, dark Calvary! 'The sufferings of Christ, and the glories that should follow' are things which the angels 'desire to look into' (1 Pet. 1:11–12); yet fallen creatures despise and reject the Lamb, the object of all heaven's worship. In eternity alone, purified and freed from the restrictions of the body of clay, shall the redeemed from among men be able to understand the full meaning of his cross of shame, and in deepest worship sing—'Worthy art thou … for thou wast slain' (Rev. 5:9)."

Chapter 7

The Message of the Cross

1898

"In me first for a pattern"—Further work on the Continent—
The Conference of the Free Church Movement in Finland—
Monrepos, Viborg

Though so little could be said, at the time, of the weeks spent in St. Petersburg, letters written by Mrs. Penn-Lewis after her return home tell something more of the depths touched and the cost of it, revealing also how every deep spiritual truth God gave this messenger of his for his people came by way of an experimental "going through" in personal suffering, so that it might be said of her, as Paul said of himself, "in me first, for a pattern."

To Miss Soltau:

Russia, beloved! No tongue must tell what eternity will reveal. How God has changed the springs of most important lives! I have stood amazed at the people he has brought to me, and the matters entrusted to me. All last year's blessing had sunk in, and this year it has gone much deeper...

The last week in Russia was a week of conflict for the land. The vessel is broken as the mighty river breaks through... There was no resistance to the message—the souls drank it in, so it was nothing outward. But God gave me to understand then, clearer than ever before, that the conflict becomes more the dislodging of the hosts of darkness from the atmosphere—taking the ground in the name of the Lord and leaving the atmosphere occupied by the hosts of light, so that the Holy Spirit is free to work unhindered.

135

That last week the pressure on my spirit grew, until I was spent ...
On the Monday the Lord said to me, "Shall a land be travailed for
in but one day?" Then the word of the Lord came "pressed down
exceedingly, inasmuch as we despaired even of life"—but "we had
the answer (that it was) death in ourselves, that we might not trust
(have any resource) in ourselves, but in *God who raiseth the dead.*"

I saw that it needed his risen life now, to raise me from the depths
to the place of victory, far above all principality and power, and that
thus the travail would be over, the ground wrenched from the foe,
and the atmosphere clear. I rose up, and the life returned. On that
Wednesday night the people were broken; on the Thursday it was
glory; and throughout those last days God swept in mighty power.

Then I understood that, clothed in the "armor of light," God
sends us to the dark places of the earth to set our foot down and
take the victory in the name of the Lord. That in the travail we may
be "pressed down" until we are "as good as dead," in order that the
resurrection life of Jesus may lift us up in triumph to the place
of victory, "far above all." Then the hosts of darkness are defeated
and the Spirit of life can work unhindered in the souls around us.
Blessed be God!

Notes from diary:

Since my return home (on March 3rd) I have been so prostrate; but
I felt the Lord was allowing the bodily frame to relax, and he did
not allow me to go to my desk. On the 10th I took our "Quiet Day"
at Leicester—so weak, but God mightily manifested his presence,
and the next day I was better and able to write a little ...

Then came the adversary, and I could not get to the place of victory. I was sorely pressed—so much so that I was actually thinking
I was to retreat from the battlefield ... The Lord then showed me
that he had allowed me to rest, but in it I had "gone under," and
picked up my own natural life again. At first God had kept me
from writing, but now he could not use me for writing, because my
body was in the way, my natural mental activities aroused. I had
been living upon my old natural life again, and this was the reason
for the old symptoms and weaknesses being manifested—exhaustion, cough, etc.

Then the Lord took me to Col. 2:10–15. I saw that, with him, so to speak, I "put off" my old body, the body that the adversary could attack, the body with the natural life in it—that he, in his risen life, might triumph. There and then I definitely dropped my "body" at the cross as never before ... Since then, blessed be God, I am quite well.

The next day I went to Nottingham and had most blessed meetings. An old white-haired saint ... came to me and said so solemnly that God had given me great responsibility, entrusting me with the mysteries of the kingdom, and begged me to be faithful and not to shrink back ... I was awed. It was like the voice of God calling me afresh to the battlefield. I told the Lord that, having dropped my weak body and its weight at the cross, I would again rise up and be his messenger. My body was set free; the risen life began to flow again. The next day I went to my desk quite fresh in mind and body, and God began to pour his light through. He took me to Job and began to light it up, and for three hours I wrote as fast as he gave it to me. I believe he has given it for print ...

But God purposed another book before *The Story of Job* was to be completed—a book which could only be written out of the depths of a personal experience of fellowship with Christ in his death and in his yearning love over sinners.[1] On New Year's Day, 1898, the word of the Lord to his servant was the first chapter of Jeremiah, especially verses 10 and 17–19. Had she been saying in her heart, as the "message of the cross" in its deeper aspects was being revealed to her, "Ah Lord! Behold, I cannot speak, for I am a child!" Was it easier to say "Yes, Lord" as the knife of the cross operated in a deep personal experience of "filling up the afflictions of Christ," in anguish over a soul sunk in sin, than to go forth with the message to God's people, that only through an experimental "conformity to his death" in their own lives could they know the manifestation of the "life of Jesus" through them, to the world in darkness and the shadow of death?

But to her a "word from God," once unmistakably received, was ever an anchor firm fixed in the eternal faithfulness of her

1   *The Message of the Cross*, afterwards enlarged and issued as *The Cross of Calvary and its Message*.

God; and to the end of her days, in all the hard places where the frail natural framework would have been utterly crushed, this anchor consciously held: "Behold, *I have made thee . . . an iron pillar,*" and her heart replied, "There is *nothing* too hard for thee."

* * *

The new year had opened, in its first hours, watching over a soul under the power of the evil one; and on returning to England in March, the close contact and hand-to-hand fight for the deliverance of this soul was renewed, even to the point of physical breakdown. Toward Good Friday the storm gathered and broke, but "God meant it unto good," for only thus could his channel be prepared for the message. "We must drink of his cup, and be baptized with the baptism that he was baptized with, if we are to speak that which we know and testify of that which we have seen."[1] And through months of awful conflict with the enemy over this soul, and the final snatching of her out of his grip, God's servant received an education in the cross as the *dunamis* of God never to be forgotten.

Writing after the annual Good Friday gatherings at Mildmay, Mrs. Penn-Lewis gives a glimpse into the inner history of this message:

> Good Friday was blessed! God never gave me such a message before—the whole day on Calvary. And he took me to Calvary in experience for a fortnight before, from the hour that the message began to open to me . . . All this winter it has been, again and again, a being "delivered unto death for Jesus' sake," and the ten days preceding the Good Friday meetings were the most awful ten days of all my spiritual history.
>
> God gave me "the word of the cross" on March 28th, and from that moment it seemed as if all hell was roused. His hand was upon me, writing all he showed me, and I wrote in the teeth of it for a week . . . I thought I had seen his death before, but it was from the *outside*—the judgment hall, the forsaking, etc., but now it was from the *inside* of his heart. It was a drinking of "his cup" I have never

---

1   *The Message of the Cross*, from the preface to the first edition.

known before; and in the darkest hour he gave me Psalm 22... I felt the anguish *to* him of that moment when all the devils of hell seemed mocking, in the voices of those who stood round the cross, that his trust in God had been fruitless—that God would have answered if he had been pleased with him, and *his God had failed him!*...

My heart was at rest if it was his pathway. And then there came to me his definite promise that the message of Calvary so deeply wrought in the experience of the cross should go forth to the very ends of the earth and carry with it the power of the cross, and "life out of death" to seeking souls...

If the real sight of the cross will come to others as it did to me, it will indeed be a blessed book. It is very sacred to me. It seems as if my very life is in it, baptized in the valley of weeping. It is more "of God" than anything I have written, and seems the outcome of six years of his deep work in me—as though all had culminated in this! But it is "*always* delivered unto death." The book will always be stamped with Calvary, to me...

The latter part of some notes, made by Mrs. Penn-Lewis, of the case through which God taught her so much of his redeeming love and power, tells the rest of the story of *The Message of the Cross*—in respect to which God has, for more than thirty years, richly fulfilled his promise that he would use it to the blessing of seeking souls to the ends of the earth:

I went back to Leicester the next day [after Good Friday] to complete the written message. I felt that everything must stand aside to get the message out; such a cost must mean that God would speak through it. It was completed by Monday, except the last chapter; and on Tuesday night I went to London, on my way to meetings at Guildford. I should add that God granted my petition ere I returned to London. It was only withheld that I might "drink of his cup," for on that Tuesday he brought the soul to me entirely melted...

At home on the following Sunday, I waited before the Lord for the last chapter; and on my knees there came to me the vision of the Lamb in the midst of the throne. The last chapter seemed to be let down from the glory—and so it was finished. The following weeks meant ceaseless labor in proof correcting, and the details of issue ere I went abroad. But the battle was over, and the Lord helped me. From the first Sunday when the message was unveiled to me, to the day before I went abroad (May 20th) when I received the first copies, the anguish was gone through, the message written, printed and issued, in just about six weeks!

The journey referred to was another visit to Copenhagen, Stockholm, and Helsinki in the service of God; and the following extracts are from the journal relating to it.

Journal: Hamburg

We left London on the evening of May 20th and had a very good passage. At 5 o'clock on the 21st we reached Hamburg... so tired after the busy days at home and this specially wearing journey... Hamburg is lovely. The River Elbe is very wide, and here it seems to have flowed out into many lakes, around which houses are built... wherever you turn you come across hidden sheets of water. I was so tired, body and mind, that it was just the tenderness of God to give me this rest before reaching Copenhagen, where I knew I should have no leisure.

Copenhagen, Tuesday, May 24th

Before I was dressed this morning, I heard a voice in our sitting-room, and found a lady come with such a joyous welcome! God had met her on the first brief visit in February, and she was overflowing to tell me all that he had done. She had moved to their country house for the summer, but had come into Copenhagen on purpose for our meetings. I was so rejoiced to hear that she herself had already translated two of the leaflets and had them printed. It was a joy to hear that she had sent *The Glorious Secret* to her brother, Count—, whom God is using in evangelistic work, and as he read the booklet, the light flashed in upon him. With joy she said she hoped he would be at the meetings.

At 3:00 p.m. the first meeting began. All were to be in a drawing-room in the house of Count Moltke, made use of by the lord for many years... It really was a meeting of believers, and God was very present with us; but the evening meeting was larger, and deepened in the presence and power of the Holy Spirit. It sounds so little just to say this, but the faces of the people, the depth and receptivity of special ones before one's eyes, manifestly receiving the message into their hearts, cannot be told on paper. A group came to beg for an "inner circle" meeting at the hotel next morning, so it was arranged.

Wednesday, May 25th

At 11:00 a.m. my group arrived, and we sat round the table, about twelve of us. One, a lady I had not seen in February, said, "You have come this time *for me!*" She had heard nothing about "conformity to the death of Jesus," but all the winter she had been passing through it, and others had said she was "backsliding." She could not think what it meant, only she had the assurance herself that she was in the hand of God. Then came *The Pathway*,[1] and she saw what God was doing. She is at the head of a large work, and is manifestly a surrendered soul. All this group *meant* dealing with God, so without reserve we traced the story of the Jordan crisis, and the opened heavens which finally led to the real Calvary, the grave, the resurrection, and the throne. We sat over this for two hours, and it was a most precious time. Three months ago they were not ready for it, but God had laid hold of some then and had opened still more to them since through the printed messages... He had indeed prepared them, and now the Lord has an inner group going on with him to become buried corns of wheat in fruitfulness for Denmark.

At one o'clock they hurried away, and at 3:00 we had the afternoon meeting, a much larger one, and such a deep hush and receptivity. God is evidently going to deepen and deepen his work. The meeting over, they gave me tea, and sent me off for a drive; and at 8:00 p.m. we had our fourth drawing-room meeting. Most blessed indeed, the attention never flagged, as I spoke for nearly an hour and a half... we did not leave until 11 o'clock.

Thursday, May 26th

We could not have any fixed meetings today as it was a holiday. The eldest son of the crown prince, who had lately been married at Cannes, was to bring home his bride and make a state entry into

---

1   *The Pathway to Life in God.*

Copenhagen. We went to a house on the route and saw them arrive. This lull gave me time to get off some pressing letters, and I made good use of my time. So did the "inner circle," for they arrived again at 4:30 for another little meeting. Some had come direct from the reception at the palace—rushing away to make use of the opportunity of learning more of the heavenly life and its King! We had a most definite time, and talked over the practical points of the spiritual life until after 6 o'clock.

A carriage came for us at 7:30 to take us to a public meeting, where my old interpreter, the Salvation Army lieutenant, was to interpret for me. When I arrived, there was such a crowd of eager faces! The change since three months ago was marked. Then, no light on the faces; all was strange to them. Now, such keen, hungry faces. They knew what they wanted and were eager to hear. So deeply did the Lord work that, as I spoke, they broke out with responses. One gentleman had nodded his head approvingly at the preceding meetings, but at this one he was visibly broken down— and so with others. The word of God was "effectually working" and had free course …

Friday, May 27th

A lady came at 11:00 a.m. to go with me shopping … then I called on one who had not been able to go to the meetings, and at 2:30 we left for our steamer to cross to Malmo, in Sweden. At the quay a number came to bid us farewell, one after the other expressing gratitude to God for all he had revealed to them, and some bringing the loveliest flowers, until I was loaded …

At Malmo a lady met us, and we went to her house to dine, before driving to the Y.W.C.A. for meetings, by interpretation. Afterwards we had supper at the same house and then took the 9:50 train for Stockholm … As we were settling in, a group appeared on the platform, of some who had been at the meeting. They were quite melted … One said she was the head of a large school and so needed the fullness of Christ. The one request was, would I go back again? I said I left it to them to speak to God about it. He would plan. Only one meeting, and then to pass on! What a responsibility!

Stockholm, Whit Sunday, May 29th

A lovely day, but cold. We find our hotel opposite the royal palace ... This is a beautiful city, spotlessly clean. The foliage just now so green and fresh and the sky so blue! Miss Roos, the president of the Y.W.C.A., was my first caller, then Baroness Palmstierna, with whom I had stayed on my first visit.

At 1 o'clock we had the first meeting, in the rooms of the Y.W.C.A.... Many were speaking with great thankfulness of Mr. Charles Inwood's visit. They had never heard so fully and clearly about the Holy Spirit, and some had manifestly received him. I shrank very much from following with meetings so soon, lest I should hinder rather than help. But God had so clearly planned the path that I could trust him to guide me very specially, and later I saw why the Lord had done it. All the time, in the messages, I kept to the manifestation of the Christ which the Holy Spirit had come to give. The Holy Spirit taking possession of us, that he may lead us into fellowship with Christ and manifest his life through us, very fitly followed.

The evening meeting was announced as for the Y.W.C.A., but it was packed with other people, every corner, men and women. Room after room was filled; as far as my eye could see through further rooms, there were people standing! With great power God moved among us as I spoke on God's vessels and how he prepares them for his own use. Tea was served afterwards, and then we had another little meeting. Many were evidently touched by the Lord.

Monday, May 30th

Whit Monday! No meeting in town, but a Y.W.C.A. outing! A little steamer took us down the broad river to one of the innumerable islands, to the Y.W.C.A. summer home, which was to be dedicated and opened. About 200 of us—a few gentlemen, a reporter of course, and Prince and Princess Bernadotte and their children. It was a typical Y.W.C.A. outing. Arriving, everyone rushed over the new house. Then from a balcony, speaking to the crowd below, the president dedicated the home. After tea, a meeting, when I spoke from the same balcony (by interpretation). I did not know what the president had said, but as I listened to her, the Lord gave me a fresh message; and when I asked her afterwards what she had spoken about, it was my first message!

At 7 o'clock we left, and reached Stockholm about 7:45. My traveling companion (Miss S. Wolkoff) and I were invited to some house for tea, with three or four others. The prince very kindly put us into their carriage, and they walked, meeting us later at the house, where we had a blessed little prayer meeting to close the day.

Tuesday, May 31st

Today a meeting at 1 o'clock. Such a blessed time, and afterwards a chat with one or two. In the evening, a drawing-room meeting in the house of Prince Bernadotte. He presided and gave out the hymns and led in prayer. God most deeply touched hearts, on "The call to the cross,'" and "what shall it profit a man if he gain the whole world and lose his own soul?" After, we gathered for a time of questions. It was most blessed. Eternity alone will tell of God's work this night. The sense of the presence of God is impossible to describe…

Wednesday, June 1st

Again a meeting at 1 o'clock… Then at night a drawing-room meeting in the house of Dr. Fries (secretary of the Y.M.C.A.); each meeting growing deeper and deeper in liberty and consciousness of God's working; and again after tea we had questions and fellowship…

Thursday, June 2nd.

The last meeting at 1:00 p.m., the best of all! To watch the deeper and deeper breaking—the clearer and clearer light on the faces—tells one much. God had given them the Holy Spirit, and now he was just showing them how the Spirit would lead them into the path of the cross.; how he would reveal to them the life of Jesus; how death with him *must needs be,* for fruitfulness. It has been so clear, and his presence so manifest, one could see how it met the souls.

The booklets I had with me, hoping to reserve some for Finland, were all taken at the first meeting; and with joy some of the older workers said, "This is what Sweden needs—we have been waiting for the message of the cross."

The new book, *The Message of the Cross*, will be translated into Swedish at once. Thank God! With such shrinking I give this message, yet it invariably meets the need of souls. Oh the cross, the cross, the cross is the power of God! "I, if I be lifted up, will draw..." Ah, when shall we learn that there is a need in hearts that only the cross will meet, and that the Holy Spirit can make simple the deepest mystery of the cross to the youngest believer! Let us not withhold God's secret of the cross because we, in our human wisdom, think it too difficult. In proportion as we give the message in the power of God, it will be made clear to souls...

Returning to our hotel, we packed and left for our steamer, en route to Helsinki. On the quay again, such a large party gathered, bringing lovely bouquets of flowers. The prince and princess, who had not missed one meeting, came also, all bidding us a hearty God-speed... Hey me! What it is to be a messenger of the King of Kings! At 6 o'clock we moved off, with deep thanksgiving to God for such grace and tenderness to earthen vessels.

On board ship, Friday, June 3rd

It is truly the love of God's fatherly heart to give me this rest. The railway journeys try one so, the shaking, close carriages... But with a two-day sea passage to Finland to attend the annual conference of the Free Church Movement, the Lord has given superb weather. It is just the needed quiet and rest between the past busy days, and the still heavier week that lies before me in Helsinki... The beauty of this sea passage between Sweden and Finland is indescribable. The islands—sometimes only rocks—mostly covered with dark fir trees; the blue sea and sky, and the sunshine...

Helsinki, Saturday, June 4th

Up at 5:00 this morning to enjoy the sunshine... I stayed on the captain's bridge a good while; and presently, steaming between the islands, I recognized the great island fortress of Sveaborg at the mouth of the Helsinki Bay. In February we drove to this fortress upon the frozen sea, and now passed it in the steamer, and presently got into calm waters, mooring at the quay at 10 o'clock.

Apartments are very difficult to get... but they had kindly given us rooms at a sort of private hospital, and agreed to give us meals in our sitting-room, a large airy room with a balcony... A funny little lad waited upon us, a typical Finn, very polite. He bows and bows when he offers us anything—but no English! We could not say yes or no or give any orders. It has been so comical, and sometimes very awkward.

Before we had even had a meal, a gentleman called, the teacher of English at the University. He had written for permission to translate all my printed messages into Swedish, so had come at once to see me. He was truly being taught of God. Converted in America many years ago, God had been leading him deeply. He knew he had the *light* of all that it meant to be "crucified with Christ," but not the *life*...

Telling me of his conversion, he said a very true thing—a fact that has come to me many times, yet I never heard it said before. He told me that God had awakened him on board ship, and in America led him to an evangelist, who preached Christ to him, and his heart drank it in. Then the devil interfered, for the evangelist said, "Now *you must believe.*" His attention was turned to his part— of believing—and he said, "How can I believe?"—and fell into years of darkness and real unbelief. His heart had received the gospel, and he was already believing, until he was told he *must* believe! Ten years or more passed, struggling to believe, instead of looking to the finished work of Christ. It has often occurred to me that, in dealing with souls, directly you turn their attention to their *act of faith*, there is a cloud and a feeling that they "cannot."

So also with God's children. Absorbed with the finished work of Christ, dwelling upon it, the heart believes without knowing it. This is God's marvelous plan of drawing the soul out of itself and its sins by giving it a Savior on Calvary—a center of attention *outside itself.* Then he enters and does the work within.

After a long talk, this gentleman left, and we were just finishing a meal when Baron Nicolay of St. Petersburg called. He had come up to Helsinki in his yacht, and was so sunburnt... He asked if I was needing some air, and would take tea with him on his yacht. So away we went, and one of his sailors rowed us out to his float-ing home. It is entirely used for the Lord's work. He takes God's messengers to the various islands where there is no spiritual help, and often preaches himself. We had tea on deck, and the air was beautiful...

At 7:00 p.m. I had another appointment... At 9 o'clock came Herr Makinen, from the conference, which had been sitting all day, to tell me about the arrangements. The light nights make one forget the time. I could read my Bible in daylight at 11:20 p.m.

Sunday, June 5th

A quiet morning, and then at 1:30 to the Alliance House, where the conference meetings are being held. The people had been sitting since 11 o'clock, and it seemed impossible to expect them to take in anything after this; and the place was so hot! Mr. Makinen was to translate into Finnish, but it seemed dreadful to speak of spiritual things when their heads must be a "porridge," as a Russian girl once said, or "a salade," as another foreigner expressed it to me! A hot, restless meeting, and—interpretation! But God, who only doeth wondrous things, took hold, and there was stillness in a measure, as I spoke on the work of the Holy Spirit. I was amazed to see the whole meeting *move* as I touched on "Calvary," as if a spring had been struck. So visibly did the meeting bend forward that a lady with me remarked it, and it showed me the key the Lord had to the hearts in this conference. I had never seen it so marked before.

In the evening I was to speak at a large meeting in another hall, this time translated into Swedish... But the lady who was the only one who could interpret for me last time was not in town, though she had hoped to come on Saturday. They found a young girl who said she would try! My heart sank. I could not touch anything difficult with so young a helper. It was a large meeting, in such a large hall. It was a real test. My little interpreter was so shrinking that she looked as if she would burst into tears, but I encouraged her, and we rose together. The Lord gave the message, and I heard afterwards that he had really spoken to souls. My young helper was wonderfully strengthened in voice and self-forgetfulness—so the Lord triumphed.

Monday, June 6th

My first meeting was not until 5 o'clock, so I had a pleasant sail in the bay, and then a quiet talk with Baron Nicolay on his yacht. On my return, to my great joy, I found the lady whom I had expected to interpret for me... It had been a real test. I could only trust and "believe my way through"; and now, just in time for the important meetings, here she was! She, too, was rejoiced, and told me that on

Sunday she was in bed, ill, and in the evening suddenly felt quite well, so was able to come. She interpreted for me on Monday evening, and God set his seal upon it in great power and liberty.

What lessons this interpretation teaches one, of God's working through the earthen vessels. The *heart* of my young helper was right, but I was *limited by her capacity*. I could not give through her all I wanted to say, because she could not understand so as to transmit the message—I could not put it through her quite like an empty pipe! She had to co-operate with her mind and voice. My other translator was a deeper channel. Because she had learned deeper things in experience, she understood what I meant more rapidly, so that I could forget her and think only of the people. Oh that our God could forget us, in transmitting his message, and think only of those he wants to speak to through us!

We closed at 6:00, and at 7:30 went to the Finnish meeting, where I again took up the "life in the Spirit"...

Tuesday, June 7th

The last day of the conference. At noon I spoke with double translation, an interpreter on either side of me. Each sentence was repeated first in Swedish and then in Finnish. God took it into his hand, and it was wonderful how he held the people through that long process, and how he held the three speakers in such quiet calm that the thread was never lost, and the people were deeply moved at the message of the cross. This seems to light up more and more as one speaks on it. The old, old story, deeper and fresher, and ever new.

In the afternoon the conference had an excursion, so my traveling companion and I went off on our own account in a drosky, a little carriage with one horse... to a most exquisite island some distance from Helsinki, connected with the mainland by a light footbridge. The beauty was indescribable... Such a rest after the noise of people and the babel of languages we are in. Part of the people speak Swedish, part Finnish, a minority know both. To get one of our meals altered one day, five languages were employed! I spoke English to my Russian friend, she spoke French to our interpreter (who knew French better than English); she repeated the matter in Swedish to our landlady, and the landlady in Finnish to the servant—my Russian friend endeavoring to clear matters by using German!... On this account Helsinki is very tiring. In Denmark we get along with English or German, but in Finland so few know English and the country itself has two languages!

This evening I gave the closing address of the conference, again with double translation.

Wednesday, June 8th

This morning we had a meeting of the delegates, and I spoke to them on soul-winning, again with double translation. There were about forty or more, from all parts of the country. How much it means!

We closed at 11:15, and at noon I had a public meeting, in Swedish only. This began three days of devotional meetings to follow the conference. It was thought at first to confine them to members of the conference; but we decided to throw all open, and those who were seeking a deeper knowledge of God would come. It was so, and day after day we saw the same faces, and watched the light upon them deepening...

Thursday, June 9th

The morning meeting at noon. The place was so hot, and no windows open because of the noise outside. My interpreter broke down as we neared the end of the meeting and could not go on. I could not have borne it, but that I had specially trusted the Lord about it... I could only motion to a minister to lead in prayer. Afterwards my helper recovered, and I asked her to tell the people I would resume at the same point the next day.

I never quite realized *how the Lord carries* me, until I was side by side with my interpreters. As I give forth the "Word of life," I seem to become more vigorous, while they seem to flag and grow weary. Even a strong man, interpreting, grew weary, though I was as fresh as when I began, and resumed at my next meeting as if I had not spoken before! This is the difference between the "power of his endless life" to quicken physically, and the natural resources...

Monrepos, Sunday, June 12th

Friday was just a repetition of the other days, with two Swedish meetings, both very encouraging... The last meeting was a very large one. God had met numbers of his children, and many were praising him for new light and knowledge of God.

We had been asked to stay over Sunday at Monrepos, a lovely country house at Viborg (Baron Nicolay's country home) and decided to go by sea... We stopped at Kotka and Fredrikshamn, and at the latter place a typical Russian priest went ashore: long hair; delicate, clear, refined face; large-brimmed white straw hat, and long blue serge gown. He was as nearly like the usual pictures of the Lord as one could imagine. Yet he smoked, and drank spirits!

At 10:00 p.m. on Saturday we reached Viborg, where Baroness Nicolay (the Baron's mother) met us, and we drove to Monrepos. Such a lovely old house, everything about it antique and interesting. Suites of rooms running one into another, and old, old pictures and furniture. The grounds are most beautiful, overlooking part of the canal leading to the Saima Lake. A nightingale was singing in the trees opposite our windows. This is a real rest, after the peculiarly trying heat and clamor of Helsinki. So the Lord cares for his earthen vessels. I had not *thought* of a rest at Monrepos on my way to St. Petersburg. It was a special kindness from the hand of the Father, who knoweth our frame, and remembereth that we are dust.

* * *

Two days at Monrepos, and a quiet week with the friends in St. Petersburg, and then HOME—arriving in London on June 20th, and in Leicester the following day, brought this fourth continental visit to an end.

August 1898 was a time of rest, spent by Mrs. Penn-Lewis in north Wales, her Russian friends with her, whilst her husband had the privilege of visiting Helsinki, St. Petersburg, and Moscow, in company with Baron Nicolay, also spending some time at Monrepos, the Baron's delightful country home. At Helsinki, Mr. Penn-Lewis met many of the friends who had given his wife such a warm welcome earlier in the year, and shared (by interpretation) in one of their meetings. At Moscow, he had the joy of seeing Gospels distributed in one of the prisons. Five to six hundred convicts, men and women, some heavily chained, were gathered in the corridor of the prison. With much prayer he stood watching their faces while a short address was given; and then the convicts passed the visitors one by one, many eagerly receiving the proffered Gospel, others utterly careless. These prisoners were afterwards scattered to prisons in Siberia and Sakhalin, carrying with them the Word of life. Little wonder that Mr. Penn-Lewis returned to England with a deep burden on his heart for Russia, and especially for the work carried on in the prisons of Russia by Dr. Baedeker, Baron Nicolay, and others, by special permission of the government.

The closing months of the year were filled, for Mrs. Penn-Lewis, with the usual succession of conferences and other gatherings, notably the Edinburgh (Annual) Convention, where her old friends, the Rev. and Mrs. W. D. Moffat, claimed her as their guest during the week of meetings. It was during this visit that the conversation took place to which Mrs. Penn-Lewis often referred, and of which she wrote in *The Overcomer* at the time of Mr. Moffat's death in 1912:

> To Mr. Moffat I owe, under God, the first understanding of the trust committed to me in the message of the cross in its deeper aspect to the Christian… With only glimmering light, I once said to him, "How can I *always* preach the cross, for there are only so many verses about it, and I cannot use them again and again?" But he kept me up that night till the early hours of the morning, explaining, urging, pleading that I would not be diverted from the message God had illuminated to me.
>
> I went away from that Edinburgh visit to some meetings for Christians at Gordon Hall, Liverpool, asking God to show me the way never to give an address on any theme without "preaching the cross"; and to my astonishment, in those days, as I was speaking on many themes concerning the Christian life, I found myself, in the heart of the message, showing the cross as the center of every theme.
>
> Then I saw that all aspects of the spiritual life could be shown to have as their basis—Calvary; and that *all spiritual truth radiated from the cross*…

"'Leaning upon her beloved!'

"To bring the soul to entire reliance and dependence upon him is the 'end of the Lord,' and the purpose of his varied dealings in the 'valley' and in the 'mountain top.'

"'Leaning upon her beloved!' This is the outcome of the life of union—what life more simple or more blessed! In this privileged position the hidden one comes forth to renewed service and activity. 'Leaning upon her beloved' to be taught of him."

Chapter 8

The Deepening of the Channel

1899–1902

To the gates of death in Russia, and the writing of *Thy Hidden Ones*—Keswick: a speaker at the women's meetings—To Canada and the United States—Preparation of *The Story of Job* and *Face to Face*—The liberation of the message—The Bridge of Allan Convention

The winter of 1898–9 marks a distinct crisis in the life-work we are tracing, the closing of one chapter and the opening of another. In the month of December a serious breakdown in health necessitated complete cessation of public work, and the Lord made it clear to his servant that he was calling her aside to hear his voice and wait upon him for light upon the future path. The first five weeks of 1899 were spent at Eastbourne, where under the loving care and ministration of a friend, a measure of restoration was slowly given. Quiet hours alone, in a bathchair by the sea, were hours spent "within the veil" while God revealed much of the meaning and purpose of the conflict of the past year—a period of strain, not so much from active service as in "a baptism of suffering" over a wandering soul that, to quote a circular letter sent out in the New Year, "has let me know in a little degree what 'filling up the afflictions of Christ for his body's sake' means."

The result of all the suffering will mean so much to the kingdom of God... I have light on sin I never had before; and all through the bitter conflict with sin in another, God spoke to me day after day. It has been, on God's part, the most marvelous experience of my life,

153

in his grace and his revelations of himself. There will be a power in the books and messages not there before, in the fuller light he has given me ... All God's light to me has been wrought out in suffering, and it has been so again. The revelation of the *holiness of God* has been almost blinding ...

To Mr. Penn-Lewis:

Eastbourne, February 4th, 1899

I have had most lovely times by the sea quite alone ... One morning Canticles opened out so blessedly; but when I get indoors, God keeps me (purposely I think) too tired to use a pen to put it down, and it is not of God to *force the brain to retain revelations made to the heart* ... I have to let it go, and bear patiently the powerlessness and the "lying fallow" that is so contrary to my heart's longing ... He doeth all things well! It is a real test to have such inward unveilings and to be content to lie still, not using my mental powers to get them on paper for others. But all is so clear, I have to obey ...

From a circular prayer letter dated February 20th, 1899:

Beloved friends in Christ,

I have no words to tell you the thanksgiving that fills my heart as I look back over the Lord's wondrous dealings in 1898 ... It was a year of fellowship with his sufferings, purely from a spiritual standpoint, that no words can express, to teach me in deep reality the message of his cross. It was his own hand that led me and his own voice that cheered me through the deep waters, in the conflict with the powers of darkness ...

On New Year's Day the Lord told me that this was to be a "year of solemn rest unto the Lord" (see Lev. 25:4–5) and reminded me of his word to Israel: "In the seventh year thou shalt release it, and let it lie fallow" (Ex. 23:11, R.V. m.), so that "the Lord's release was proclaimed" (Deut. 15:2) and I could, with a quiet heart, go and rest awhile. I had forgotten—but God had not—that I had just concluded six years of active and ceaseless service on the Canaan side of Jordan ...

For months I have had God's messages in writing, and through pressure of correspondence and innumerable small matters claiming ceaseless attention, they have never gone to print. I have endeavored to keep the correspondence in check, sometimes writing late at night; but even with the help of a secretary it has been impossible. My heart has been grieved over the unfinished booklets.

Then came God's withdrawal of power to go on, and the imperative necessity of rest. This was my release ... He showed me that I must be severed from all conscious links if I was to fulfill his purposes. Intercession must be only "in the Spirit," moved by the Holy Ghost who knows my needs and can indicate them to those who know him in Spirit-prayer; but I must not waste precious hours in providing material for prayer when he needs me at his feet to receive his messages. He showed me that if I was to write what he gave me, I must be entirely withdrawn aside with him, even as Moses in the mount with God, and let the business of the camp alone.

"Be thou for the people GODWARD ... the small matters they shall judge themselves ..." (Ex.18:19, 22).

A letter from Baron Nicolay to Mr. Penn-Lewis quaintly puts the matter in another way:

I am sorry to hear of your dear wife's illness. May she consider that the earthen vessel is not a "heavenly vessel" in this sense, that a poor earthen vessel does need careful handling, not to break before the time. It is a favorite dodge of Satan, if he cannot keep us below the mark, to push us beyond the mark and make our activity consume us ... Maybe St. Paul had, for the same reason, to be put in prison for two years. We should have grieved over the "lost time," but certainly it was not lost in God's sight, who ordained it so ...

On February 22nd, restored to a great extent to her usual health, Mrs. Penn-Lewis crossed once more to St Petersburg, this time for rest and quiet, away from the constant calls which seemed unavoidable in England. Then was revealed the purpose of God in enforcing a year of release from public work.

"I had not been many days in St. Petersburg," says a letter written some months later,

...before the Lord began to open up to me the *Song of Songs* as I had never seen it before; and for a month I wrote, in the light of his face and in indescribable peace, the message that flooded my soul with joy. It would have been quite impossible, in the midst of active work and the pressure of desk claims, to have sat at his feet for such an unveiling.

To Mr. Penn-Lewis:

St. Petersburg, March 7th, 1899

God is pouring light upon it [Canticles] and my pen is running without halting. I know now why I have been sent here, because it is perfectly quiet and I *can* be wholly given up to writing... The light is so full, and the "bubble-over" of life so strong, that I can hardly lay it down. I wake up in the morning and scribble notes with a pencil, and even dress with the Bible open—I have never had an experience like this... If this is the fruit of all the deep waters, I am well content. It will be my first book really written with delight...

March 15th, 1899

I think it is quite clear that this unveiling of the Song of Songs as union with Christ is to be a large book; it is so fresh to me, and is opening so fully. I am able to write quite six hours a day, and am only half way through yet...

No meetings were taken during this visit, and the only relaxation from close writing was the daily drive in the keen bracing air.

Yesterday I drew a personal salute from the emperor.[1] As we crossed the wooden bridge leading from the fortress on the other side of the Neva... in the middle of the bridge I looked up, and coming toward us at walking pace was an open Victoria, and on the side next to me, the emperor—we were practically face to face. The empress was on his right. We looked at each other, and I bowed of course, and slowly his hand rose to his hat in a military salute... They were going to the fortress church for the Lenten Requiem...

But alas, just before Easter, when apparently quite well, Mrs. Penn-Lewis was suddenly struck down with a sharp attack of

1   Nicholas II, the last of the Romanoffs

pleurisy. That afternoon she had driven out in 17 degrees of frost, and the keen air aroused a dormant inflammation in the delicate lungs. With little or no reserve strength, she rapidly sank to the lowest ebb of life, and "...for ten days and nights, four Russian women of God, ladies of 'honorable estate,' literally held up their hands to God in prayer for the threatened life. When they flagged, 'the enemy prevailed,' and when they held on in faith—with an open Bible before them—the foe was driven back, until, on Easter Eve, the knowledge came in spirit that the battle was won."[2]

"I have no fear about the issue of my illness," says a letter to Mr. Penn-Lewis written on April 26th:

> ...my *work is not yet done!* God is in it, and he is only equipping for better service by and by. The first week was the worst ... One night I felt myself becoming unconscious; it seemed as if my spirit was slipping away, when with such a "pulling together" I said, "I *will not die!*" and then I came back to consciousness. God is bringing me into deeper and deeper rest. It would be much easier to the flesh to be suddenly healed! But I see that I must leave absolutely all question as to time—otherwise there is no surrender ... It will not go one point beyond his limit, and he will do his work in the very best way ...

For more than three weeks the fight of faith never relaxed, and from that moment of assurance on Easter Eve the patient began to regain strength. On May 3rd, after six weeks in bed, the temperature was normal for the first time, and immediately berths were booked for the journey home a fortnight later, in faith that the Lord would continue to answer the prayers of his children. The tide had turned.

"Who is this that cometh up from the wilderness, leaning upon her beloved?" came the voice of her Lord from the Song of Songs; and the following day the power to write returned, as she recommenced her meditation upon the book at chapter 8. "Today and henceforth," says the diary, "my keynote will be 'leaning upon the beloved' as never before."

2 Quoted from *The Overcomer*, December, 1914

* * *

Among the large number of books accumulated by Mrs. Penn-Lewis through the years, it is easy to distinguish those which specially met—or interpreted—her own experience, by their heavy underscoring and many marginal notes. A two-volume edition of Madame Guyon's *Autobiography* contains many such glimpses into a similarity of experience, with, on the part of Mrs. Penn-Lewis, a deep added understanding of the danger of counterfeits from the ever-watchful enemy, which was to a great extent hidden from God's servant of old. In speaking of her literary labors, Madame Guyon again and again describes how she wrote, under the hand of God, many things which it was not in her own mind or spirit to write. May we give two brief extracts to illustrate this:

> While writing I saw that I was writing ... treasures of knowledge and understanding that I did not know myself to possess ... I had no book except the Bible, and that alone I used without searching for anything. When, in writing on the Old Testament, I took passages from the New to support what I was saying, it was not that I sought them out, but they were given to me at the same time as the explanation; and exactly the same with the New Testament ...
>
> I still continued to write, and with incredible quickness, for the hand could hardly follow the Spirit ... The places which may be defective are only so because sometimes *I wished to write as I had the time,* and then it was not grace at the fountain head ...

"So it was with *Thy Hidden Ones*, and other books and articles—always *from the 'center*,'"[1] runs a penciled note. "This is exactly how I have always written. J.P-L."

With unspeakable thankfulness Mr. Penn-Lewis received his beloved wife home at last on May 19th, and the work of getting the message on the Song of Songs through the press occupied the remainder of May and June in order to have it ready in time for the Keswick Convention in July.

Year after year Mrs. Penn-Lewis had been present at the convention, and knowing the tide of blessing which God gave

1   e.g., the central depths of the spirit indwelt by the Holy Spirit.

through her proclamation of his Word, many were the voices urging that she should speak at the public gatherings; but hitherto the Lord had not so led. Now, in 1899, for the first time she became one of the speakers at the ladies' meetings, by invitation of the trustees, and very tender was the welcome she received from many old friends on this her first public appearance since God had so marvelously raised her up from the edge of death. The brief account of these meetings given in the Keswick number of the *Life of Faith* will be of interest:

The words from Mrs. Penn-Lewis were very blessed, full of the tenderness of one who had learned in suffering and had been face to face with God. Her first message (Wednesday) was that glowing passage of Hebrews 12:18: "Ye are not come unto the mount which might be touched." The very reading of it was an inspiration, as "ye are not come" was repeated between each point. "Ye are *not come* unto blackness; ye are *not come* unto darkness," and so on, until it rang through all hearts with a triumph echo. "But ye *are come* unto Jesus!" It seemed to need little more—so calming, so satisfying, so conquering did it sound. She dwelt much on the next points: "Ye *are come* unto the blood of sprinkling—ye *are come* unto the mediator of the new covenant." The foundation truths of the ground of a sinner's acceptance with God were forcibly dwelt on; and no one could wonder at the stream of prayer, brief and intense, which flowed from the audience after it, and the new yielding of heart and will and life to him who had poured out all for us.

On the next day this was followed up by her dwelling on words from Heb. 6:17–20: "The immutability of his counsel" and "anchored." How there could be no sure growth, no steadfast walk unless the soul was anchored on "the immutable counsel," the unchanging Word of God, and on the living person of our forerunner "within the veil." Anchored thus, the rested, settled soul will stand whatever shaking (12:26) our God shall choose to send. And what a joy to remember, about that "immutable counsel," that it is what God is *"willing to show!"* "Willing to show to the heirs of promise," if they are willing to see.

Some other blessed truths were brought out and many searching things said. The home relationships were much dwelt on—child to parent, parent to child, sister to sister, sister to brother, and mistress to servant. The light of God was turned full and strong from his Word on home life and witness-bearing.

This gives the outward story, but the glow of joy over answered prayer, and confidence in the working of God in this testing of her renewed powers, is seen in a letter written after reaching home. "God kept me weak and 'invalidish,'" she writes:

> ...up to the moment of my first message—and then he poured in his life, and I was suddenly free, as if I had emerged from a long tunnel. All the weakness disappeared ... I am just my old self. It is all he promised for Keswick, but he did it *only as I stood up to speak!* The first message came like a voice from heaven and laid hold mightily. "Ye are NOT come to blackness ... but YE ARE COME to Mount Zion, and to Jesus, and to the blood of sprinkling."
>
> I received such a welcome from everybody. It has been a wonderful time ... The new book *[Thy Hidden Ones]* went rapidly. Marshall Brothers said, more than any other ...[1]

Present at Keswick this year was Professor W. R. Newell, assistant-superintendent of the Moody Bible Institute, with whom Mrs. Penn-Lewis had several interviews at his request. Of him she wrote, "He is a prepared soul and so ready to hear." And in the wonderful out-working of the purposes of God, this contact became the first link with the North American continent, as Professor Newell took back to his work not only a vision of the deep need of the church of God for the proclamation of the cross of Christ as the crucial message of the gospel, but also a quantity of the books and booklets to give to students and workers with whom he was in touch.

After Keswick, by the clear leading of God, Mrs. Penn-Lewis once more retired from the much-owned public work, and went abroad again, for the Lord bade her take her rest "as solemnly and faithfully as her service." "I saw then," she wrote, "that to maintain a deep stream from God in public work, the messenger

---

1   Mr. Marshall wrote, in a personal letter, that it was "by far the most popular book at Keswick this year."

needed to watch as keenly for the voice of God crying '*Halt!*' as for the word 'Go forward.' I learned again that to follow the Spirit of God, and be blind and deaf to the voice of man, meant being led into richer and fuller service than before."

One happy summer month was therefore spent with her beloved husband in the Channel Islands, and the autumn in Switzerland with her Russian friends, afterwards joining Mr. Penn-Lewis at Eastbourne for the Christmas season.

Canada and America

In the following summer came a call to visit Canada and the United States; immediately after Keswick, Mr. and Mrs. Penn-Lewis sailed for Canada, spending the August vacation together there, the latter remaining behind on the service of the King until the end of October. The following account is culled from letters.

Niagara Falls, August 16th, 1900

We are enjoying our holiday very much, and have every indication of being in the Lord's prepared path, and that is surety for all going well. Unless he made straight our paths, we might well be worn out instead of rested, as we are strange, and do not know the easy ways of getting about...

On Friday, August 11th, in the most exquisite sunshine, we entered the Straits of Belle Isle... On the Sunday there was a church service in the saloon at 11:00 a.m., and I asked permission for a meeting in the steerage in the afternoon. Will [Mr. Penn-Lewis] led it, and some of the saloon folk came and looked at us! A gentleman from Montreal, who presides over a Sunday afternoon men's meeting, read the Scripture. A clergyman from London spoke beautifully, and I followed. We felt that a real work had been done, not only among the passengers, but in taking our stand for God before the others. I had good talks with some of the women, and then found a Swedish woman, knowing English, and asked her to collect all the foreigners for a meeting after tea.

A gentleman at our saloon table owned that he could speak Swedish, so he went back with me. There were thirty or so Norwegians and Swedes, and I spoke to them by translation. Some of the women sobbed, and my translator had to talk to them. I do not think he had ever found himself in such work before—I do not know if he was even a Christian! He was fairly taken back at being thus used ... We had a real good time after this; everyone seemed easy to approach. Men I had had no word with told me their troubles, and books could be given easily. I think it was the most delightful Sunday I ever knew.

We reached Montreal early on Tuesday morning, and the first few days were very strange. It was "England," and yet not England! Everything big, bold, and noisy. At the railway we were in a tumult of great bells, apparently calling one to church all day long. I discovered that they were swung on the engines to give notice of the approach of the trains! On Thursday we left for Toronto, where we made our way to the China Inland Mission Home, which is to be my Canadian home after Will leaves me; we had such a welcome. They pressed us to stay with them, but we felt we could not burden them with baggage, etc. The next day we crossed Lake Ontario to Niagara Falls, Mr. Frost, the head of the Canadian C.I.M., traveling with us as pilot. The falls far exceed all I had expected, and the surroundings are so beautiful that every point seems more lovely than the last ...

Yesterday I had to dress up in oilskins to go under part of the Canadian Fall. When I found it meant partial disrobing I protested; but the young lady was so nice, fetching me a new suit of oilskins and putting warm towels round my neck, so I went on with the business, and followed Will down the elevator—a pretty picture truly! The guide took special care of me and led me inside the mass of falling water—the spray poured over us like a shower bath. It was with mingled feelings I went back to the dressing-room, thinking myself a silly creature to go—but in that room I had such a blessed talk with the girl in charge as I would go down half a dozen times to get. I asked if she could recognize Christians, and she quickly said "Yes," and before I knew it, I was telling her that a real Christian meant one with the life from heaven imparted to them—not one who tried to patch up the old life and struggled to make it climb up to heaven. That God's way was to send down, as a gift, a bit of heaven's life into us, to take us back to heaven. The girl drank it in, and said she had never seen it like that. So I had my reward for my "experience" ...

At the hotel we are waited on by a Negro, a veritable "Uncle Tom." He waits on us with such grace and gentleness, and his face lights up when I thank him—I am quite charmed with the man... I spoke at an endeavorer's meeting in a Presbyterian church on Sunday, and had an hour's talk with the minister today. He is truly a faithful witness here...

Mr. Penn-Lewis sailed for England on August 25th, and the days of real service now began, first with three days of meetings at Ottawa, then on to Kingston for two meetings, followed by three days in Toronto at the Missionary Training Home of the China Inland Mission.

The first piece of work in the United States was the conducting of four Quiet Days in a country house some five miles from Peekskill-on-Hudson (New York), the home of Mrs. C. de Peyster Field, at whose invitation this visit to America was undertaken. Thirty guests were accommodated in the house, and a stage coach came up daily from Peekskill bringing others, so that there were fifty present for dinner each day. The days were very full, commencing with morning prayers at 7:45, and meetings during the day, interspersed with many interviews with souls seeking personal help. The Lord was present in manifest power, and a deep intensive work was done in the lives of the Christian workers there gathered, so that, when the last day came, there was not one guest but had really been met with by the Lord in a very vital way.

"I have seen God deal with *some souls* out of a group," wrote Mrs. Penn-Lewis:

> ...but never before with every soul present. We shall none of us ever forget it. Yet during the two days preceding, I had one of the keenest conflicts I have ever known—I almost fled!
>
> > Tho' hot the fight why quit the field?
> > Why should I either fly or yield,
> > Since Jesus is my mighty shield?'

These words just brought me through, and then the Lord broke forth upon us with visions of God. During the four days I had practically four meetings each day and was carried beautifully through.

After a brief rest, Chicago was next visited, arriving on September 24th in time for the closing meetings of a ten-day workers' conference at the Moody Bible Institute, under the presidency of Dr. R. A. Torrey, in which Mrs. Penn-Lewis was to take part, followed by some special meetings in the lecture hall of the institute, under her entire charge. Extracts from letters home will give a glimpse into this work.

From Chicago, en route to Northfield. 1st October, 1900

At Chicago I stayed at the Moody Bible Training Institute. Miss Strong, head of the women's department, had been helped by *The Message of the Cross* and was most kind to me. The first evening I stepped into the workers' conference meeting, to see the working of it—and heard myself announced *in a very American way* (which I feel too shy to repeat), to speak the next morning.[1]

It was 7:30 breakfast here again, and at 10 o'clock I appeared in the church (Moody's) and went to the platform. A large gathering. I spoke on "the fire shall try every man's work," and then on the wise and foolish builder depicted by the Lord. I was asked to speak again, and at 2 o'clock Professor Newell came in to sketch out our arrangements. Such is American speed that by 7:00 p.m. the bills were in the hands of the conference audience!

On Thursday I began alone in the lecture hall. All the men and women students were there, and many others. I spoke of Job, and the Spirit of God held that gathering as I depicted Job as he was, and then the gradual creeping in of the "I" and his *"good* self" etc. A man in the front seat fairly broke down ... The Lord kept saying to me, "dig deep," so in the afternoon I spoke on "let him *disown himself* and take up his cross." On Saturday we had the "grain of wheat" sacrificing its life for fruitfulness. A most blessed time, and very crowded meetings.

I have had prayers and a Bible reading among the students each morning and numbers of serious interviews with workers.

---

1   The announcer was Dr. R. A. Torrey, and the remark that so embarrassed his unseen hearer was, that she was "one of the most gifted speakers the world had known!"

One minister asked me if I would go on his theological college in Tennessee, and earnestly laid before me the possibilities of a tour, only among the theological colleges, which he could arrange. The meeting in the lecture room on Sunday afternoon was crammed, with people standing in the doorways and along the passages, and I was given a good hold of a most difficult meeting.

This morning (October 1st) a young Japanese student came in, who had been on a mission tour in the district. He heard I was here and traveled back all night to catch me before I left. He had read all the books and made up his mind to get to England to see me sometime! So we had our talk, and I hurried into a large meeting at 10:30, and from that straight into a cab for the train. I had my section (sleeping arrangement) made up at once, and after lunch in the buffet, lay down and slept soundly for two hours! I had traveled 24 hours from New York, then for five days worked from seven in the morning, with scarcely an hour's break, day after day—out to meals, talking; back to appointments, on to meetings, and after every one, numbers pressing for a talk. I scarcely remember five days so packed with vital work, for here at this center are workers from almost all parts of the world. Miss Strong and I had one drive, along the lake shore and through Lincoln Park. It was all I saw of Chicago, except that I went one morning to see about my train ticket.

New York, October 15th, 1900

From Chicago I returned to New York via Northfield. I could only spare two days, but was glad to use them in this way; and it was with very great interest I looked upon the group of buildings so familiar to many of us through the work of the late D. L. Moody. I stayed at Revell Hall, one of the girls' seminaries, and in the morning was driven to the Northfield Hotel, used during the winter as a Bible training school, where I spoke to the students. Then to the 497 girl students gathered in the Chapel next morning at 9 o'clock. Such a mass of girl faces! I spoke for twenty minutes, and it went home. One girl scrambled on to the platform to tell me, with tears on her face, that it had helped her. But I keenly felt the brevity of my opportunity and the great need.

Mrs. D. L. Moody sent me over to the Mount Hermon Seminary in the afternoon, in the buggy with the old family horse, Dan (probably the one Mr. Moody used as he drove about the country he loved so well). Professor Cutler would not hear of my leaving without speaking to the men, so 400 students gathered in the chapel for their usual Wednesday evening prayer meeting, and I spoke about Paul. It was beautiful afterwards to hear solemn words from many: "Lord, I will not be disobedient to the heavenly vision."

Of course I visited "Round Top," and as I sat on a seat near Mr. Moody's grave, I thought of the wondrous honor accorded to him in his earthly record—that of being a true winner of souls—and of the glory of his "coronation day."

Returning to New York on October 9th (after a few days rest at Peekskill) I had the opportunity of giving a message at the convention being held in the Gospel Tabernacle (Rev. A. B. Simpson). The Lord gave me so keen a message on "how Saul lost his crown" that it made me almost sick to have to give it—a stranger, and to strangers! But I obeyed, and God sealed the word. I lunched at their home, and returned to Hephzibah House quite exhausted with the severity of my message. Speaking again at the Gospel Tabernacle on the following Sunday afternoon, I heard that the severe message on Wednesday had done execution; some in real crises had been helped, and thanked me for my faithfulness.

New York, October 26th, 1900

Two days' meetings for workers at the Harlem branch of the Y.W.C.A. were followed by a week of Bible readings in the large drawing-room of Hephzibah House (October 16–19), where God was with us in marked power ... On the Tuesday morning my message was "our God is a consuming fire ... He shall sit and purify ..."; in the afternoon, the man with the eyes of fire saying "I know ... I know ...", and his call to "overcome." On Wednesday, "love not the world," and the world "crucified." By Wednesday afternoon the meeting had grown, and the third drawing-room began to fill. The message was "the sacrifices of God are a broken spirit ...", and this reached its climax on Thursday morning with "God forbid that I should glory, save in the cross of our Lord Jesus Christ." The Lord had laid hold of the people, and they sat in each meeting as if they did not want to move. By Thursday afternoon every chair in this great house was brought in, three rooms full, and the halls out toward the main entrance. I saw that the Lord was really working. Then came the message of LIFE "from the heavenlies to the kitchen," in Col. 3. Oh what a week it was! I was enabled to speak the truth fearlessly; we shall never forget it. Souls who had resisted God for seven years were melted, and few passed out but had met with God. When I put the question one afternoon as to whether it should be the cross of Christ or the "world," by a spontaneous move many broke out with the answer, "The cross, the cross!"

On Saturday (October 20th) I went to South Nyack on the Hudson. First I had tea with the Rev. A. B. Simpson and his wife, and then was driven to the Missionary Institute on Nyack Heights, where I spent two very full days with the students. Returning to New York, I had one large meeting of women in the beautiful auditorium of the City of New York Y.W.C.A., another among forty deaconesses engaged in the parishes of the New York churches, and on October 24th and 25th addressed a few meetings in the church of Dr. D. M. Stearns at Germantown (Philadelphia).

God has given me wonderful openings. If I had known the whole country I could not have planned a more effectual use of a brief visit, touching, not the fringe of things, but the vital centers—and all brought about by God's own hand. I brought a very big box of books, but they were not half enough; and I had to write for a fresh box to be sent out, and again another.

Tonight, to descend to earthly matters, there is almost pandemonium outside—New York gone wild! This house (Mrs. Field's private town residence) is in the heart of the city, facing Madison Square, and I have seen from my window a typical bit of American electioneering! Roosevelt, the governor of New York, is running for vice president and is to speak tonight. A parade of 75,000 men, a seething mass of people, crowd the square, and street after street. Magnificent fireworks—the sky alight the whole evening with stars of all colors. Small platforms erected along the side of the square. People shouting and tearing along, waving flags, torches, and colored lights. An indescribable babel of bands, cannonading, shouting, noises of all kinds. Roosevelt passed slowly in an open carriage, standing up and bowing. When they will stop tonight I do not know!

I left for England by the *Oceanic* on October 31st. The one word rung in my ears during the whole of my visit was *"Foundations."* I was reminded that the wise builder "digged deep," and this briefly describes the need of the Christians in the United States, for crowds are easily drawn and quickly moved. *Deep subsoil work* is the one great need. May God equip his instruments in that land, and all whom he sends forth to bear his messages there, making them wise master-builders, laying a good foundation, so that in the testing day when the floods come and break upon the buildings, they shall be found to have been "well builded" (Luke 6:48).

The Liberation of the Message

The years 1901 and 1902 were mainly years of literary labor, as the winters were spent abroad. As has been seen, Russia was the birthplace of *Thy Hidden Ones*. *The Story of Job* was written during a protracted stay in Davos (Switzerland) in 1901–2, under medical supervision, in hope of staying the progress of the lung weakness which was still more manifest after the serious illness in Russia two years before. *Job* was written under the hand of God with the same wonderful liberty and heavenly unveiling as the message on the Song of Songs, and was so manifestly "gold out of the furnace" that a writer in *The Christian* spoke of it thus:

> Mrs. Penn-Lewis … proves herself not merely to have intellectually and intelligently comprehended the book, but to have entered spiritually and experimentally into its inmost thought, and to have in spirit passed through, in some degree, the sorrows of the patriarch … From first to last, the terrible experiences of the sufferer, and the restoration and the joy at last, are shown to be the dealings of the only wise God our Savior with his child, whom in love and faithfulness he afflicted and exalted. These illuminative pages contain, not so much a study as a meditation. Though full of thought and of Christian experience, they come from, and appeal to, the heart rather than the intellect; and yet there is more enlightened and enlightening intellectual discernment than in many commentaries …

The little book *Face to Face*, an exquisite cameo meditation upon the inner life of Moses, with whom God spake "face to face," was written (the actual matter in one week), at Eastbourne in May 1900, at the request of Messrs. Marshall Brothers, to form one of their Quiet Hour series. Two thousand copies of this book were sold in the first four months of its existence, and it was the means of making much more widely known the other writings of Mrs. Penn-Lewis; for up to this time all had been issued privately, without advertisement, and chiefly circulated among those who heard the writer speak at conventions and other gatherings. The publication of this message through ordinary business channels, and the prominence given to it in the advertisement columns of the *Life of Faith*, led to a spiritual crisis in the experience of the writer, as God showed her clearly that the agonized shrinking of her natural temperament from any kind of publicity, which had never been wholly overcome, was narrowing God's work through her, and she was brought to a fresh point of surrender as the word of the Lord came to her one day: *"Let them stretch forth* the curtains of thy habitation" (Isa. 54:2). "But Lord, they will advertise!" she cried; and he answered, "LET THEM."

"Every time I open *The Life of Faith*," she wrote to a friend:

> ...I hear his voice again, 'Let them,' and I have a deep peace over what I should once have winced at... I could never do it over a book I published myself, and that is why God took this one from me. I always knew I had no right to withhold the messages he gave me from being made known, because of my sensitiveness. It is the greatest victory of God for me to be at rest in this... Now the books are going to people I may never meet, and who have never heard of me, because I have never encouraged reports of meetings. A writer must be known, and this was God's way of doing it. He *gave* me this message for Marshalls—it was settled with the Lord before it was written—so how can I question it?

A still keener fight, and greater victory, came over a request from the late Richard Cope Morgan, editor of *The Christian* and head of the great Christian publishing house of Morgan and Scott, for permission to publish a photograph, and a sketch of her life and work, and the way in which God had led to her present position as a teacher of the deep things of God. He wrote:

The experiences of thoughtful, spiritual, and experienced Christians, wisely given under the guidance of the Spirit of the meek and lowly one, cannot but be helpful, and are much needed in these shallow and superficial days ... I quite understand your feelings. To some the publication may be a gratification—to you a torture. But HE knows!

After a time of deep heart-searching, God convinced his servant that this request was also in the current of his will, as opening a door for the message of the cross to a far wider circle of believers than she had yet reached. While resting at Davos in August 1903 the paper was written for *The Christian* under the title, "The Leading of the Lord," and another letter gives us an insight into the conflict preceding the victory:

I have been through deep waters over that paper. It was pure obedience to God, with a very Gethsemane of anguish, until the Lord showed me that it was an abnormal sensitiveness that needed his touch ... In the face of suffering from such a temperament as this, I have done all my public work, but this paper was the climax, and nearly overwhelmed me. I would never have dared to say "Yes," but that, in the mount with God, he told me he could do no more with me until I removed my last restriction. Then he showed me how I have given him *carte blanche,* with one reservation—the least possible amount of publicity! I have even sought to "help him" by stopping, wherever possible, reports to the papers—and never saw that I was making a reservation ...

Now God has shown me that I have limited him through this anguished shrinking, and it has had to be more than "consent"; I have had to seek deliverance, that I may hinder him thus no more ...

This is the story of the paper, "The Leading of the Lord," and how few will know what the suffering has been ... Pray for me, that God will hide me in himself while they read my heart's history, that as the message goes out he will veil me, and make all to glorify God.

The brief visit to America was also the means, in the hand of God, of widening the scope of the proclamation entrusted to his servant, by creating in that country a great demand for everything that could be obtained of the printed messages. Week after week, the American mail brought a flood of letters that taxed all the resources of the editions then in print. "Books, books, books, are all the time wanted for America," Mrs. Penn-Lewis wrote in January 1901, "and the Lord is blessing them on every hand … Many papers in America are reprinting the leaflets, and *such* letters are coming! God is answering prayer—to him be the glory."

After a series of meetings at St. Peter's Church, Islington, (Rev. F. Trevelyan Snow), Denmark, Sweden, and Russia were revisited in May 1901, returning to England early in June, to fulfill an engagement to take part in the annual convention at Bridge of Allan, Scotland. In accordance with the custom, which still prevails at Keswick conventions, the Lord's handmaiden was invited to address special meetings for ladies—though in other lands, and in smaller conferences in our own land, her more public ministry had been so blessedly sealed by the Spirit of God. Even in these centers of evangelical light and truth, the greater part of her time between the meetings, and at the meal table, was occupied with important interviews on spiritual matters with many who were giving the Lord's message in the public gatherings. An aged minister who was present year after year at the Scottish convention, at times being in charge of the evangelistic work on the Sunday preceding the special gatherings, writes the following retrospective notes:

"I believe it was in June 1901 that Mrs. Penn-Lewis was first present at the Scottish Keswick held annually at Bridge of Allan, to address meetings for girls and women—a number of the more conservative members of the committee objecting to the ministry of women in the general, mixed meetings, in those days—much as the convener, the Rev. W. D. Moffatt, M.A., desired to arrange otherwise.

But God has his own way of bringing his purpose to pass (Isa. 55:8–9) and one day the clerical speaker planned for the general meeting failed to appear! Just as Mrs. Penn-Lewis was commencing her meeting in one of the rooms in the Museum Hall, a friend entered and said to her, "You are requested to come and address the general meeting. The speaker has failed to come."

It can readily be understood how strong was the temptation to decline … but after only a few moments hesitation, the will surrendered and the call accepted, our sister went forward.

The array, in the tent, of Presbyterian divines, doctors of divinity, and ministers of all denominations, might well have caused a sense of bondage; but with a strong realization of the presence of God—as one of old who said "The Lord, before whom I stand"—Mrs. Penn-Lewis gave such a message on the cross of Christ as resulted in at least one minister saying, "That is the message for the church in these days"… In after years there was no suggestion of a limited ministry whenever our sister was able to come to Scottish conventions … Oh that God would send puir auld Scotland such a breath from heaven once again, in these dry and dead days of formalism …

Some who read this story will have heard Mrs. Penn-Lewis tell how, as she walked up the aisle of the tent behind Mr. Logan, with nothing but a deep, deep sense of her own emptiness and utter insufficiency for such an occasion, the thought came to her: should she give an ordinary Bible reading, as she so well could, on some beautiful, pleasing theme from the Word? Or should she—*dare she*—be faithful to her commission as a crucified messenger of the crucified Lord, and tell out to that concourse of ministers and white-haired divines the oft-times unwelcome message that the cross, in its personal application to the servant of God, means a deep experimental circumcision of the heart, a laying down of the "natural" gifts of the soul, the "own" eloquence, the "own" power for service; that out of the depths of the spirit, where Christ dwells, may flow to others the life of the risen Lord, unchecked and unhindered by the human channel. Then, as she mounted the platform, the Lord himself poured through her lips the message he had for that gathering, in a faithful proclamation of Paul's gospel of the cross.

The Bridge of Allan Convention of 1902 found Mrs. Penn-Lewis in the midst of the final proofs of the new book, *The Story of Job*. For more than six months she had "lived every hour for that book: sleeping, eating, resting, walking, all with the aim of being fit to write." After such a season of discipline and obedience to the hand of God, it was natural that the Book of Job should be the subject of her addresses at the convention; and so intense was the presence and power of God that on the third day, numbers of the ministers came into the ladies' meeting to share in the blessing—for "where the Spirit of the Lord is, there is liberty," not bondage! Lunching with a group of speakers and ministers after the meeting, they sat long at the table asking questions and seeking to learn the secret of such revelation to *"babes"* of the deep things of God so often "hid" from the wise and prudent. In response to her protest that she was "no theologian," a learned doctor of divinity turned to Mrs. Penn-Lewis and said, "You have the very best kind of theology—the theology of the Holy Ghost!" And the convener himself, whose help and encouragement Mrs. Penn-Lewis so often warmly acknowledged, seems to have felt that the debt was largely on his side; for Mr. Moffatt wrote to her after some meetings in London, where he had proclaimed with new power the message of Calvary as deliverance from the *bondage* of sin:

> Sub-soil work had not been done and I was driven to do it...but the stillness was awful! You know it—"a sharp threshing instrument having teeth"...I sent them home to their knees, to deal with God alone...
>
> Of course I write thus to you because *I am your son in this service.* You have seen what I did not see, and believed for what I did not think to be possible, and have cheered and helped me when all was dark and blank. Someday, in the glory, we will talk over it all. One thing I entreat—do not cease to pray for me. Do you remember your last prayer for me in my room here? It was like the "mighty ordination of the pierced hands." Please take me still as one of your burdens to the master's feet...
>
> It is difficult to explain the influence of your teaching on my mind, but somehow it is *teaching that teaches,* and I find that few do that now...

It must be remembered that these were days in which the "message of the cross" was rarely preached, except in its first application to the forgiveness of sins through the blood of the Lamb. That the cross *"breaks the power* of canceled sin" through the identification of the sinner with Christ *in his death to sin and to the world;* that, "crucified with Christ," the believer is led into a fellowship with Christ that alone enables him to obey the Lord's injunction to "take up the cross and follow me," with all that this involves in conformity to the likeness of the Lamb—this was the half-forgotten truth which God ordained Mrs. Penn-Lewis to proclaim by lip and pen, to iterate and reiterate, until it has permeated the teaching of the church of God, even in circles where her name is scarcely known.

In the early days, the messenger was truly "crucified by the message," as she rang it out wherever the Spirit of God gave her open doors, refusing to be diverted from her specific commission either by criticism or by popularity. And how overwhelming was her joy when she saw God laying upon others the burden of the same proclamation—always with the same unction of God upon it! "I tested the 'cross' in my Sabbath services in these huge congregations," wrote Mr. Moffatt in 1901, "and saw how it 'caught on'… but I cannot preach it yet as I must preach it, *from the deeps!* I am clear enough in my *vision* of it, but my *insight* is not deep enough. Vision and insight go together in the prophet, if his message is perfect."

In the year 1903, seven years after the issue of the small book *The Message of the Cross*, there came from the press book after book on the atonement, showing, as Mrs. Penn-Lewis wrote some years later, "that a specific message given of God and witnessed to under his hand, *produces effect in the unseen realm*"—*liberating* men to proclaim with "insight" that which they see before them in the Word of God, but which remains mere "words" until illuminated by the Spirit of God in its working power.[1]

The message of the cross also swept through the Keswick Convention of 1903 like a mighty wind from heaven. In her brief history of the spiritual awakening in Wales, Mrs. Penn-Lewis, after a rapid survey of the remarkable prayer movement of 1898 to 1902, which girdled the world with prayer for revival, speaks of this "marked renewal of the preaching of the cross" as part

---

1   *The Overcomer*, December, 1914.

of God's hidden preparation for the outpouring of his Spirit in power:

> Early in 1903 the records in the papers showed on every side that the messengers of God were being led by him to proclaim afresh the message of Calvary. At annual meetings, opening services, and special conventions the keynote again and again was the "need for direct preaching of the cross"...
>
> In the light of this, how significant to find that at the Keswick Convention of 1903, when the windows of heaven were opened, and the Holy Spirit swept as an overflowing stream over the huge gatherings of five thousand men and women ... *the cross of Calvary was unveiled in fresh and vivid power;* for almost every servant of God entrusted with his messages proclaimed with one accord the "word of the cross" as the power of God to save from the bondage as well as the guilt of sin, and "crucified with Christ" as the secret of deliverance and victory was the theme.[2]

A writer in a contemporary issue of *The Life of Faith* reported the same movement "back to Calvary" in the following words:

> Two great truths were set forth among us—first, that Christ died for us; second, that we are identified with him in death. To thousands of Christians the second point was an aspect of the work of Christ that had hitherto escaped their notice. Here was the secret of rest and power presented in a word.[3]

"A most wonderful Keswick," Mrs. Penn-Lewis wrote to her Russian friends:

> ...God answered the prayers of seven years, and all with one accord preached the cross. *F. B. Meyer was mighty!* He gave only Galatians 2:20 in all his messages... People were amazed and there was mighty power... I spoke every day,[4] and also had a packed meeting on Sunday afternoon, arranged by Mr. Hogben of the One by One

---

2 From *The Awakening in Wales.*
3 Rev. S. A. McCracken.
4 That is, in the ladies' meetings, but the men would not be denied, and numbers of ministers and others quietly filled up the back seats of the pavilion day by day.

Band. They say hundreds were turned away … God has truly poured out his Spirit, and the souls were thronging …

It will be seen later how this liberation of the preaching of the cross was the Lord's preparation of a group of his servants who should carry the message to Wales, where also the stream of blessing became "waters to swim in." We must now return to the beginning of the year 1903.

"Let us see whether the vine hath budded, and the tender grape appear, and the pomegranates be in flower."

—*Song of Songs, 7:12, m.*

"She has always had a keen passion for souls, but formerly her 'own' activity used to draw her out of step with her Lord. Now she fears to move without him, and if she will always ask his will, he will keep her in the way of his steps. She may 'look on the fields … white already unto harvest' (John 4:35) when she looks with him; and in union with him, she will see the grace of God and be glad; she will be able to discern the first tokens of fruit."

Chapter 9

Foreshadowing of Revival

1903–1908

A visit to India—*The Word of the Cross* booklet—The Llandrindod Wells Convention and the Revival in Wales—A contributor to *The Life of Faith* and *The Christian*—The spiritual conflict with the powers of darkness

At the close of the year 1902, the Lord, in a remarkable way, pointed the path to India. A letter reached Mrs. Penn-Lewis from a lady then unknown to her, with the words: "God has shown me you are to go to India," offering to travel with her and help her in every way possible when there. Much exercise of heart took place over this letter; but after very careful sifting of the evidence whether it was of God or not, all doubt was removed, and the early months of 1903 found Mrs. Penn-Lewis in southern India, giving the Lord's message in Bombay, Bangalore, Madras, Coonoor, and other places.

A letter from Mrs. Penn-Lewis, which appeared in *The Life of Faith* of March 25th 1903, gives a condensed report of this visit:

Coonoor, S. India, March 3rd, 1903

For the sake of those who are so faithfully upholding me in prayer, and with whom I have no other means of communicating, I must write again to say how graciously the Lord is answering their prayers.

I am now resting in this most beautiful spot, after a very full time of service in the heat of the climate of Madras. It is peculiarly difficult to me to write of any work in which I have the privilege of

179

sharing. Moreover, I have found the work itself often hindered by too full accounts of it in our English Christian papers; so that I am not free to say as much as I would wish to those who are sharing in it by prayer.

They will be content to know that the Lord gave many tokens of his presence with us, and in many gatherings we had what an old Quaker used to describe as a "heart-tendering" time, the very best evidence of the brooding over hearts of the Holy Dove.

On arrival at Madras I found that meetings had been arranged in a large central hall; but, after prayerful consultation with several of the leading workers of Madras, we decided to divide the time at my disposal for several series of meetings in widely apart districts of the city, which is about nine miles long. I felt also that the European and English speaking community had so recently had the help of Dr. Torrey's meetings that my own heart was more drawn out to the work among the Indian Christians, for I feel assured that India can alone be truly evangelized by her own people.

Accordingly I gave the most of my time to special gatherings for native pastors, catechists, and workers, speaking to them by interpretation into Tamil. These gatherings were all held in the Christian College church belonging to the Free Church of Scotland Mission.

After some days a special request came that I would hold a meeting in North Black Town, in a native schoolroom right in the heart of the native quarter of Madras. Here we had a truly blessed time. The danger is *nominal* Christianity without a true change of heart; and an added danger that European education induces the native to aim at a government or *mission* appointment as a means of livelihood, rather than the Spirit of Christ constraining them to preach the gospel for Christ's sake alone. Some missionaries of long experience feel deeply the need of a fresh tide of divine life in the native church. It is not as yet fully a reproductive church, and our prayers for India should be directed to this end, that is, that the present Indian church should be quickened into abundant life so that every professing Christian should become a channel of life to others.

But to revert to our Madras gatherings. Morning Bible-readings were held in the Y.W.C.A. room on several days. Two other meetings in English were held in the Wesley College Room at Royapettah, and a morning meeting in a drawing-room near by.

On my last Saturday I went to the native church at Royapuram, and closed the work in Madras on Monday, February 23rd, by a visit to the Orphan Homes at Tondiapett, founded and carried on by a native worker, Mr. G. J. Israel. Here we had another gathering of workers and the very manifest presence of the Lord in our midst.

One matter of worldwide importance I hope to write about again, and this is in connection with the remarkable Mission Press under the superintendence of Rev. A. W. Rudisill, D.D. I had the privilege of going over the works early one morning and of addressing the large number of native workmen after they had answered the roll-call for the day. The foremen and principal workers are Christians, but the majority of the men are heathen. I shall never forget their riveted attention as for twenty minutes I spoke to them on "the place called Calvary." Never did the gospel, with its glorious message of deliverance from the burden and power of sin and the *fear of death,* shine out more to me in its beauty and power, and never did I see more clearly the truth of Paul's words that "the preaching of the cross is the power of God," as I saw the way it laid hold of these heathen minds.

Dr. Rudisill exclaimed afterwards: "Ah! The power of the cross; did you *see* how it held them?"

Of this work in the Mission Press I have much upon my heart to write about again.

Meanwhile I shall be grateful to those upon whom the Holy Spirit lays the burden for continued upholding in prayer. Further work on the plains is not possible, as the heat is daily increasing; and it is yet early for the missionaries to come to the hills. But some meetings are proposed here and at Ootacamund ere I leave for Bombay to join my steamer.

Jessie Penn-Lewis

One result of the journey to India was the issue of many of the printed messages in Tamil and other dialects, from the Madras Mission Press mentioned above. *The Bombay Guardian* also gave in its pages a full report of the Bible readings given in Bombay, and afterwards issued them in booklet form; and a Hindu scholar, who had already translated some of the writings of Dr. Andrew Murray, obtained permission of Mrs. Penn-Lewis to translate some of her books and send them to three different Tamil papers for use in serial form. At that time there was very little Christian literature available for the native Christians of India, and thus the ministry of these days was infinitely wider and deeper than any mere account of meetings taken can show. The first printed message, *The Pathway to Life in God,* was indeed directly responsible for the many open doors in Madras; for the Rev. John Stewart, of the Free Church of Scotland Mission, told Mrs. Penn-Lewis that some years before they had received a copy of *The Pathway,* and it had been lent round *"until it was in pieces"!* And many others came to tell of blessing received through the ministry of the printed page.

Mrs. Penn-Lewis in India, 1903

But the very fact that *The Pathway* and other booklets had preceded the coming of the writer herself meant that there were souls going on with God who needed both "instruction and reproof," in all tenderness and love and the Spirit of Christ. All error is "truth pressed to extremes," and there was discovered in some earnest and truly eager souls a tendency to hold and exercise the blessed truth of Romans 6 and Galatians 2:20 as a *"line of teaching,"* in the power of the natural mind—and therefore in the power of the flesh and the "wisdom of man." This "human conception of a divine reality" caused some to use language about it which at times went "beyond that which is written." If there is a possibility of "knowing Christ after the flesh," it is also possible that the very truth of God may be "taken hold of by the flesh and the fleshly mind" (Andrew Murray), and preached in the "wisdom of men," thus making it powerless. "The letter killeth, but the spirit giveth life" (2 Cor. 3:6) is equally true of the gospel as of the law, and the most precious message of "life out of death" can bring an atmosphere of "death" instead of life unless preached in "words which the Holy Ghost giveth," so that the faith of the hearer stands "in the power of God" and not "in the wisdom of man."

Not by a stringent "cutting off" of exterior things, nor by seeking a mental apprehension of "death with Christ" *in the conscious life,* but by a simple reckoning upon his death as yours—shall you experience in the inner depths of your life, servant of God, the divine spiritual reality that "Christ in you" is in truth *your very life,* displacing the old life of nature and continually "making to die" its inclinations and habits (Rom. 8:13; Col. 2:20–23; 3:1–4).

We therefore quote the following extracts from solemn words of warning written by Mrs. Penn-Lewis to one and another before leaving India, with the earnest prayer that the Spirit of God may make use of them again for the help of any who, having received the message of the cross with joy, have not found it "work" as they hoped.[1] This is doubtless because they have sought

---

1   that is, in the deeper aspect of Gal. 2:20.

to "perfect in the flesh" (or natural mind) that which was "begun in the Spirit," and can only be wrought out in the spirit and perfected in the life by the indwelling Spirit of Christ.

India, March 29th, 1903

I have seen the work at —, and met all the souls concerned, and I see how the human presentation of the blessed Calvary deliverance has blurred the message and thrown many off the track.

I feel most deeply that the 'experimental' side has hidden the power of the divine side and prevented the Holy Spirit from showing the work of Christ alone as the basis of faith. In every soul I have dealt with I have seen the disastrous confusion and despair produced by preaching an experience instead of the work of Christ. I can only cry to God to enable you to lift up CHRIST instead of a dead self.

I have taken every soul I have dealt with to the Lord, and sifted before him all the fruits of [your teaching] in these confused ones; gone over the Scriptures concerned, and watched and prayed to see where the error is, and clearer and clearer God has shown me it is the danger of preaching an experience instead of Christ. Of preaching a "death" that is not the application of Christ's death by the Holy Ghost, but an experimental "death" beyond that which is written.

"I fear lest … as the serpent beguiled Eve by his subtlety, so your minds should be corrupted from the simplicity that is in Christ." It is the mind, not the heart, that is the trouble. The mind beguiled from the simplicity of Christ. Your experience may easily be of God and yet the mind not able to interpret it clearly…

Dear friend, it is with deep yearning and many tears that I am jealous with a jealousy of God concerning you. It is a solemn thing to hinder the Christ from reaching his own, however unconscious we may be of it. It is heart-breaking to see you frustrating the very longing of your own heart to help God's servants … Surely he can illuminate your mind and heart, to give you a deeper sympathy and love in dealing with souls. How terrible it is to appear hard when your heart is full of love! How terrible to put iron chains of bondage on others—souls whom God has made free! "Where the Spirit of the Lord is, there is liberty."

But God will bring you through into a large place, where your vision will be of God, and you will carry to all around you the vision of God that brings self to the dust and does not occupy the souls with their own miserable selves. Then souls will be drawn to the glorious Christ within you, and never see the earthen vessel at all. That is his way—and souls then know that they have met with him ...

And to a leading missionary in S. India she wrote:

... It could hardly be possible for me to be here without hearing of the painful divisions of last year. I think you know that for quite eight years my own service has been entirely at conventions and amongst workers, and I have had to deal with every phase of the experiences and expressions along the line of Romans 6. This long time of continual service in many countries, among the most deeply taught of the servants of God, has made one acute to see at once where the line of expression is off the fine balance of the written Word, and to discern where the Holy Spirit does not bear witness. Where we are perfectly in line with the Scripture, rightly dividing the Word of truth, the Holy Ghost commends the message to every man's conscience as coming from him. What is from God, God seals with his Spirit. Is it not so?

Alas, alas, for the souls in despair and confusion, looking for an experience of "death" instead of resting on the work of Christ, which brings glad freedom and the positive inflowing of life from the risen one.

And then this question of "separation." It is my deep conviction that "separation," as God wants it, can only be truly brought about by the Lord himself as the inevitable outcome of his manifested presence. It has been sad to see souls thrown back from the fuller knowledge of God through "tennis" being emphasized as "unlawful," instead of the glorious Lord being lifted up, who will make his will known to every surrendered heart. May the Lord keep us from touching other lives by dealing with exterior things instead of preaching the fullness of Christ ...

Christ alone is the answer to each need. If we could only unveil HIM, it would not be long before the souls would cry "woe is me," and not need to be told of "separation." God forgive us for emphasizing the negative, instead of him who is all in all, and is the drawing power unto himself ...

It was during this visit to India that Mrs. Penn-Lewis compiled the little booklet, *The Word of the Cross;* and it is possible that the whole purpose of God in the long voyage was concerned mainly with the bringing forth of this tiny messenger of the cross, in the very words of Scripture, which was afterwards issued in many millions, and in over one hundred languages and dialects, carrying the vital and central truths of the gospel world wide. The story is told by Mrs. Penn-Lewis as follows.

The Story of the Bible Booklet

God has been calling his people to their knees, and in response to the movings of his Spirit upon them "making intercession according to the will of God," they have been pleading for a world-wide revival. Surely in answer to these petitions we may now expect to see the Lord coming forth in the glory of his power to answer the prayers inspired by him.

Since the petitions have been so large, asking nothing less than revival throughout the whole world, we may expect the omnipotent Lord to respond with large answers, revealing to his servants divine schemes, far above our thoughts, as the heaven is above the earth, for the world-wide proclamation of the gospel of his Son.

The conviction is increasingly growing upon me that the message which will bring the mighty working of the Holy Spirit in a world-wide revival will be the renewed preaching of the cross of Calvary as Paul the Apostle preached it. The *essence* of the gospel, so to speak, as summed up in his words, "Jesus Christ, and him crucified."

But we must remember that the gospel as Paul preached it included not only reconciliation to God through the blood of the cross, but deliverance from the *power* of sin by the believer's fellowship with the Lord upon his cross, through which he is "crucified to the world," and the world crucified unto him. Then is made known to him the riches of the glory of this mystery, which is "Christ in you, the hope of glory."

This message of the cross must be proclaimed anew ere the revival will come, and the church be prepared for translation at the Lord's appearing.

The adversary of souls knows this, and he is devising all manner of devices to hinder the *preaching of the cross,* knowing that his time is short. Multitudes are being ensnared in "doctrines of demons"— one and all revealing their source by their rejection of the cross. Whilst, alas, alas, in many churches professing the Christian name we have silence over the gospel of the cross, and sometimes direct antagonism. "Do speak about the cross and his sufferings; we never hear about that now," said one to a worker conducting a meeting. Alas that it should be so.

Since Calvary and the great sacrifice offered there for the sins of the whole world is the very pivot of all things in God's sight, surely the most high God will not behold all these devices of the evil one without giving his people a *renewed and mighty testimony to the gospel of Calvary,* and in his own omnipotent way devise means whereby the prince of darkness shall be defeated, and the gospel of the death and resurrection of the Son of God be proclaimed throughout the world and borne witness to by the Holy Ghost as in the days of Pentecost.

One such world-wide plan, bearing unmistakably the marks of the divine mind in its conception and preparation, came before me in my visit to Madras, India, in February 1903.

It is impossible in a short space to tell the story of the long preparation of the M.E. Mission Press in Madras, under the superintendence of Rev. A. W. Rudisill. I can only briefly say that in the press are a set of eight machines given to Dr. Rudisill in a remarkable way. They were invented by a gentleman in Pennsylvania, U.S.A., and kept solely for his own use for advertising a patent medicine which he was selling in enormous quantities. By these machines he was able to issue a little book consisting of sixteen pages of the size of two inches by three, at the rate of one hundred thousand per day, or twenty-eight millions per year.

The inventor had refused to have his machines duplicated, but of his own accord *gave a complete set* to Dr. Rudisill, who accepted them rather dubiously, not knowing clearly what use he could make of them.

After they reached India, and were set up in the press, it came to Dr. Rudisill that the wee booklet could be filled with verses of Scripture and the Word of God thus be scattered in millions throughout India; then, by a device of his own added to the machines, he found that he could print in ninety-eight languages at one time!

As the year 1903 dawned, it found Dr. Rudisill with specimen booklets prepared, asking for the co-operation of the people of God in this possible million-scattering of messages from his Word, and giving specimen pages in several languages; but as yet Dr. Rudisill had not seen the actual message from the Word of God which the booklet was to contain. In February 1903, by a chain of events which he relates in a pamphlet telling the story, the purpose of God was revealed to him, and he saw that the Lord had given him the Bible booklet machines for the express purpose of scattering throughout the world, in every language into which the Bible is translated, the gospel of Calvary—the precious message which tells the soul of freedom from the guilt and power of sin and the indwelling of the risen Lord...

Do we really *believe* with all our hearts the statement that "the word of the cross... is the power of God" (1 Cor. 1:18, R.V.)? The Greek word translated "power" in this passage is "*dunamis*," and it has been pointed out that this word does not mean *latent* power, but *power* in *action*.

The word of the cross is God's power in action to all who believe. It is God's "instrument to energize a dead world, for through it Omnipotence can manifest its power."

Have we messengers of God dared to believe that divine energy is in the "word of the cross," or have we limited omnipotence by thinking that *his* "word of the cross" needs many words to explain it? Is it not rather the key devised by the all-wise Creator to unlock the hearts of men?... We are shown this in the story of the way Philip preached the message of Calvary from the prophecy of Isaiah to the eunuch in the desert. The energy of God was in the message, so that the man of Ethiopia went on his way rejoicing.

That the Lord himself has devised and prepared this worldwide plan for scattering the message of Calvary through the Bible booklet we can have little doubt. Since this is so we may believe that it "shall accomplish" that whereunto he sends it. The "word of the cross" will not return unto him void, but it will prosper in his hand.

"Amen, O Lord," so be it throughout the whole world, that the crucified and risen Lord may see of the travail of his soul and be satisfied.

Dr. Rudisill himself has told how the Little Press was given its message:

I was not fully satisfied that I had understood all that God purposed in the wondrous growth of the press... after all the years of tenacious carrying out of the plans laid upon my heart, I could not but ask, "Is this all?" I now spent much time in prayer, seeking the mind of God. Alone in the press before daylight, I would claim the promise of the Father and believe that I had received the gift of the Holy Ghost. I expected to receive such a flood of light that, filled with praise, I should cry, "He has come! The Comforter has come!"

But in spite of all this, a feeling of weariness over the press would come, and joy in it I had not. The tempter would say, "This is all you have after praying for the fullness of the Holy Spirit"...

But I was brought lower and lower, until it seemed I could not even pray, and the press was a greater burden than ever. Still lower down I had to go; and the climax came when, at the first Communion service of the New Year, kneeling in full faith that God would help me, I seemed to see before me an ugly, horrible figure on a cross. I cried, "Lord, I am a vile sinner! Have I followed thee to the cross, to see thee there in such horrible guise? Have mercy!"

For days afterwards I struggled to shake off this terrible thought. What did it all mean? I was so humbled in the dust that I walked in dread of myself and felt almost in despair. "Does this come of daring to believe for the fullness of the Holy Spirit?" I said. "Where is the light I thought would stream from heaven?" One afternoon the powers of darkness raged so fiercely that I thought all was lost. I had not only glimpses of that awful image on the cross, but the press itself seemed to be passing under a curse. Hell raged around it. I could endure it no longer.

At this time of crisis I attended some special meetings conducted by Mrs. Penn-Lewis. The first Bible reading she gave struck me as being free from human speculation to a degree that at first interested me, and then riveted my attention. This led me to read one of the small books she had written, and to my delight I found that also free from human speculation, and pointing the soul to the cross with an earnestness and directness that impressed me deeply. I read other books written by her, and in those too, "Jesus Christ was openly set forth crucified," and I saw how the Apostle Paul had gloried in the cross, not only as a means whereby he had peace with God, but also as the instrument of his own crucifixion. "Through which the world hath been crucified unto me, and I unto the world," he wrote to the Galatians.

I saw the "word of the cross" to be, indeed, the *power* of God, not only to the unsaved soul, but to the child of God. Light began to dawn, until one morning early, pondering over the awful picture I had seen at the New Year Communion service, the Spirit of God whispered to me: "*It was yourself*"—and deep peace filled my soul.

I went to the morning Bible reading, and the message was, "I have been crucified with Christ; yet I live; and yet no longer I, but Christ liveth in me: and the life which I now live in the flesh I live in faith, the faith which is in the Son of God, who loved me, and gave himself up for me" (Gal. 2:20, R.V.).

Broken at the feet of the Lord, I prayed and praised. "But Lord, I have been seeking the fullness of the Holy Ghost."

"Do you not know that the Holy Ghost reveals the cross, and your place as *crucified with Christ*, ere he can have room to dwell in all his fullness in your life?"

Enough! This covers all. "Lord, what wilt thou have me to do?"

Now the light streamed in, and in his light I saw light. I saw clearly "one increasing purpose" shining through the years from my boyhood until it rested upon those Bible booklet machines. The hand of God had not wrought all these things except for some purpose in his eternal counsels.

And what was that purpose? It is remarkable that I never was free to make the selections for the Bible booklets myself, and had no inclination to ask others to do so. Verses had actually been suggested by some, but I had always felt a staying hand upon me, as though the time had not yet come. The sample pages printed were only tentative … I saw now that the Lord had an object in the delay.

But the fullness of time had come at last! With the full message of Calvary illuminated to my own soul as I had never seen it before, I saw that the little book must carry only the story of the cross. My mind went back to the strange way in which the press had been given the booklet machines. They had been devised to send to many thousands the news of a remedy for one of earth's diseases—surely they were prepared of God to carry to all people and tribes and nations the proclamation of the healing power of the death of the Son of God …

I now became deeply impressed with the thought that, as Mrs. Penn-Lewis had been so signally raised up of God to spread the message of the cross, if she would select verses bearing directly upon this message, and devote each page to some particular phase of the wonderful teaching of the cross, this little booklet might indeed become a message to the world. She agreed to do this.

The message for the little book was sought of God and given to the press. The hour had come! The press was given its message! It is easy to see that this was not brought about by a *man-made* plan. God used a number of agents who saw not what it meant, nor its beginning, nor its end. As we glance back over what has been wrought and see the links in the chain, we must surely exclaim, "It is the Lord's doing, and it is marvelous in our eyes!"[1]

In a letter to Mrs. Penn-Lewis, Dr. Rudisill wrote:

Oh wise interpreter of the deep things of God, you have shown me *God's plan for me,* and henceforth I shall *make no plans for God!* I see that I have nothing to do but to keep in his plan, and keep step with him in that plan, no matter where it may lead . . .

But how very little is the insight you have given me compared with that other infinitely greater mission of enlisting this press for proclaiming the message of Calvary, as it assuredly will, in many tongues. You have set the press free, you have liberated it! It is as much yours now, to proclaim your message—or rather the message God gave you for it—as though you owned it. The focal point of all these machines will be to tell out the word of the cross . . . they have become messengers of the glorious gospel of the Son of God. And you—you were the messenger of God to harness these to God's purposes, to guide them into his plan . . .

You have come with the sword of the Almighty to strike at this stronghold of Theosophy (Madras), and this press is your servant for the Lord's sake.

God loves little things, and he loves to use them for great purposes—a rod, ram's horns, broken pitchers, an old garment fallen from the fiery chariot, and a sling with a few smooth stones from

---

1   From *The Story of a Little Printing Press*, a pamphlet by the late A. W. Rudisill, D.D.

the brook. No wonder, then, that God can use a little printing press and a little book.

So wrote Dr. Rudisill in the preface to the pamphlet from which we have taken the above story of God's wondrous leadings. "It is God's telegraphic dispatch to a dying world," remarked the late Rev. D. M. Stearns, editor of *Kingdom Tidings* (U.S.A.); and the saintly Bishop of Durham, the late Dr. Handley C. G. Moule, wrote, "I greatly like the *Word of the Cross* Bible booklet; it gives the very soul of the divine message."

The booklet was issued from the Mission Press in Madras with none of the usual organization deemed necessary for the furthering of vast schemes, yet its circulation rapidly reached millions in Indian dialects alone. When the story became known, the Lord laid it upon the heart of a Jewish missionary in Jerusalem to prepare the booklet in Yiddish and Hebrew.[1] Thus it came about, with no human forethought or plan, that almost the first translation issued from the press was in the language of God's ancient people, in accordance with God's own principle "to the Jew first" Other translations poured in upon Dr. Rudisill from all lands. The British and Foreign Bible Society asked for 100,000 booklets in Tamil. The Salvation Army, and other societies working in heathen lands, were not slow to see the value of the little printed messenger; and before very long the booklet was available in no less than one hundred languages and dialects.

Space forbids that we give details of the extraordinary way in which God has worked through this tiny "missionary," but it is of interest to note that the *Word of the Cross* booklet was the first gospel message to enter Tibet when that "closed land" was suddenly opened by the British forces under General Younghusband. An army officer undertook to have a copy of the booklet in Spanish distributed to every Spanish-speaking household on the Rock of Gibraltar. The demand for the Bible booklet throughout Great Britain was beyond all expectation, and the Lord laid it upon the

1   The Rev. Samuel Schor.

late Mr. Thomas Hogben, founder of the One by One Band, to organize a systematic distribution throughout our own land and the Colonies, through the agency of the praying bands associated with the One by One work.

Many are the romances of God's working told by missionaries and evangelists using the wee booklet in their daily work, of which the following is but an example. An evangelist wrote of his use of the booklet:

> Souls in batches of thirty, forty, fifty have been led to Christ, convicted and converted through the message of the booklet. Yea, hundreds have thus been won for Christ during the last three months, and scores of Christians have been led into the victorious life through its means. I asked one young man: "How long is it since God's Spirit spoke to you?" And he replied, "A young man gave me a Bible booklet. I read the first page, and then the second, when I reached John 3:16, and since then I have had no rest. I know God can save me"—and he did.
>
> Seven young men came to my room knowing nothing of the blessed life of victory—no holy boldness for the Lord, no passion for souls. We just got together and read the message in the booklet, then knelt silently before the Lord until one after the other just sank prostrate before him. We were there three hours, and since then each one of them has been marvelously changed.
>
> Hardly a week but they have been used of God to win souls. Two of these young men are going into the ministry...
>
> At a free breakfast to the very lowest in a certain town, five remained behind to seek the Lord; and as I prayed that God would break them down, an ex-convict's wife said about the booklet message, "That's the message to break them!" And it did. There was a desperate prisoner in the prison, and I asked the warder to let me see him. I went to the cell, and got him on his knees, then read to him a few verses out of the booklet. It was the old message of Calvary in all its power, and he was brought to Christ...

During the Welsh Revival it was said that souls were given such a revelation of Calvary to their spiritual vision that their whole lives were changed. As we ponder the story of the Madras "Bible booklet," just preceding the marvelous outpouring of the

Spirit of God in Wales, and bearing—in the dealing of God with Dr. Rudisill—the marks of long preparation in the purpose of God, we cannot but feel that here was another step in the divine movement toward the calling of the people of God to a spiritual awakening and a renewed preaching of the cross of Christ. And is it not, even now, a call from God to his children to seek from him a deeper unveiling of all that "Calvary" means to their own souls, that they may be equipped by the Holy Spirit to enter into God's world-purposes concerning its proclamation?

Closely associated with the compilation of the Bible booklet, in the leading and teaching of the Holy Spirit, was the rewriting by Mrs. Penn-Lewis, on her return from India, of the small book *The Message of the Cross*, which had already run out of print. With the fresh evidence before her that the "word of the cross" is indeed the *dunamis,* the energy of God, God's "power in action" for the salvation of a lost world, there poured from her pen a fuller and richer opening up of the same theme, in which was incorporated the earlier message which had been so definitely given of God.[1]

"An old doctrine in a new light," was the heading of a very hearty commendation of the book by the Rev. Griffith Ellis, in a Welsh magazine; but a personal letter to Mrs. Penn-Lewis from the late Oswald Chambers shows the value of the teaching as it appeared to one himself deeply taught of God. Writing from Dunoon College, Scotland, on November 2nd, 1903, Mr. Chambers said:

> Your *Cross of Calvary* is pre-eminently of God. The splendid treasure of pain, your pain, has merged into the greatness of God's power. Your book teaches clearly and grandly what the Spirit witnesses to in the Bible and in our hearts, viz: that "the way of God" flatly contradicts common sense, and by utmost despair the Holy Ghost leads to resurrection triumph. The *breakdown of the natural virtues* seems to be the point wherein most regenerated lives are cast into despair. Your book will help these to understand that this despair must end in death to natural goodness and self, and be raised by

1 *The Cross of Calvary and its Message.*

the power of God into inconceivably glorious power and peace and liberty of life ...

You are clearer and clearer each time you write, and each day you grow from those past days of mysterious crucifixion, which is an open secret to those of us who have the witness of the Spirit ...

This book, which has become a "classic" on the atonement in all its aspects, has been translated and issued in many languages. Dr. Andrew Murray wrote a foreword to the Dutch edition, published in South Africa. Truly prophetic were the words of Mrs. Penn-Lewis in her preface, dated October 1903, as she spoke of "the conviction growing in many hearts that the Holy Spirit is bidding the messengers of God go back to Calvary, and then will come the worldwide revival for the calling out of his redeemed ... for which we look." For the "preaching of the cross," in its power to deliver and separate from sin and the world, and its victory over the power of Satan, is the "preaching" God used (and will still use) for the bringing about of revival among his own children, and a great ingathering of the unsaved.

The Llandrindod Wells Convention

With the renewed commission for active service in the fall of 1902, and just before the call to India was received, the Spirit of God began to move toward bringing into existence the Llandrindod Wells Convention, in the same spontaneous way as the inception of the Y.W.C.A. branch at Neath ten years before. At Keswick that year were two Welsh Ministers (the Revs. J. Rhys Davies and D. Wynne Evans), who told how thirteen Welsh people had met one day at the 1896 convention to pray that God would give Wales a convention for the deepening of spiritual life; and from that time on, they had been holding this petition before the Lord. Now the "fullness of time" seemed to have come. "Let us go and see Mrs. Penn-Lewis and confer with her," Mr. Rhys Davies said to his friend; and every succeeding step evidenced that the Lord was going before, to bring into being the convention which afterwards became one of the channels for the rivers of life to Wales—an important factor in the outbreak of revival in the principality in 1904–5.

Later in the summer of 1902, Mrs. Penn-Lewis, being in south Wales, laid the project before the aged Dean Howell of St. David's—beloved of all sections of God's people in Wales as "a man of God, a patriot, preacher-orator, and bard"; and encouraged by the co-operation and wise counsel of this mature servant of God and others, the details of the long-prayed-for convention rapidly took shape. Mr. H. D. Phillips, who had recently organized a series of meetings at Llandrindod Wells for the Rev. F. B. Meyer, accepted the local secretaryship. Other help was gladly given for dealing with the local arrangements, and the Albert Hall at Llandrindod Wells was booked for the first week in August the following year. By January 7th, when Mrs. Penn-Lewis sailed for India, the greater part of the arrangements were in train. The part taken by the venerable Dean of St. David's proved to be his last earthly service for his master, as news of his death reached Mrs. Penn-Lewis on her arrival at Bombay.

Mr. Albert Head, writing to *The Life of Faith* in August 1903, said that "the desire for a Keswick for Wales had been in the minds of several who had attended the annual meetings beside Derwent Water, and it was evidently the Master's commission to Mrs. Penn-Lewis, herself a native of the principality, to bring the desire to fruition. The Wells was chosen as a place of meeting, as many Welsh ministers and workers gather [there] during August; and apparently no better place could be chosen for securing the attendance of so large a number, representing various congregations and colleges, and evangelical and evangelistic agencies."

The speakers at that first convention included the Rev. J. Stuart Holden, the Rev. Evan H. Hopkins, Dr. Charles Inwood, Dr. F. B. Meyer, and Mrs. Penn-Lewis, with Mr. Albert Head as chairman. The conference bore upon it the marks of Spirit-born preparation ... So noticeable was the ministerial attendance that a well-known missioner involuntarily remarked, "Wales may be the cradle of the evangelists for the coming revival!"

And again it was the message of the cross, showing the experimental aspect of the Holy Spirit's work in the believer, the putting away of all known sin, *deliverance through identification with Christ in his death,* and the definite reception of the Holy Ghost as a necessity for all in the service of God. This was carried home to hearts by the power of God in such intensity that on the last two days it was manifest to all that the Spirit of God had come down in Pentecostal power...

In August 1904, the second convention at Llandrindod took place, when a testimony meeting revealed how deep a work had been wrought in 1903. A minister, writing to a Welsh paper, said that many "saw a door of hope for revival in Wales in the near future." Referring to the testimony meeting, he said:

> It was a luxury to hear ministers and laymen giving expression to the change that had taken place in their ministry and in their personal lives since the convention of 1903... It is manifest that better days are about to dawn, and blessed are those believers who are willing now to consecrate themselves as instruments for the Holy Ghost in the next revival.

> It can be seen, therefore, how all through 1903 and 1904 the underground currents were quietly deepening, and sometimes breaking out to the surface, until the time drew near when the floodgates opened, and the Spirit of God broke out upon the land as a tidal wave, sweeping all things before it...[1]

Six Welsh ministers who entered into the Spirit-filled life at the first Llandrindod Convention agreed to meet once a month through the year for a quiet day with God, and at the 1904 convention held a midnight prayer-meeting when they "consecrated themselves afresh to God for his use and definitely asked the Lord to raise up someone to usher in the revival!" They returned to their respective churches burning with a new zeal and a new message; and in each place the flame of revival sprang up shortly after, resulting in a great ingathering of souls, and through them

1   From *The Awakening in Wales and some of the Hidden Springs,* by Mrs. Penn-Lewis.

and their quickened people, spreading from district to district, until it was said, "Wales is on fire."

In the *Life of Faith* for November 9th, 1904, there appeared a contribution from Mrs. Penn-Lewis telling of the "cloud as a man's hand" which had risen over Wales, quoting a letter received from a well-known evangelist; and three weeks later another, which began: "We have prayed for revival. Let us give thanks! The 'cloud as a man's hand' about which the Rev. Seth Joshua wrote in October is now increasing. God is sweeping the southern hills and valleys of Wales with an old-time revival..." And from that time onward, Mrs. Penn-Lewis became the chronicler of the revival, contributing a page to *The Life of Faith* each week, tracing the course of that movement of God, first throughout Wales, and then through many lands and by many channels, reviving the sleeping church of God and harvesting a great host of souls for his kingdom.

It was said by some who perhaps only saw the emotional aspect of the work in Wales that the Celtic temperament was the great factor in the whole movement, and particularly the Welsh singing. The Lord answered this suggestion by manifesting the same melting power among Christians of different race and temperament in India, China, Korea, Japan, and other missionary countries, and also in parts of Europe. A typical instance, in which Mrs. Penn-Lewis herself was the Lord's "channel," occurred in May 1905, at a conference for Christian workers in Germany. The Spirit of God came down in mighty power as his servant spoke of Calvary as the place of *unity* between Jew and Gentile (Eph. 2:11–18), that there can be no divisions *in Christ*, for Christ cannot be divided. The presence of God was intensely felt, as a worker rose and said something in German. Then a brother rose and shook hands with another with whom he had been at variance; then men and women from all parts of the gathering rose, confessing to one another "hard thoughts" and a spirit of division and disunity. In the next meeting the message was on the power of Calvary's victory to deliver from the bondage of sin, the spirit of the world, the spirit of division, the power of the devil, and the life of self-pleasing; and the Lord did his own work among the 250 or so Christian workers gathered, not one soul remaining untouched.

At the close of the conference, the greater part of those present rose and pressed to the front to yield all to God and to receive the fullness of the Holy Spirit. Again was heard the chorus of prayer, as numbers prayed together without confusion, and on the following morning, for two hours, there was a stream of public testimony from old and young, to what God had wrought in them.

"God *can* work, whatever the nationality or the temperament," wrote Mrs. Penn-Lewis in the *Life of Faith* afterwards:

> In this conference we have seen that the "melting" was done by the Holy Spirit himself, *through the Word of God,* with no persuasion or pleading, as it might have been had the messenger known the language of the people. Blessed be God for this evidence that the Holy Spirit can melt without the use of any means save the Word of God wielded by himself, even in broken words translated into another tongue... Undoubtedly what God has done this week will prepare the workers for revival, and we can only pray that all the surrendered ones may be as "coals of fire" scattered over the land...

* * *

For three years (November 1904 to the end of 1908) Mrs. Penn-Lewis continued as a weekly contributor to *The Life of Faith*, first as recorder of the times of revival, and afterwards with messages from the Word to the awakened souls in the church of Christ, so that the record of the revival passed on into a record of the advancing spiritual growth of the body of Christ that followed the awakening. In response to the expressed desire of Christian workers, many of these articles, giving a bird's eye view of the movement of the Holy Spirit throughout the world, were reissued weekly on a separate sheet for broadcast distribution, under the general heading, "England, Awake!" In a letter dated February 27th, 1906, the Rev. C. G. Moore, then editor of the *Life of Faith*, remarks: "About the sheets—every one of them has been sold out, and last week I think 7,000 were printed; so that evidently there is a demand for them which is most encouraging"…

For some two years Mrs. Penn-Lewis also contributed articles to the pages of *The Christian*—a ministry which seems to have arisen out of a visit to Egypt in 1904, when a deep fellowship in the things of God was established between herself and the editor and founder of that paper. In her book, *Glimpses of Four Continents*,[1] Mrs. R. C. Morgan refers to this time:

> Mrs. Penn-Lewis' visit to Egypt coincided with ours, and we were brought a good deal into contact with her. "I have long been wishing" said my husband, "to be at leisure for a long talk with Mrs. Penn-Lewis, and in order to be so I had to come to Egypt!" The ten days spent together at Mena House, close to the Pyramids, were to me a continual "Keswick" in which two kindred spirits represented the platform, and I the audience. Between the "meetings," or while they lasted—for neither our friend nor Mr. Morgan thought it ever out of season to speak of the things of God (which were a perennial subject to them)—we made excursions…

The contributions to *The Christian* fulfilled an important service to the church of God when, in 1908, they took the form of a series of articles under the title of "An Hour of Peril," in which Mrs. Penn-Lewis sought to place before the people of God a brief outline of the then arising Pentecostal movement, based upon letters written by eyewitnesses in many parts of the world. The articles were not written in a spirit of opposition or adverse criticism, but with an earnest attempt to enable believers to discern for themselves the points of danger, and an urgent appeal to all to "try the spirits, whether they be of God," wherever supernatural manifestations were taking place. As the introductory article put it:

> The tactics of Satan as an angel of light have been so subtle, and his imitations of the working of the Holy Spirit so close, that however deep the inner conviction has been that false powers were at work in the movement, the fear of touching anything that *might be* of God

---

1   Morgan & Scott.

has checked the bold outspokenness which many faithful servants of God felt to be their duty... Nevertheless, as fresh reports kept coming in from land after land where this movement was reaching it was seen, almost without exception, that everywhere it brought division and separation among Christians. In some cases, unhappily, where there had been a true "revival" by the Spirit of God...

In reference to these articles—the precursors of the teaching afterwards developed in *The Overcomer* against the subtle tactics and counterfeits of Satan as an "angel of light"—Dr. F. B. Meyer said, in a letter written from S. Africa:

> I think that the letters in *The Christian* are of high value just now. There is nothing else to guide these perplexed souls. What a strange thing it is! But surely the watchman should blow the trumpet and warn the people...

Satan's war against the saints is summed up, in Ephesians 6:12, in one word—"wiles." The inroad of counterfeit workings of the enemy which gradually mingled with the true working of the Spirit of God during two years of almost world-wide revival, found the people of God unprepared. Through ignorance of the "deep things of Satan" and what he was able to do among them by guile, and "ignorant of his devices," almost all that was supernatural was liable to be accepted as divine. It was "a warfare belonging to the time of the end, and therefore practically unknown and unprepared-for in the literature of the church, although clearly to be discovered in the Word of God."[2]

It is remarkable that for some years God had been leading Mrs. Penn-Lewis to deal with the believer's conflict with the powers of darkness from the Scriptures, and from knowledge gained in dealing with souls. In 1897, at a day of waiting upon God at the China Inland Mission Hall, London, she gave a series of addresses upon spiritual conflict, particularly in regard to those who had been brought by the Holy Spirit into the experience of union with Christ in the heavenly places. Notes of these addresses were issued in a small booklet, *Conflict in the Heavenlies,* which

2   Mrs. Penn-Lewis.

was afterwards incorporated in the larger work, *The Warfare with Satan and the Way of Victory*, a "brief treatise dealing with a vast, and to a certain extent, little known subject." An extract from this book, issued in 1906, when the Welsh Revival had already subsided, will show something of the spiritual background of the revival, and also some of the underlying causes of its cessation:[1]

If we look back at the history of the past decade, up to the time of the awakening in Wales, we can see how the Prince of Darkness was working insidiously among the people, undermining their faith in the Scriptures as the Word of God, silencing the preaching of the cross to the utmost of his power, and drawing off great numbers into Theosophy... Christian Science... and Spiritism.

At the same time, the church was to a great extent powerless. Divisions, worldliness, and carnal ease on the whole marked her condition... until the Divine Spirit broke forth in Wales in Pentecostal power. The church throughout the world was more or less awakened... and now all who know anything of the Spirit-filled life find themselves in a spiritual conflict with the hosts of wickedness in high places, and are discovering that every manifestation of the Holy Spirit is being met by a counterfeit of the evil one. In fact, the more "spiritual" a man is, the more open he is to the spirit-world—either of good or evil powers... Let the believer seek an *"experience"* without the cross and all that it means in continuous crucifixion of *self*, and the evil one will give him all that he desires... Alas, it is terribly possible for a deceiving spirit... to enter and speak through children of God who have unwittingly given place to the devil in some subtle way...

A clergyman wrote: "In my case I found that any doubt, fear, agitation, want of love, self-exaltation, especially the feeling that God was going to do great things through me because I was so surrendered... brought false power and deception." The continuance of

1   From *The Warfare with Satan and the Way of Victory*. It may be mentioned here that a concise summary of this book was selected as one of the papers for insertion in Vol. 10 of *The Fundamentals*, a series of volumes restating the fundamental truths of the Christian faith, issued free by the generosity of two Christian laymen in the United States to 250,000 Christian workers throughout the world. An unabridged edition was also issued in cheap pamphlet form, and many thousands distributed among Christians in India and China.

supernatural manifestations at first pure and of God, with a change of source unperceived by the ensnared believer, is the most subtle of the latest workings of the enemy, and is the key to the strange and terrible inroad of spiritualistic manifestations among the most spiritual and surrendered souls in the church of God.

The story of the revival itself is more fully told in the book we have already quoted.[2] From it developed the joint witness of the collaborators of the book *War on the Saints*. Through the strain and suffering brought upon him during eight months of daily and continuous meetings in crowded, ill-ventilated chapels, one of the chief figures of the awakening in Wales completely broke down; and thus it came about that, by the invitation of Mr. and Mrs. Penn-Lewis, Mr. Evan Roberts went down to the country home near Leicester where they were now living, for a time of rest and recuperation. His recovery, however, was slow and intermittent, lasting many months; and during the long period of convalescence, he began to open his mind to his hostess on many experiences of supernatural forces witnessed during the revival. Since her own mighty endowment of power for service, Mrs. Penn-Lewis had learned the path of the cross, and seen the dangers attendant upon souls who, having experienced such a breaking-through into the supernatural realm, do not know *identification with Christ in his death* as the place of safety from the wiles and assaults of the devil.

"In the years since my wondrous experience," she wrote about this time to her old friend Dr. F. B. Meyer, "I have been given by the Divine Spirit the interpretation of the cross to the Christian... Through my long years of walking with God, and the consequent deeper and deeper revelation of the depths of the fallen creation and the need of the cross to sever us from it in every subtle action, I know that only the knowledge of the cross can save such from spiritual wreckage..."

This God-given knowledge and experience, together with the insight into the devices of the enemy gained by Mr. Roberts in

2   *The Awakening in Wales.*

his experiences during the revival, are conserved to the church of God in *War on the Saints*. Issued only after seven years of testing, proving, and praying-through the truths given therein, this book has been the means, by the grace and power of God, of the deliverance of hundreds of his children from the wiles and deceptions of the great adversary of God and man, which, when recognized, can be resisted and defeated in the victorious name of our Lord Jesus Christ.

"In integrity and truth, covered with the whole armor of God, hidden in him who was manifested to destroy the works of the devil, she is to look and see that in the conqueror of Calvary she is 'far above all principality and power' (Eph. 1:21), for in his cross, he triumphed over 'principalities and powers,' and put them to open shame.

"The lions' dens (Cant. 4:8) are far beneath his feet; in him she may tread upon the young lion and the serpent (Ps. 91:13); for the God of Peace will bruise Satan under her feet as she learns to overcome through the blood of the Lamb (Rev. 12:11)."

Chapter 10

The Overcomer

1909–1914

The founding of the magazine—The London and Matlock Conferences—A "working holiday" in Finland—The world war and the closure of *The Overcomer*

Meanwhile the "Bible booklet" work was increasing on every hand, and a whole-time secretary was engaged in its distribution and the correspondence that arose out of it with servants of God in many lands. A circular letter was sent out at intervals to give fuel for prayer and praise to those interested in the work; and this led, in 1908, to the issue bimonthly of a small eight-page occasional paper with the title *The Word of the Cross*. The following notes, taken from early issues of this little paper, reveal still further the deep need of the spiritual church which later called forth the testimony of *The Overcomer* to the "victory" aspect of the work of Christ at Calvary:

> It is dawning upon us that the *Word of the Cross* booklet was fore-given of God for this time … It was only in 1903 that it was given, just a few months before the Spirit of God broke forth at the first Llandrindod Wells Convention, and then in the year after, in what is now known as the awakening in Wales. Then in 1906 came what may be called the "hour and power of darkness" upon the church of Christ. All over the world, believers who had been pressing on to the "heavenlies" found themselves attacked by the most subtle "deep things of Satan." Lonely groups of believers who knew nothing of what was occurring in other parts of the world, and isolated workers unaware of the experiences of others, became conscious of the most

extraordinary attempts of Satan to *imitate* the Holy Spirit in his workings ...

It was at this very point that ... the *victory aspect* of Calvary was revealed to many souls, and through the darkening months that followed ... has proved a key to victory in the face of Satan and his hosts. And now, blessed be God, just as the enemy seems to have triumphed in misleading so many ... there is most clear indication that God is setting his hand to reunite the disintegrated ranks under the banner of the cross. There is a quiet turning to the "place called Calvary," and the precious little booklet is now proving a special weapon in the hands of believers for the "lifting of the standard" of the cross ...

The prophet Isaiah wrote, "When the Adversary shall come in like a flood, the Spirit of the Lord shall raise up a standard against him." What standard will the Divine Spirit lift but the standard of the cross? Not the wooden cross, or the cross without the Christ— but the *death on the cross* of the Son of God, which not only atoned for sin but conquered Satan, and delivered his captives out of his power ... (From the *Occasional Paper,* 1908).

In the last issue for the year there appears a little note that it is intended to increase the size of the paper and to record, "not only the ever-increasing blessing attendant on the distribution of the booklet, but messages on the preaching of the cross, which may stir to renewed prayer and action all who have proved in their own lives the victory of Calvary." But in January 1909, the magazine made its appearance, not only enlarged in size and number of pages, but as a monthly paper, entered at Stationers' Hall, and with a new title, its scope being enlarged to admit of articles on the purpose and conditions of revival, on the various aspects of the message of the cross, and the maturing of the body of Christ to be "overcomers" in the sense of Revelation 2 and 3.

Two extracts from the editorial notes of that first year, one from the January, the other from the December number, tell the story of the founding of the magazine.

Step by step the Lord has led on, and made clear his will to meet a definite need among the children of God in such a paper, which is now sent forth in his name to accomplish that whereunto he sends it. *Its title* is a true one, for it goes forth, first and foremost, to proclaim with no uncertain sound the atoning work of the God-Man on the cross, and all that Calvary means in its height, and depth, and breadth and length, to meet the deepest and entire need of an utterly fallen creation. And to preach the cross today... demands nothing less than being *an "overcomer" indeed!*

For... only those who know, not only the power of the sacred blood of the Lamb, but their identification in death with Christ, and therefore joint-life with him in his risen and ascended power, *can* overcome so as to "sit down" with him in his throne (Rev. 3: 21) and finally "inherit all things" as co-heirs and co-rulers with the Son of God, the firstborn of many brethren. (*The Overcomer*, January 1909).

The welcome given to the little paper was altogether beyond the anticipation of its editor. The first number, prepared in one week and sent out with very little previous notice, was soon out of print; and so insistent were the calls for further copies that a second edition was printed six months later!

Very quickly the Lord confirmed the venture of faith, for as soon as the editorial preparation of the first number was begun, it was manifest that the little paper was to be carried forth on a current of life from God; for the Spirit of God poured life and power into the work—verily "the waters were risen... waters to swim in"... Then the frail barque was launched. No trumpet blast hailed its appearance, but human hearts cried welcome, and letters soon came telling of blessing to souls and eager acceptance of the victory message.

The powers of darkness, however, were alert, and every succeeding issue was prepared in conflict such as only those know who understand the resistance of the arch-foe of hell to the Calvary message. But we have, by the grace of God, reached the issue of the twelfth number, and we cry with thankfulness, "Ebenezer!" (*The Overcomer*, December 1909).

In January 1910, the paper was again enlarged, from sixteen to twenty pages, with the addition of the now familiar cover; and in this form it continued until its cessation during the years of the European war. Every year—indeed every month—the circle of its readers was extended, and eternity alone will reveal all that the magazine meant to those members of the body of Christ who desired to "press on into full growth." A correspondent in another land put the ministry of *The Overcomer* very concisely when he wrote to its editor:

> The "why" of defeat and the "how" of victory is the glorious ministry which has been entrusted to you for the church... If I understand you aright, you have a definite goal in view. You want to remove *ground of attack* in the worker, so that the Holy Spirit may burst forth in revival power. John 7:38 would mean revival breaking out all over the harvest field... They who know their Lord would call it the restoration of the *normal* life—what we now find is the *abnormal* life, a life atrophied...

Without doubt, entry into the "heavenly warfare" of Ephesians 6 must needs follow the acceptance of the message of the cross in its fullness; for Romans 6, "crucified with Christ," if it be experimentally known, means that the spirit becomes truly *"joined to the Lord"* as "one spirit" (1 Cor. 6:17), and the believer then becomes conscious that his wrestling is not against flesh and blood, but against unseen spiritual foes in the spiritual realm to which he is now introduced. It is a conflict "in the heavenlies," unknown to those who have not passed experimentally through Romans 6 and Galatians 2:20 to Ephesians 2:6—"hath raised us up together, and made us sit together in the heavenlies in Christ." In the last days of the dispensation, the powers of darkness are pressing upon the church to keep her, if possible, from rising to her glorious place "far above all" in Christ; and it is increasingly necessary for every member of the body of Christ to understand the spiritual warfare of Ephesians 6 and 2 Cor. 10:4–5, that they may triumph in *Christ* over Satan and his hosts, as well as over sin and the world.

Speaking of the "pressing on from faith to faith" in the opening up of truth during the first sixth-year issue of *The Overcomer*, Mrs. Penn-Lewis wrote in December 1914:

This aggressive warfare which was developing … at last showed that it would demand all the spiritual strength and time which up to this period had been usable for other service. It showed, also, that the character of the commission demanded a severance in service from others not called to such a witness, lest they should be hindered in their own specific work, and the witnesses be hindered in their testimony.

It was no small thing, therefore, when the Spirit of God indicated that my service in the *women's meetings* at Keswick was finished, and in 1909 a letter of withdrawal was written …

The cost of this step of obedience was very keen. The Word of God deeply severed soul from spirit, as I saw … how the *soul* could unknowingly feed upon the "fellowship" side of Spirit-given and Spirit-anointed service for God.

In 1911 came the same clear guidance from God to withdraw from the Llandrindod Convention. The day before going to the convention a letter of resignation was written in faith that the Spirit of God would show the meaning of his leading. The message of the cross and of the warfare was given and borne witness to by the Spirit of God, in light to souls in need of deliverance from the oppression of the foe … God had opened for his people a marvelous realm of truth, which to withhold from the church of God would mean not only eternal loss to the church, but unfaithfulness to God on the part of those to whom it was given. The truth to be unfolded needed *the full time of a convention for its elucidation,* and it could no longer be faithfully made known in occasional addresses and side meetings. So once again the step was taken. The letter, written under obedience to the Spirit, with no outward evidence of its need, was handed in to the council; and we parted, they giving unto me "the right hand of fellowship," that I should go unto the saints with the warfare message, and *they* unto the saints who needed other aspects of truth (Gal. 2:9).[1]

God withdraws his servants when they have finished their work in one sphere, and thereby closes one door of service; but he opens another before them until they finish their course. The Matlock Convention, begun at Whitsuntide, 1912, had just the same

---

1 Mrs. Penn-Lewis still continued as one of the trustees of the convention. She retired from the leadership of the women's meetings and from the heavy organizing work.

spontaneous rise as the one at Llandrindod, in the "happenings" which brought it about, for the specific purpose of unfolding the warfare message to the church of God. Three of these conventions [were held], the numbers increasing year by year as the message was understood and the need of fuller knowledge of its application to the present period of the church's history grew upon the spiritual children of God.

* * *

Mr. Mrs. Penn-Lewis in the garden at Cartref, Leicester, 1912.

Photo: Ramsden, Leicester

Monthly conferences for Christian workers were held at Eccleston Hall, London (lent for the purpose by the late Lord Radstock) during these busy years; and for several successive years a two-day conference was arranged in Leicester. This latter eventuated in the Matlock Conference already mentioned. These gatherings initiated a unique and original form of convention work, in that they became literally "conferences," where workers from many fields of service met to "confer" upon the deep things of God and upon the difficulties and obstacles besetting their ministry.

The vision of such an "open conference" had been upon the heart of Mrs. Penn-Lewis for some years, and was only fully realized when she commenced to convene conferences herself, without the help of council or committee, in dependence upon God alone for the supply of every need, both financial and spiritual. As this form of open or "mutual" conference afterwards became the pattern for all gatherings in connection with the testimony of *The Overcomer.* Some extracts from the magazine in reference to these early "experiments" will give valuable insight into a form of meeting which has been proved to give true liberty to the Holy Spirit to guide and control, and to be of inestimable value to workers needing light upon the problems of their daily walk and work.

In announcing the first conference at Matlock, in the year 1912, Mrs. Penn-Lewis set forth their aim and basis as follows:

Large numbers of Christians attend conventions for the purpose of earnestly seeking a victorious life; but, for lack of *personal application of the truths proclaimed to their individual difficulties, they* do not emerge into a life of steady victory. The conference at Matlock is specially arranged with a view to helping such believers, not only by giving a sequence of teaching on the basic truths of victory over sin and Satan on the ground of the finished work of Christ at Calvary, and the imparted power of the Holy Spirit, but also that believers needing spiritual help may meet with workers able to counsel them and lead them into victory.

In view of the conference we think it well to reiterate some statements we have from time to time expressed in *The Overcomer,* viz.: that we are deeply convinced that it is not our commission from God to initiate or lead *a "movement"* in connection with *The Overcomer* and its distinctive message. We have for many years deprecated the harmful tendency among God's children to either form or join "movements" which, under the idea of advance, tend to separate the members of the body of Christ the one from the other at a time when unity, on the basis of the finished work of Christ and the sharing of one life between all who are joined to him, is most essential in the face of a united foe ... We are deeply convinced that the great need of today is the building up of the body of Christ so that it reaches maturity and readiness for the Lord's appearing...

Our aim in *The Overcomer* is this simple ministry of the Word, giving the measure of light we have upon aspects of truth we have learned through deep suffering, and proved as yet in small measure, but sufficiently to know that they are of God for his people. We are aware that they do not meet the need of all believers, but there are those to whom they have come in delivering power, and who testify that their lives have been lifted to another plane.

The conference at Matlock will be upon the simple lines of opening up truth which all the children of God need for aggressive service at the present time, and for the leading of those in bondage into a life of victory...[1]

From the report of the first Matlock Conference we cull the following:

In many respects the conference was a remarkable one ... in the unconventional character of the proceedings, the mighty purpose of God that bound them together, the entire absence of waste in time and talk; the abiding, ever-deepening seriousness of it all; and the tremendous, far-reaching power of the Spirit of God in speakers, hearers, and in the truth itself ... The debatable, the collateral things of the spiritual life were acknowledged but practically untouched. The first "principles of the gospel of Christ" were left, and speakers and hearers alike pressed on to "full growth." In accordance with the Word of God, they gave and received "strong meat" prepared for those who are "of full age"...

---

1   Mrs. Penn-Lewis in *The Overcomer*, June, 1912.

In the mornings, Mrs. Penn-Lewis led open conferences on the themes announced... when questions were freely asked and dealt with, the liberty of utterance and the vital terseness of all that was said showing the deep need of those who had come. So vital was the grip of need that the "open conference" overflowed to other meetings, and scarcely any "addresses," in the usual sense of the word, could be given. The convener indeed remarked once that, just as medical men have a "congress," so it appeared that these gatherings might be described as a "spiritual clinical congress" for those who have the cure of souls. The Word of life was ministered as opportunity came... With great emphasis defeated ones were told, *"There is victory for you* by taking hold of the VICTOR with a new faith—in *him* you can win your way to triumph"...

To give light to perplexed and troubled servants of God was the primary purpose of the conference—a biblical, spiritual interpretation of doubtful situations, of counterfeit guidance, of mistaken activities, as well as to renew faith and hope and courage by clothing the believer in the whole armor of God...

When the conference proper had closed, an impromptu "students' class" of Christian workers came about in the Rest Room, which proved to be one of the most valuable times of the week. About thirty workers—evangelists and others—stood the test for three hours of probing questions on their efficiency of service and prayer-life... "Expression" of truth in public speech, misconceptions in the mind, tactlessness in dealing with souls, etc., were dealt with as they arose in the questions, with a keen desire on the part of all present to put aside all "personal" sensitiveness for the sake of greater efficiency in the service of God...[2]

Of the third Matlock Conference, Mrs. Penn-Lewis wrote:

The conference this year was far in advance of the preceding ones... The guidance of the Spirit of God from first to last, in leading the conference as a united whole, hour after hour, with no program, yet with no sense of a break in the "cable" of his leading, rejoiced those who watched over the proceedings with jealous prayer, and showed how deepened in spiritual maturity and understanding of how to "walk in the spirit" those present were...[3]

2   *The Overcomer*, July, 1912. (Report by "Our Own Commissioner.")
3   *The Overcomer*, July, 1914.

The outbreak of the Great War in the August following, and the consequent difficulties in the carrying on of all Christian work, brought this series of conferences to a close, after the gatherings at Whitsuntide 1914.

It will readily be understood that the editing of a monthly magazine, in which the greater part of the matter given was from the editor's own pen, made frequent visits abroad impossible, and limited the time and strength available for the constant convention work in which she had hitherto been so greatly used of God. It may have appeared a turning away from a great ministry, with loss to the church of God; yet through her steadfast obedience to the "leading of the Lord," by means of *The Overcomer,* the message committed to her reached believers who were pressing on with God in every corner of the world in a way that not even the books and booklets of earlier days had done.

In the midst of the heavy literary work of these years, numbers of invitations were of necessity refused, from such distant places as Australia, Palestine, America, Germany, etc., though a considerable amount of platform work was undertaken nearer home, in addition to the Whitsuntide conferences at Matlock. At Keswick also, for many years, open meetings were addressed on the Sundays preceding and concluding the convention week, accompanied by rich and far-reaching blessing. In August 1913, however, an invitation was accepted to spend a few weeks in Finland and Sweden with her friend Baroness Kurck, and address a number of meetings for Christian workers at Ruovesi, a lovely spot amid the pine woods of Finland, and at Helsinki. The following are brief extracts from the voluminous record of this "working holiday," sent home in sections from time to time.

Journal: Paarlammi, Ruovesi, Finland, August 9th, 1913

I posted my first record on August 5th, and had not then had time to reconnoiter my surroundings. I am in the home of an old lady of 83, Madame Aminoff. Her son owns the estate around here, and lives in the "big house" named Pekkola,[1] about an hour's walk away.

---

1   This beautiful mansion was burnt down in 1918 by the Red Army, and its

It is impossible to describe the beauty of the place. Not a person to be seen—utter stillness, wander as you will along the pine wood paths or the lake shore...

In the household, three daughters, and at present five guests: a Swedish missionary and her mother, Madame Forselles (president of the Finnish Y.W.C.A.), Baroness Kurck, and myself. Madame Forselles I met fifteen years ago, on my first visit to Finland. God met her then, and she has been praying for fifteen years that he would send me back to Finland with his message. She was even then very delicate. She tells me that she obtained *War on the Saints* last spring, and through light received from it she has fought through her work and kept on her feet physically, or she would have been obliged to give up her work through ill-health... She is president for all Finland of combined associations for work among women.

At 12:30 each day we start off in a one-horse drosky for a five mile drive through the pine woods to Ruovesi, drawing up outside the church (Lutheran) where the meetings are held at 1:30. I go into the church to the chancel steps, where I begin with a few words of prayer, and then open my Bible and speak until 3:30—about two hours—each sentence translated into Finnish... Then we walk to the schoolhouse nearby for dinner... and at 5:00 p.m. return to the church for a Question Hour. This has been the best way of getting at the *need* of the workers.

I have rested in the mornings, whilst Mme. Forselles has been at Ruovesi with the workers. It is beautiful to see the faces changing day by day, one after another getting the needed light. Many are really receiving the fullness of the Spirit, and numbers are seeing what *"walking after the Spirit"* means. The "grip" has also come in the meetings, especially when showing the working of evil spirits in counterfeiting the human. The dark, weary look has gone, and the spirit has been liberated, as the worker has said with such thankfulness, "Oh, it is such a relief to know that it *has not been oneself!*"

In brief, it has been a wondrous time of liberating all round, and the tide of joy and thankfulness is rising. The whole conference has been kept in one stream of openness to truth. I have had full liberty in dealing with every aspect of the spiritual life. The "will," the human spirit and the Holy Spirit, mind and spirit, Ephesians 6, the devices of the powers of darkness, etc., etc. All simple and clear and unhindered...

owner shot.

We leave here on August 13th and I have two clear days, then three public meetings in Helsinki … I do not yet know God's plan for me at the close. We may get a day on a steamer, coasting down to Viborg to Baron Nicolay's place "Monrepos," or we may go direct to Stockholm and go to see Prince and Princess Oscar Bernadotte—or we may go at once to Baroness Kurck's home at Rynge. I expect and hope that Miss Wolkoff will be in Helsinki on Thursday, and I wait to see her plans. Fare ye well.

Hotel Kamp, Helsingsfors. August 14th, 1913.

On Monday (11th) we were told that Mr. Aminoff, of Pekkola, was sending his private steamer to Ruovesi to take us, via the lake, to Pekkola, and then by lake again to Paarlammi, where there is a private landing stage in the grounds. When the conference closed at 6:00 p.m., the Paarlammi house-party walked down to the Ruovesi landing stage and boarded the little steamer; and we were nearly two hours steaming in and out between islands, and round fresh turnings of the lake, until we saw a sort of pagoda on an eminence and a landing stage below. The steamer hooted, and we slid in to a little pier. Down came some bonnie children, and a gentleman behind them. We landed, and after introductions—no Finnish or Swedish, alas, by the English lady—we walked some distance to the house. The grounds looked like a park—lawns, standard roses, huge cactus and palm trees, and loveliest of all, a broad avenue of silver birches facing the front of the house as far as eye could see.

Then, with Swedish courtliness, we were led into the house for tea. It was interesting to see these private homes, which tourists do not see, and to watch the customs of the country. When we had finished tea, Madame Forselles arose and, turning toward the host, gave a sweeping curtsy with the words, "tacker se mycket" (thanks very much); and he drew his feet together and with a graceful bow responded. All the others did the same, except the "English lady," who just gave a little bow! This custom is followed at every meal.

Then we went out of doors. Mr. Aminoff led the way to show us his cattle—one hundred head—in their stalls for the night. A most interesting house and farm, and worth seeing; but the darkness was coming on, so we hasted to the little steamer, and in half an hour reached Paarlammi, about 9:30 …

August 12th

The last conference meeting at 1:30. Finns are usually so dumb and shy and reserved, but what a miracle we saw! After half an hour's talk, I asked for testimonies, and all over the meeting they arose—they had learned that "the spirit-life must be expressed," that "God seeks an outlet." Then we turned it into a class, and I told the workers how to use their voices! Then we got to the "universal." Every person said where they came from, and we took the places to God in prayer—then the whole church, and the whole world! And they learned to say "Amen" to every petition and every testimony. There were about 150 workers from all parts of Finland—many chief workers, and some foreign missionaries ...

August 15th

To Helsinki, where my friend, Miss Wolkoff, with her companion and her Russian maid, had just arrived ... The following day was very wet; and I sat nearly all day with my Russian friends, until 5 o'clock, when I left them to prepare for my first meeting ... It was now fine, and we had a large attendance. I spoke on Romans 8, the spirit-life; and Ephesians 6, the spirit-warfare. It was like being back in Russia to see Baron Nicolay and his sister come in, and with them Baroness Wrede—far famed for her prison work in Finland ...

I had great liberty in speaking, and then returned to the hotel with Miss Wolkoff. She was leaving for St. Petersburg at 11:25 p.m. It was a great sorrow to me that she had to leave so soon, and meant rather a "battle" to rise above it and give myself to the work ...[1]

On Monday at 4 o'clock I had a very important interview with a Finnish worker, and then received Baron Nicolay for a vital talk over *War on the Saints*, etc. He has known me for fifteen years, and has not seen me for seven. He was especially struck with the vigor and "life" that I now have, which was more of a testimony to many than even what I said. All these old friends told Baroness Kurck

---

1   Mrs. Penn-Lewis never saw this beloved friend again. The constant interchange of correspondence continued until the end of 1915, when, after a postcard of loving greeting written on Christmas Day, silence, impenetrable and unexplained, enveloped the fate of this—as of many another—Russian saint. The younger sister was, in the providence of God, called home very suddenly in December 1908.

that I was "younger than fifteen years ago!" (Amen). Then came the last meeting in the church, which was again very large and very responsive. So my work here was ended ...

Stockholm, Saturday, August 23rd

At 12:50 we started by train for Prince Bernadotte's country house. At the station their car was waiting, with two leather coats for us to put on for driving. Then we sped through the lovely lanes and forest scenery for five kilometers, and stopped before the veranda steps of Malmsjo, to find the prince and princess and two daughters waiting for us ... The princess and the baroness have been intimate friends since they were girls, so it was quite a home-party and most pleasant, with no formality ...

After dinner we went for a walk in the grounds, giving opportunity for personal talk over spiritual things ... then we went indoors. In a corner of the large hall was an old-fashioned fireplace with pine logs piled. The prince lit the wood to get a blaze, and then we broke up into groups as the eldest daughter arrived—a trained nurse from Stockholm, dressed in nurses' costume and bonnet. The doctors say she is one of the best nurses they have. She now has charge of a ward in the hospital and takes her night duty and operations, etc., with all the rest ...

The arrival of the nurse-sister for her weekly half-holiday took away the two younger daughters, and then we got together in a corner of the hall for a talk over various aspects of the spiritual life until the supper bell rang. So to the dining-room we went, and then resumed our traveling garments and entered the motor car for a train at 9:14—the nurse returning with us. It was 10:30 when we arrived, but away she went alone in a hired taxi to the hospital.

Sunday, August 24th

A quiet day. Baroness Kurck and I had a long talk on the issues of the truth of the spiritual "warfare" to the church of God ... Although I have said very little about it, this journey has *confirmed in point after point* all that we have been learning ...

Tuesday, August 26th

To Rynge... How glad the Baroness was to get home. It is such a lovely spot. Facing one side of the house is a piece of water, on either side avenues of trees. The grounds are most extensive... After a rest we wandered out into the south garden—warm and fragrant with fruit and flowers...

Yesterday morning I spent in writing and prayer... Afterwards we went fishing in the lake for crawfish! Two long sticks, a piece of cord, and a lump of meat. We dropped this *bonne bouche* at the crawfish's nose as we saw him lying in the water. He clutched it, then a boy slipped a net under him and he was landed in a bucket. But we got bolder!

The boy had gone away, so the Baroness played her cord until the clutch was tenacious—and hey presto! The poor clutcher was landed on the bank. Then I went one better and played my cord until two took hold; and as they clutched their *bonne bouche,* I swung them both to the bank! At supper they appeared in their red clothing and renewed our acquaintance...

On Wednesday we go to Copenhagen, staying two nights to see friends, and I sail on Friday morning for England. I sorely needed this quiet rest, for it has been incessant traveling since the conference at Ruovesi. Farewell.

* * *

Twelve months later—in August 1914—the First World War broke upon the nations; and at the end of the year, the issue of *The Overcomer* as a monthly magazine came to a close—not for lack of readers or support, but in spite of an ever-increasing circulation, by a leading of God as clear as that given for its inception. How true the guidance of God was, after events abundantly proved; for it would have been circumstantially impossible for his servant to continue the publication during the difficult years of that protracted struggle.

Looking back over the six years of strenuous editorial labor (seven if we include the *Word of the Cross* magazine of 1908), Mrs. Penn-Lewis wrote the following brief sketch of its career in the closing number of *The Overcomer* (first series), December 1914:

When the paper was commenced six years ago, by very clear command of the Spirit of God, everything was humanly against it. No "ordinary" steps were taken to announce its advent, for no publisher would have taken the risk of its issue. In fact, when the simple handbill announcing its advent appeared, a publisher of repute wrote as a personal friend to the editor, in deep concern, anticipating nothing but failure for the paper from a financial and circulatory standpoint.

Therefore, as we look back upon its history, we clearly see that nothing but the hand of God carrying through a definite purpose ordained by him could have upheld and steered the paper; and only the Holy Spirit of God could have guided it to the sorely tried children of God scattered all over the world and used it to minister to deep need unknown to all but him ... It penetrated in an extraordinary way to some of the remotest places on the inhabited earth, reaching isolated believers in land after land, to whom it came as a message directly sent of God, lifting up the crushed and, in some cases, almost wrecked workers on the eve of being driven off the battlefield ...

The danger of going beyond the measure of the Spirit in a given piece of spiritual service, because it has become *prosperous,* is a real one to those who seek to co-work with the Spirit of God. The knowledge of this danger has been of great value in guarding the *Overcomer* from being diverted from its ministry. Again and again it could have become involved in the network of twentieth century machinery. Offers of large sums of money as "capital" to develop it as a journal meeting a deep spiritual need have been made by some who saw its potentialities; while other workers of repute have offered to organize prayer-circles in connection with it. But from these, as well as from many other propositions, we have, by the grace of God, turned away. We had no commission from God to found or to conduct a magazine developed and worked on ordinary lines, or to build up an organized "work," or to institute a "school of teaching," but only to minister the truth of God to the spiritual people of God and to remain simply witnesses to the end ...

The *Overcomer* had no ordinary beginning, neither has it been an "ordinary" paper in the preparation of matter for its pages. It has not contained "mental" matter, that is, matter which is merely the product of the mind, even *a spiritual mind!* It has been filled with truth gained by fresh and living experience of the written Word of God … The work of editing the paper, and of all who have contributed matter to its pages, has been done "without money and without price," as labor given freely to the church of God.

Of the personal sacrifice involved for herself and her "fellow-heir of the grace of God" in all this, nothing is said; but the next paragraph gives a glimpse into a selfless devotion that withheld not even their "home" from the service of God:

Readers generally may not know that *The Overcomer* has been published from an office opened in my *private residence*.[1] When the little paper was launched, no such arrangement was anticipated, any more than the rapid growth of the magazine into a world-wide circulation. But when the arrangements made for the first year's issue proved unworkable, as a small book room already existed, in the charge of a secretary[2] who had assisted me in literature issue for twenty years, the work was transferred to the book room, little realizing all that would be involved in the sending forth of such a paper. As the work grew, inquiries were made among business agencies as to the practicability of release from the business burden; but there had come about a *personal correspondence with the readers,* which made it impossible to transfer it to other hands without injury to the paper and the removal from the editor of much valuable insight into the spiritual needs of the readers.

As the years went by, capable and devoted helpers were sent of God to give assistance in the office; and the small staff grew in efficiency within the limits of its power. But—and herein lies the crux of the circumstantial aspect of the leading of God in the closure of the paper—no staff of workers, however devoted and capable, could lift the burden of the responsibility, and business machinery which has been fast growing around the editor, and which could only now be continued by entire devotion to its demands and a cutting off of all other *spiritual* service to the Lord's people.

With deep gratitude to God for his sustaining grace in carrying through a service for the church of God which has taxed the

1   Cartref, the house on the outskirts of Leicester to which Mr. and Mrs. Penn-Lewis moved in 1906.
2   Miss Butterwick.

enduring power of spirit, soul, and body to the utmost limit, I therefore recognize that the time of release from the business burden of the publication of *The Overcomer* has come.

The issue of the literature through the little book room, which was in existence before the advent of *The Overcomer*, carries with it none of the burden of machinery surrounding the issue of a monthly paper. The office therefore ceases, but the book room remains ... Our readers, therefore, can be reached by circular post, in the event of any special issue of an occasional paper which the Spirit of God may lay upon us; the announcement of any new book or message in print, from a large number of yet unpublished MSS; or the resuscitation at any time of *The Overcomer* in another and less burdensome form.

"Make haste, my beloved, and be thou like to a gazelle ... upon the mountains."

—*Song of Songs 8:14*

"She longs for the day of his appearing to the world, for that glorious day when he shall be marveled at in all them that believe; therefore, in unison with the eternal Spirit, she makes intercession according to the will of God, and prays with deep desire, 'Make haste, my beloved,' for she is 'looking for, and earnestly desiring (hastening, m.) the coming of the day of God,' and is, according to his promise, looking for new heavens and a new earth, wherein dwelleth righteousness' (2 Peter 3:12–13, m.)."

Chapter 11

Respite Years—an Interlude

1915-1919

Prayer Messages—Editing the *Friend of Israel*—The Ministry of Women

The four years of the Great War lie like a gulf across the lives of those who passed through them as adults, sharply dividing past from present, while they lived and worked and prayed in an ever-present "now" which belonged to neither, and seemed as though it would never pass on into the calm waters of ordinary life. To Mrs. Penn-Lewis, in spite of the national suffering and anxiety, which she keenly shared, these years brought a measure of respite. *The Overcomer* closed, traveling becoming ever more and more difficult, there pressed upon her the urgent need of rest and recuperation after six years of heavy, continuous desk work such as few businessmen could have carried through without reaction. The monthly conference for Christian workers in London was continued without a break[1] and became a "place of prayer for all nations" indeed; and when, through the necessity of wintering in a warmer climate, the convener was unable to be the messenger, the breach was generously filled by other servants of God.

After spending the first winter of freedom from editorial work in the Channel Islands, Mrs. Penn-Lewis returned to Leicester in May 1915, hoping to pick up some measure of desk work; but

1 But removed to the Hall of Sion College, Eccleston Hall being required for government purposes on account of its proximity to Victoria Station.

after one month, disquieting symptoms showed the necessity of a medical examination, and it was found that there was a recurrence of the lung trouble which had been quiescent for some ten years. The physician remarked that the *Overcomer* work had been closed down "only just in time," and urged the need of wintering away from the cold and damp of England. Under the most favorable condition, he said, the disease might run its course in *two years;* failing which, her life might be cut off still more quickly.

"I have had similar medical verdicts from time to time during the past twenty years," she wrote in a message to the London Conference:

> ...and they have always served God's purpose in calling me aside for a period of retirement, for entering into a deeper knowledge of God, and deeper preparation of my own soul for the carrying out of fresh revelations of his will. God has always brought me forth with renewed health and power in due season. I want you to know that I have the assurance that he will do the same again, should he tarry. The message he is ringing in my heart is—"Alive from the dead." "Behold I am ALIVE for evermore." "Faith ... is the victory that overcometh the world"...
>
> If the Lord will, I hope to write you a message from time to time; and I trust you will become mighty in prayer, and personally more and more victorious in life as you gather month by month in the conference hall...
>
> With much prayer for each of you, whom I love in the Lord, Yours in expectation of his coming.
>
> Jessie Penn-Lewis

Of these written messages to her "spiritual children" in London during those days of world-wide agony and sorrow, the following extracts are of more than passing value:

Guernsey, November, 1915

I awoke on Monday morning with these words ringing: "There'll be no dark valley when Jesus comes"... Blessed be God, *none!* I am convinced that to keep the heavenly spirit, we need to sing the songs of heaven. An empty mind will soon become an earthly one. We must fill our minds and hearts with the things of heaven if we are to walk through these days as "heavenly people."

Paul knew this when he bade the Philippians THINK of true, of honorable, pure, and lovely things, and "things of good report," if the peace of God was to guard their thoughts. Take heed, dear friends in God, to *shut your minds* to all things that are contrary to God—think of the lovely things of heaven, and you will become heavenly.

Lastly, just a word about the War. Looking back over the months since it began, how marvelously prophecy is being fulfilled! God is on the throne. No man nor nation can stay his hand in this controversy with the nations... Lift up your heads, for your redemption draweth nigh.

Guernsey, December, 1915

"What manner of PERSONS ought ye to be, in all holy living (or conversation) and godliness?" (2 Pet. 3:11, 14, R.V.). Not "what manner of position or service"—but PERSONS! You, yourself, what sort of person are you in conversation and life? We who "look for these things"—let our personality be stamped with them. "Persons," the Lord looks for—take heed to your personal manner of life, that it speaks of him.

Just a word of grateful thanks for your prayers. I am decidedly better and stronger, and am wielding as a weapon the Lord's word, "ALIVE...", and trusting him to fulfill all that it means. I *"lay hold* on eternal life." May we each know more and more the *power* of his resurrection to keep us above the atmosphere of death that is filling the world. LIFE, LIFE, eternal life is ours...

Guernsey, January, 1916

"PRAY... and not faint" (Luke 18:1). Ask God to teach you how and what to pray, so that you may be in line with his will. Pray that the awful war now raging may rapidly work out to a close, having accomplished God's purpose in permitting it—that is, pray it to God's end! Ask God to teach you to pray from his standpoint, the standpoint of eternity, not time; the standpoint of the spiritual, not the natural, vision.

"Pray... and do not faint" seems to me that the pressure in the atmosphere is so great that one can only get power to breathe, in a

spiritual sense, by perpetual prayer, because prayer keeps the spirit open God-ward. It seems as if we who are expecting the Lord to come are like divers down in the ocean bed! We are *encased in Christ*, with just a "pipe" of the spirit open to the atmosphere above, through which our heavenly "air" can reach us. The weight of the ocean would crush and kill the diver, were it to break through his casing, or if the pipe were broken or choked. The Lord is truly our "casing," our covering, as we abide in him, and the awful ocean-weight of the world's atmosphere cannot get in as we hide in him, and keep the spirit open by prayer to the heavenly air by which alone we can breathe and live through these awful days. Therefore—"pray... *and do not faint.*"

A vital spiritual link with our allies across the Channel is revealed in the next letter:

March 1916

I want to ask you to pray especially for the passing through the press this month of *War on the Saints* in French. I hear that a pastor in Paris is giving a series of lectures on "Satan and the warfare with the saints" and using the English book as a text book! In Switzerland also, I hear of valuable work being done. A well-known missioner writes that all over Switzerland he has been able to form prayer groups to pray against the forces of darkness. This means, in Switzerland and France, a steady aggressive against the supernatural evil powers. An intelligent, steady prayer-warfare of a similar character is sorely needed in England. Will you pray that God will awaken all who know anything of this warfare, to active prayer, under the guidance of the Holy Spirit?

April 1916

Exodus 17 was given me one morning: "Then came Amalek... and Moses said... I will stand on the top of the hill with the rod of God in mine hand" (Ex. 17:8–9). What had not God done with that rod? At every crisis Moses had gone first to God, and then he had come out and stood with that rod stretched out, typifying the sovereign power of God...

But the power was *not in Moses*, nor could he lift the rod without first dealing with God. In his conflict with Pharaoh, he had to go again and again, as it developed, and *cry to God;* and it was only after such times of dealing with God that he went out and wielded the "rod." Back and fore Moses had to go between God and the conflict. That "rod" was stretched out in judgment upon Egypt's king, and stretched out to open a way across the Red Sea for God's redeemed ones. Now comes WAR! And Moses ascends the hill to watch the conflict, and hold up that rod. This time the rod had to be held up until the victory was won—you know the story.

Now read it with Rev. 2:26–29. "Power" over the nations! And he (the overcomer) shall rule "with a rod of iron"—"even as I received…"—even as Christ himself received power to rule! Extraordinary words, but very clearly depicting those who are to reign with Christ.

The message to you and to me is just simply the need, at this time of stress, to abide in the Mount of God and hold up the rod. It is only another word for PRAYER—not so much the prayer of intercession, but the *attitude that follows intercession.* Trace out these two threads in the life of Moses: the times when he cried to God, and the times when he held out the rod of victory in the faith that his intercessory prayers were answered.

Back and fore, back and fore, as you see the conditions in the world, go you between God and the need. May God teach you how to thus have "power over all the power of the enemy," and in your spirit life learn to "rule" over nations.

God be with you and keep you living in Psalm 91 as a real "pavilion" in these days of peril …

May 1916

Under a heavy burden concerning the lack of a national turning to God. I was given Exodus 32 with emphasis on verses 10–14, and Numbers 14:13–14. I saw in this instance that Israel *as a nation* did not cry to God, but yet the nation was saved through *the intercession of Moses.* The intercessors who will not "leave off praying" (Chaldee paraphrase of "let me alone," v. 10) can save the country. Then I saw the basis of Moses' cry to God—"Wherefore should the *Egyptians* speak and say"… (v. 12), and "Then the *Egyptians* shall hear it"… (Num. 14:13), that is, GOD'S NAME WILL SUFFER! I thought of the native chiefs in Africa and the people of India and other lands, to whom the name of Britain stood for all they knew of liberty, both of soul and body. I though not only of Britain's sins, but what *Britain's saints* have done for God! I remembered that, even on the continent of Europe, England's messengers had carried to many of the born-again souls the deeper truths of God. What does not Russia owe to the late Lord Radstock? What do not Sweden, Norway, and Denmark owe to the Keswick Convention? Will God only look at England's *sins* and forget *England's saints?* Nay, like Moses in the Mount, let God's intercessors cry to him for Britain, that whilst he judges her, he will mingle mercy with judgment, and save her testimony to the heathen...

Let me also say to each of you, turn to God as the all-sufficient one. (Gen. 17:1, Schofield note). Do not *lean upon any one on earth* for help, or light, or succor. Rely only on GOD as the one who is enough for you. Use all that you have ever learned of him, and TRUST HIM as the one who cannot fail you. Cease from man, and prove in these darkening days that God is your refuge and strength, and underneath are the everlasting arms...

I have received a letter concerning "divine healing" which may also express the thoughts and prayers of others. It is important that the Lord's praying ones should not be diverted from their world vision in prayer by undue concern for persons. I therefore take this occasion to bear my testimony to the truth of Matt. 8:17 and Rom. 8:11, and say that I am standing by faith upon these divine facts. But I am also clear that by continued "weakness" (2 Cor. 4:10–12; 2 Cor. 7:9; 2 Cor. 13:4) the Lord is... opening up to me prayer service within the veil which I *see to be as effective in results* as active service. Released from the ceaseless labor connected with the editing and publishing of a monthly magazine, I find my spirit liberated into a realm of perpetual prayer where the truths of *War on the Saints* are powerful.

The *need* of today is undoubtedly a "revival of *prayer*," so as to "make up the fence" and close up the "gap" through which the hosts of darkness have rushed in upon the church and the world. (Ezek. 22:30).

In January 1917 an *Occasional Paper* was sent out to those readers of *The Overcomer* who had registered their names and addresses in the hope of some such after message, for letters from all parts of the world showed that a large body of believers who had received help through the magazine were sorely missing the "portion of meat in due season." "Nothing has ever taken its place. It supplied a great and pressing need which no other literature has ever attempted to meet, even in smallest measure," wrote one of the leaders of a large Bible school in America; and many others wrote to the same effect. Other *Occasional Papers* followed at intervals, bearing welcome news of steady improvement in health, with increasing power given of God for his service; and dealing in masterly fashion with the "modern attitude to the Bible" and the "camouflage" of the doctrine of the atonement—since become a landslide of apostasy from the faith which throws a lurid light upon the question uttered by our Lord: "When the Son of Man cometh, shall he find the faith on the earth?"

In the editorial letter of the second of these papers we get a glimpse of the leadings of God during this period:

Leicester, January 1918

My dear Friends in God,

I deeply regret that a full year has gone by without my being able to issue another occasional paper, for many have been the letters from other lands, as well as the homeland, asking why.

The one hindrance has been the clerical work of issue in the absence of the staff which so ably handled the sending out of *The Overcomer* in the past. But now by the suggestion of one of God's honored servants, it has been arranged for this special issue to be sent out as an inset in *The Christian*. And so I am able to communicate directly with you in print once more, as well as to share the message with a larger circle of the Lord's children all over the world.

It is with deep thankfulness to God that I find the seed sown through six years of costly labor in the issue of *The Overcomer* is still bearing more abundant fruit. The 6,000 copies of the *Occasional Paper* sent out in January 1917 brought back letters of such gratitude to God for the message of past years that it is evident, were it possible to resuscitate the closed magazine, it would receive a response deepened by its absence. Numbers now write and say that at last they *understand* the truths which they at first so dimly apprehended, and have been driven to read again and again the bound volumes in their hands ...

I also would thank those of you who have been much in prayer for my restoration to health, and thankfully tell you that those prayers are being answered. The renewed strength has come through the light on life triumphing over death, as unfolded in the fifth to the eighth of Romans. Obliged to spend last winter on the south coast, I found that the "reign of death" was strong in my bodily frame. As no taking hold of God for "healing" availed for more than intermittent periods, I became deeply convinced that God had something to show me I had not yet known. Then slowly light came, until one day the Holy Spirit suddenly drew, as it were, a veil off the four chapters in Romans referred to; and from that hour the *reign* of death ceased, and I find the reign of life becoming established as I steadily meet every phase of "death" which I become conscious of, with the weapon of the Word, that the "reign of life" must triumph. Now counting the Spirit of God to make true what he has made known, I am spending the winter in Leicester, expecting to be enabled for full service in all the will of God until the Lord comes.

You will be glad to know that I have been able during the last few months to visit south Wales twice. At Porthcawl in September the Lord gave signal blessing in an atmosphere full of the Holy Spirit of God.

The old sweet "revival" touch was there in revival hymns and testimony, but in a far deeper and purer way. Conferences at Stockport, Matlock, Brighton, and Southsea have also had marked witness of the unhindered working of the Holy Spirit.

I am also happy to tell you that, in the absence of the editor for an indefinite period on mission work in South Africa, the Lord has placed in my hands the editing of the quarterly magazine *The Friend of Israel and The Time of the End*. This is the organ of the Prayer Union for Israel founded at Mildmay in 1880, with prayer union circles in many parts of the world. I am glad to have this service in connection with *prayer* for the Jews at the time when, as one has said, "the Royal Mail of the elect church is nearly through on the main line, and already the Jewish train (which has been on the siding all these years of Gentile opportunity) has got steam up and is about to come on the main line again." ...

The literature continued to circulate in a quiet way during the years of war, and through the Free Distribution Fund (founded on the closure of *The Overcomer*) some 45,000 books and booklets went forth to missionaries and workers in other lands—a special censor's permit to send printed matter abroad being obtained from the government! The following extract from the letter of a missionary is typical of the thankfulness aroused among God's hard-pressed servants for the practical teaching upon life in and for God, given through the medium of *The Overcomer* and other literature:

> If my witness as a missionary in a Mohammedan land is worth anything, I can testify that I count my great spiritual victories over spiritual hosts of wickedness, both in heavenly and in earthly places, from the day when I learned quite simply, and *aloud,* to deny "ground" in my ransomed body and soul and spirit to the devil and his agents; to reassert my freedom from the power of sin on the ground of Rom. 6:11; and to reaffirm my trust and confidence in the *"law* of the Spirit of life in Christ Jesus" according to Rom. 8:2; and all this I did—sometimes in the operating theater as I stood giving anesthetics in the insufferable heat for five hours. Sometimes busy in storerooms with madly irritated nerves demanding an outlet; often and often in walking about the great hospital compound in the blazing sun; or just before presenting the gospel in my halting Persian to a hall full of dispensary patients. And— *I am not the only one* who has profited by the message of *The Overcomer* in Persia. May you come behind in no venture of faith to his glory until he come…

In addition to the editing of *The Friend of Israel*, a new book, on the message of the cross "for the time of the end,"[1] was issued in 1917, and in the spring of 1919 a pamphlet dealing with the ministry of women. Of the latter we find this note in the *Occasional Paper* issued about the same time:

> I would like to tell you, in connection with the preparation of this book, that I have never had more clearly the expression of the Lord's mind concerning some writing he wished me to do, than I have

1 *All Things New.*

had in this matter. I am therefore assured that he has some definite purpose in its issue…

In some sense it would be true to rank Mrs. Penn-Lewis with Mrs. Josephine Butler and other courageous women who, with their whole trust and confidence placed in the Lord of Hosts, went forward in his name and at his call, in the face, not only of the prejudice of their generation, but the prejudice of their own desire and inclinations. We have seen how, from the commencement of her ministry, Mrs. Penn-Lewis had to conquer her innate shrinking from any kind of publicity. Some words written by her in the year 1919 throw further light upon God's dealings with her in this matter in the early days of her service for him:

> I saw that God had given me a specific commission to proclaim the message of the cross at a time when it had almost ceased to be referred to in the pulpits. I saw also that God miraculously opened doors before me to proclaim this message, which no man could shut, but that the one objection was the fact that I was a woman. There was no quarrel with the message; there was *no denial of the Divine seal;* and there was no getting away from the evidence of the results. But none of these things did away with the fact that I was a woman; and therefore I could not but see that, whilst God opened doors for me in some quarters, others were fast closed to the message I bore, purely and only because I was a woman.
>
> The great cry of my heart, therefore, was, "Why did not God commit this vital message to one who could have open access to deliver it without restriction?" So deeply did I feel this that for years I cried to God that he would raise up a man to whom he would entrust the commission he had given to me… Many tears did I shed over this; and with anguish of heart I would go into the open doors that were plainly set before me; until at last, when I saw and could say with the Lord, "I beheld, and there was no man," I had to settle it that for some unexplained reason, God had committed this message to me, and at whatever cost I must go forward.[1]
>
> Not only did I question the evangelical leaders with an eager desire to see that the hand of God laid hold of them to proclaim the

---

1   That is, the experimental out-working in the believer of his identification with Christ in his death and resurrection life (Rom. 6:5; Gal. 2:20).

full message of Calvary, but I labored in the delivery of my message, watching with eager eyes to see whether there was not some hidden and chosen instrument to whom I could transmit *this burden,* who would rise up in God's time to proclaim it to the church and let me step aside...

I knew only too well what the letter of the Scripture said, in just three passages of the Apostle Paul's writings; but I was certain in my mind, as I walked with God and found his will and guidance, and as his message came to me, that if we only knew the exact original meaning of those passages, they were bound to be *in harmony with the working of the Holy Spirit* in the nineteenth century...

Now at this time, when it is widely admitted that we are at the close of the times of the Gentiles, and at the very edge of the complete fulfillment of Joel's prophecy (Joel 2:28–29)... I am strongly impressed that, for the strengthening of the position for the Lord's handmaidens' freedom for use by the Holy Spirit in proclaiming the wonderful works of God, I must now set forth in print the evidences that this is the purpose of God, as I have proved it in my own life.[2] I no longer say to the Lord, "Why hast thou made me a woman?" My spirit is now at rest; and I see why, in spite of all my endeavors by prayer and action to retire from the commission which was directly laid upon me, I was not able to get free; for *God had a deeper intention* in making me a woman, and giving me the marked approval and guidance of his Spirit in the service he had called me to.

A woman who is called to preach is likewise called to an understanding of the Word which will agree with that inward voice. It is *the Word* and the Spirit by which we must be led...

With this burden upon her spirit, Mrs. Penn-Lewis published the small pamphlet giving light from the original Scriptures upon this subject, so vitally affecting the authority and infallibility of the Word of God, and its divine fitness to "meet the need of every generation." Nor is this booklet, as would seem probable, out of harmony with her other writings; for the message of the cross is its motive and its end, showing how, for the members of the body of Christ, the "enmity" was "slain" at Calvary, not only as

2   This was written with the intention of embodying it in the *Autobiography* she hoped to write.

between Jew and Gentile, but between "bond and free" and "male and female" (Ephes. 2:11–19, Gal. 3:28)—both having died with Christ, that "out of both" might be made a new creation, that is, the spiritual body of Christ, of which he is the head.

> In the home sphere she is woman, wife, mother, sister; but in the church and in service for God, praying or "proclaiming godliness" (1 Tim. 2:10, lit.) she is a "partaker of the divine nature," a messenger of the Lord of Hosts, a member of the heavenly body, the church—in both spheres seeking, with a meek and quiet spirit, to do the will of her head in heaven.[1]

A gentleman with strong prejudice against the ministry of women came to the Overcomer Conference at Swanwick and was present at a meeting in which God spoke with mighty power through his handmaiden. In conversation with her afterwards, he confessed: "I would not have believed it possible, had I not seen it, that God would use a *woman* like that!"

"God never does use a woman like that," was her quick response, *"or a man either!* God only uses the NEW CREATION."

---

1   *The Magna Charta of Women, According to the Scriptures.*

"Thou art a fountain of gardens, a well of living waters and flowing streams."

—*Song of Songs 4:15*

"When walking in unbroken communion through the power of the blood of sprinkling, and in entire obedience up to light, the believer ought to carry no care about the 'flowing streams.' The Lord knows how to bring needy hearts in contact with the overflow of his life, which breaks forth spontaneously from his hidden one just as she remains restful in his keeping."

Chapter 12

The Renewed Commission

1920–1925

The Overcomer, Second Series—The Swanwick Conference—The removal of the work to London—The Home-Call of Mr. Penn-Lewis

The spiritual outlook upon the church and upon the world immediately after the war was grave in the extreme, and the passage of years has amply confirmed the vision of those who so interpreted it. The "perilous times" had indeed set in. "Spiritism is in the air," said a speaker at the Church Congress in 1919. "It is more than a craze; it is a wave of psychic passion upon the people." With thousands of bereaved hearts seeking communication with their lost loved ones in the unseen realm, is it any wonder that the door was set wide open for a tremendous influx of "teaching spirits" with "doctrines of demons" (1 Tim.4:1) into the world of men?

Deeply burdened with the necessity of a ringing challenge to the oncoming tide of apostasy, Mrs. Penn-Lewis felt that the time had come for the resuscitation of *The Overcomer*, with a supplementary message urging the children of God to continue to "stand fast in the liberty" wherewith Christ hath made them free, and not to be "entangled again" with any "yoke of bondage," either through Satanic counterfeits of the things of God, or through the multitudinous teachings of the apostasy which were beginning to penetrate even evangelical forms of Christian service.

In January 1920, therefore, the magazine was sent forth once more, in the "less burdensome form" referred to in the closing issue of 1914 as a possibility, should the Lord tarry; that is, as a quarterly paper supported by the free gifts of its readers. The heavy clerical labor of registering thousands of yearly payments was thus obviated, and the way made clear to send the magazine freely to all who desired it, in spite of the greatly increased cost of publication and the heavy financial pressure upon many of the Lord's servants in post-war days. God set his seal upon this method by moving his stewards to cover the cost quarter by quarter, even when the circulation rose, as it rapidly did, to *five* figures; and in the same way the magazine continues to go forth, until the Lord shows that its ministry is finished.

The three months that followed the issue of the first number of the new series were crowded with evidences of a real spiritual "move" through its resuscitation. "I must confess," wrote the editor in the second number, "that I had not fully apprehended how deep and widespread was the response to the testimony given in the six years' issue of *The Overcomer*. It seems almost as if we had resumed our paper-fellowship just where we left off at the end of 1914! This is a proof of the work having been of God. No work of human origin would have survived all the testings of these last years..." A Christian worker in California wrote: "It was with almost a sob of relief that I welcomed the first copies of *The Overcomer*—it was as if reinforcements had arrived to aid in the battle against sin and error..." And similar letters poured in from all parts of the world, expressing deep thankfulness for the renewed witness to the power of the cross and the blood of the Lamb.

We read in the first of the new series:

> The standard of the cross must be kept uplifted... and the body of Christ set free from all that would hinder its readiness for the Lord's appearing. For this we must "war a good warfare" and be active co-hinderers with the Spirit of God against all the plans of Satan to silence the preaching of the atoning cross and to entangle believers in the counterfeits and errors of the day...

What, then, is to be done to "counter the apostasy and the working of lawlessness"? "Proclaim the Lord's death till he come" (1 Cor. 11:29). Ring out the witness to the blood of the Lamb and the atoning cross, right up to the moment of the Lord's appearing. Let us send forth the message of truth to counter the devil's lies. By voice and pen let the messengers of the gospel *proclaim* the message of Calvary..."

In obedience to this vision of the need of the hour, a conference in connection with *The Overcomer* was convened for four days in April 1920, in succession to the Matlock Conferences of pre-war days—this time at the beautiful conference centre at Swanwick in north Derbyshire. The announcement of the conference in *The Overcomer* explains the deep heart purpose and burden which lay behind its inception:

> We seem at the present hour to be advancing to conditions in the world similar to those in which Paul proclaimed his message. Not yet is there open persecution in Britain, but it is surely on the horizon should it be that forces which now appear to be gaining the upper hand ever reach full sway.
>
> There is therefore need for a gathering together of those who hold the faith of the gospel of Calvary to mutually confer over the "present distress," and in the presence of the Lord to strengthen each other's hands to stand in the battle in this evil day. It is also necessary for the effective proclaiming of the message of the cross, that the messengers should know the message in all its aspects so that it works in power in their own lives. *Only those who live the "cross" can preach it effectively.* For mentally apprehended, and proclaimed only in words which "man's wisdom teacheth," the very message which is the *dunamis* of God is made of "no effect."
>
> In view also of the grave perils of the present hour in the spread of the great apostasy, and the tidal wave of spiritism, with its parallel influx of counterfeit workings of Satan as an angel of light among the very front ranks of spiritual believers, it is urgently necessary to confer as to how the standard of the cross should be lifted afresh in mighty power to stay the onrush of the foe.
>
> Such a consultative conference we hope the conference at Swanwick will be. To make this more possible, we have arranged

a timetable, giving themes for each day, to be considered *in their relationship to the cross* as the center and basic cause from which all true spiritual "effects" must spring.[1]

This was followed by the timetable, and a request that:

All who purpose joining us may ponder and pray over each day's theme, and search the Scriptures, so as to be prepared to contribute any light the Spirit of God may give them for use at the proper hour.

The "pattern" given of God for the former conferences was adhered to, and no program of speakers arranged. In each of the principal meetings, Mrs. Penn-Lewis gave the opening address from the Word of God, which formed the basis of messages which followed from one and another of those present. The "message" was the message of the cross, as of old, in all its aspects, from substitution and justification, to the dividing of soul from spirit, and the conflict in the heavenlies of the mature believer. With a deepened experience and richer illumination of the message, every aspect was elucidated in its relation to the whole doctrine of the atonement, with a rare appreciation of the *"balance of truth"* in giving the objective position and its subjective issues in life and service.

Preliminaries and formalities were reduced to a minimum, that every moment might be given to the vital matters under consideration, to which any member of the conference was free to add his or her "quota of light," if given such a word by the Holy Spirit at the time.

In response to the expressed wish of many who were present, the "singularly lucid and Spirit-breathed opening up of the Calvary message" given by the convener was afterwards issued in book form.[2] The following extracts from the brief account of the gatherings given in *The Overcomer* might serve as a general description of other conferences at Swanwick which were to follow, and which came to be regarded more as an annual house party or reunion than a convention in the usual acceptance of the term.

---

1   From *The Overcomer*, April 1920

2   *The Centrality of the Cross*. (First edition entitled *The Logos of the Cross*.)

We were in number about 250 servants of God.[3] The majority were *workers* in the very forefront of the battle, keenly putting to the proof, in hand-to-hand fight against the forces of evil, the truths of the Word of God as set forth in the pages of *The Overcomer*. There were also between forty and fifty clergy and ministers of the gospel, as well as lay-evangelists and missionaries—most of whom were heavily burdened over the spread of the apostasy from the faith of the gospel ... Some were facing in their churches problems caused by the inroad of supernatural workings of Satan, which were manifestly "counterfeit" as judged by their fruits in producing confusion in the services and division between the children of God. Many of the ministers had come hoping to get light upon these problems, as well as to have their own hearts strengthened in their purpose to be faithful to the gospel of the atoning cross ...

The last day of the conference, when *The Proclamation of the Cross* and its message had been considered, saw a high tide of the moving of the Spirit of God. It was only then, as we looked back over the week, that we could see how rich and full had been the unveiling of the atoning cross of our risen and glorified Lord, and how marvelously it had been proved that ministers of many denominations, lay workers and spiritual teachers of all stages of growth and knowledge, could meet together in one spirit, and without controversy over divergent points of view, *on the basis of the cross*. Also it was plainly visible again and again as the days went by that in the full unveiling of the cross, all manifestations and workings of the "flesh" were eliminated and the pure working of the Spirit of God made possible. More than once the melting presence of God was so felt that those present sat in silent awe; and when we left the "holy mount" on the Saturday morning after a 7:30 a.m. praise meeting in the conference hall, it was with the united testimony that it had been a unique object lesson of the "word of the cross" as the *dunamis* of God in every aspect of the Christian life.

* * *

One meeting of this remarkable conference especially lives in the memories of many who were present, when the message of

3 The housing capacity of The Hayes, Swanwick, is 317, and this number was reached, and occasionally exceeded, at later conferences.

John 12:24 was the theme: *"Except a corn of wheat fall into the ground and die it abideth alone, but if it die, it bringeth forth much fruit."* With burning intensity Mrs. Penn-Lewis poured out the message of God which lay at the roots of her own "hundred-fold" ministry, passionately desirous that others might catch the vision. As the moments sped by, the hearers seemed to lose sight of speaker and place, hearing only the voice of the Spirit of God, calling to a higher plane of life and service than any yet dreamed of as possible. The Holy Spirit "filled all the house where they were," submerging all in a flood-tide of life from God. When the voice of the messenger ceased, a long silence fell upon the gathering, until at last an aged clergyman rose, and in a hushed voice laid before the Lord the inexpressible longing of the hearts before him, to be made willing for this pathway of the cross, for "life-out-of-death" *fruitfulness* in his service, through a life "tinctured" with the very life of God in the human vessel.

The results of this conference proved to be far-reaching and abiding, and led to the establishment of small conferences on the same lines in many centers up and down the land, arranged by ministers and others burdened with the need for a fuller and stronger proclamation of the foundation truths of the gospel of Calvary. From the editor's personal letter in various issues of *The Overcomer* we cull the following glimpses of the way in which the Spirit of God bore witness to this special emphasis upon the proclamation of the message of the cross:

> In Rev. 13:8 we read that the only ones who did not "worship" or bow down to the world-wide power of the Dragon, working through his super-man (described as "the Beast"), were those whose names were in the "Book of Life of the Lamb slain"—that is, those who *held to their faith in the crucified Lamb of God,* having eternal life through him. It broke upon us at the Cardiff Conference that the work God is now doing is preparing and strengthening his blood-bought children thus to stand in the peril of the present hour. The witness to the cross at the present time has a deeper relation to the Lord's return than we had realized. It means more than the defense of the faith, and even the salvation of those who will receive it. It

means the preparation and equipment of the only ones who will be *able to stand* as the influence of the deceiver ensnares and engulfs the whole of the inhabitants of the earth.

In this light, the conferences on the cross which we are holding are of vital significance. [I have] referred to the increasing blessing manifested in the monthly conferences in London. During the last three months this has again increased. On March 3rd the hall was thronged to the doors, many unable to obtain seats; and there were some striking cases of strangers who had come in and been met of God. A very remarkable case came to my knowledge of a young girl under a strong delusion (which the physicians considered incurable) being fully delivered by the light entering her mind on the meaning of Romans Six... To God we give all the glory.

Reports from other parts of the country and abroad show that the Spirit of God is drawing together a cohesive force of those who are determined to know nothing among men but Jesus Christ and him crucified...

There is undoubtedly a movement of God in every part of the world, and a raising up of the standard of the cross by the Spirit of God. "The subject of the cross is receiving widespread revived attention," writes the leader of a world-wide prayer movement in America [the late Thomas E. Stephens], saying that he had received a paper from Los Angeles telling of an all-day prayer meeting there, in which some of the most prominent evangelical pastors took part, and every address bore on some aspect of the cross in relation to intercession... It is evident that America is responding to the message of the cross... *"Pray,"* writes the leader of the prayer movement referred to, "that this new interest in the message of the cross may not be hindered or side-tracked by the devil, or by *unwise friends"*...

The principles of warfare prayer are penetrating the church... The Rev. Gordon Watt, for instance, tells how he used *War on the Saints* for seven years in his northern parish; and now the truths learned then are meeting the deepest need everywhere he goes. At the American "Keswick," a series of talks on prayer warfare especially opened eyes and gave a real stimulus to many. Mr. Watt adds that "the Christians in every place where the message is being delivered *are finding a new weapon to meet the onrush of modernism;* for they are beginning to see the real enemy, and to understand what prayer warfare can accomplish." Truly, the Spirit of God is raising the standard against the foe.

Concerning the testimony of *The Overcomer,* I am especially thankful for the way in which the Spirit of God is using the truths set forth in our pages to equip *ministers of the gospel* for their most difficult position today. Lonely witnesses to the gospel of Calvary ... write to us asking for our prayer-upholding in the warfare they are in, whilst others say they have entered new realms of the glorious gospel of Jesus Christ through the message we proclaim, and tell of its effect in their churches.

These letters send me to my knees with a great and intense yearning that the numbers of hard-pressed ministers of Christ, in positions growing more and more untenable every day, might only *know* the realms of victory truth which have become blessedly familiar to thousands of the rank and file of our readers. It is borne in upon me with deep conviction that many who have been reckoned "modernists," even in the mission field, are not really so *in heart.* Many are in deep personal need of fuller equipment for their ministry, and have never had a real insight into the *Message of Calvary.* It is for us to pray for these servants of Christ, and to labor to help them all that is in our power ...

Some of the early conferences at Swanwick were held in the midst of extraordinary industrial upheavals, and were only carried through by an intensive putting into practice of all that the conference stood for in aggressive "prayer warfare" against the powers of darkness, and a real proving of the victory of Calvary over them. This was especially true of the 1921 conference, of which Mrs. Penn-Lewis wrote thus in *The Overcomer* in the following July:

> "We went through fire and through water, but thou broughtest us out into a wealthy place" was the experience, metaphorically, of all who were able to reach Swanwick for *The Overcomer* Conference, announced to be held April 18 to 25. For the gravest crisis which England has had to face since the close of the war ... came to a head just the week before the conference was to take place. The long threatened strike of the combination of trade unions known as "The Triple Alliance" was actually fixed for April 15th. Had this

strike taken place, it would have been impossible to travel, and no conference could have been held.

The "prayer warfare groups" in London and elsewhere were also in a crisis.[1] Could their faith come unshaken through such a test, and triumph? For months, prayer had been focused on this conference, asking that the issues of it should be world-wide, and a mighty witness be given to the "principalities and powers in heavenly places" of the victory and power of the cross of Christ.

And now, just a few days before the long-looked-for gatherings, it appeared as if the "god of this age" had succeeded in bringing about such conditions that the prayers of the saints could not be answered! The outward and visible circumstances looked as black as they must have done to the Israelites on the borders of the Red Sea ... We dare not cancel the conference and thus nullify our faith—and it seemed impossible to go forward. "BUT GOD ..."

Those responsible for the actual arrangements can never forget the dense darkness and conflict which surrounded them during that crucial week. A message from Swanwick came: "Wire if conference is to take place," and the word of faith replied, *"Expect to hold conference as arranged"* ... Then the prayer groups gave themselves anew to prayer. It seemed as direct a conflict between God and the devil as it was in Egypt, with Pharaoh contesting the liberation of the people of God.

Late on the Thursday night (14th) came the challenge of faith: "Lord, if *thou* hast planned this conference, and it is *thy purpose it shall be held,* give us proof by utterly overthrowing the schemes of the adversary."

And it was done! At that very hour a trade union official was speaking to a meeting of members of Parliament, when *unexpectedly*—and apparently unintentionally—he suddenly said words which proffered the olive branch of peace! The Friday that was to see Britain in the grip of a national strike saw instead the virtual break-up of the Alliance and the way clear for the people of God to go forward ...

After such a prayer-battle and such a victory for those "on the Lord's side," the conference of 1921 proved indeed to be the

---

1   Groups of "two or three" meeting for prayer in private homes—an outcome of the monthly conference in London.

"Mount of God" to the preachers and Christian workers there gathered, and a deep work was done—but who can describe all that is meant by the manifested presence of God? "The memory of that wonderful week," we read in *The Overcomer,* "is not so much of the addresses, nor of the speakers, but of the tender, melting atmosphere, wherein the Spirit of God seemed to search the depths of every heart and life and bring each one low at his feet. One blessed result of this was, as someone noted, "the marvelous unity and love which prevailed throughout the whole conference..."

And again:

> The conference was an example of what the Holy Ghost would do when he could get a company together of "one accord." There was not a discordant note throughout the week, nor, what is often a subtle danger, any breaking off into small companies for the discussion of other "lines of truth" than those arising out of the theme of the conference. Many of the Lord's children do not realize how they *hinder the full working of the Holy Spirit* in a conference when they divert the minds of the attenders to other aspects of God's fathomless truth not specifically in line with the objective of the gatherings they are attending. The "I of Paul" and the "I of Apollos" spirit was absent, and consequently the Spirit of God was able to lead all who were present into one accord at the throne of God. The Thursday evening meeting reached high-water mark. One who had been in the Welsh Revival from its beginning said that he had not seen one meeting in Wales, at that time, of greater power.

This same note is struck again and again in the reports of these conferences, and the vital secret of this blessed oneness was the earnest appeal always made by Mrs. Penn-Lewis that, while many present necessarily held divergent views on prophecy, on sanctification, on healing, and other matters, all these should be put aside for the time, in order to meet at the place of unity—the cross of Christ—and to concentrate upon the great objective for which they met. "While the word 'overcomer' is a Bible word," she said, *"there is no such thing as 'overcomer' teaching'!* We simply proclaim the gospel of Calvary, with all that it implies... and that is far more than victory over sin, over the world, over circumstances. It includes victory over the powers of darkness and the defeat of Satan."

To those who asked why *The Overcomer* and its conferences did not take up questions of the interpretation of prophecy and other "lines of truth," her answer was always the same in substance:

> As our ministry lies in spiritual service to the whole body of Christ, in the unfolding of the unsearchable riches available to the believer through his wondrous death, resurrection, and ascension into glory, we have sought to keep *unidentified* with any system of prophetic teaching, believing that controversy on themes which are not fundamental to *salvation* tends to hinder the very purpose for which men strive. The need today is supremely the UNITY of the body of Christ in view of his soon return...
>
> The cross alone is the center of light as well as of unity. In the degree that each believer actually experiences the inworking power of the cross, whereby the old Adam fallen life, manifested in the *fallen intellect* as well as in the sins of the flesh, is really put to death—to that degree the Spirit of truth is able to reveal the inner meaning of the fathomless truth of God.

The physical battle did not grow less with increasing years, and early in 1922—just a month before the annual conference at Swanwick—another severe test came. The 'Editor's Personal Letter' in the April issue of *The Overcomer* gave its readers (whom Mrs. Penn-Lewis always regarded as beloved personal friends) the story of the Lord's wondrous love and power:

April 1922

My Dear Friends in God,

I am thankful once more to be permitted by God to speak to you through the pages of our little paper, for it appeared a brief while ago that I might not be able to do so again. But our wonderful living Lord has raised me up from a dangerous physical attack, and I am looking forward by his grace to being at Swanwick. I told you in my January letter that I was conscious of the physical frame being so spent and worn that only the grace of God would enable me to get through the winter. The climax came early on March 9 with a hemorrhage from my lungs which lasted several days ... and I had to face at once my position. Did this signify that my ministry was accomplished (Acts 20:24), or was it only a new call for faith? Once I was clear on this point, I had to decide what course to take. I was away from home, staying in the cottage on Matlock Moor, cut off from all external help. Should I at once return home to be "nursed," or stay and prove "El-Shaddai"? I then saw that the first path would be the one of unbelief, and that there was "no other way but through" in faith in a living God. For just a brief half hour I faced the question whether I was prepared to be suddenly taken to the heavenly home. From this "mount of vision" I could see you all in your battle on the plains. Was I never again to help strengthen your hands with the words of life, and share in your faith victories? For myself it was absolute peace and readiness to "depart and be with Christ which is very far better"; but so much the Lord had promised me I should finish before that time came, rose to my vision ... I turned from the blessed prospect of relief from the conflict of these days; and looking into the face of the Lord, I told him I must go back to the work if he would permit me. And he did.

Others also went to the throne of grace, and on the fourth day there came the touch of God on the danger spot. Suddenly every trace of hemorrhage passed away, and then all I had to do was to rest and regain strength after such a testing. Since then I have been steadily recovering.

This issue of *The Overcomer* is being prepared, in much weakness, in my "writing cottage" on Matlock Moor. You will bear with the personal tone of this letter, but the bond in Christ with the thousands of my readers all over the world is a very real one. For many years now we have shared our joys and sorrows through the medium of our pages. Your conflicts have been mine, and I have rejoiced in your advance in the deep things of God ...

A note of praise in the July "Letter" tells of yet another proving of the risen life of her Lord (Rom. 8:11) as all-sufficient for the human vessel when called to be "poured forth" in his service. After speaking of the conference as "the best of the three" yet held, she continues:

How can I describe to you what God wrought for his frail messenger! In answer to your prayers I was carried in a tide of life which never flagged for the seven days, nor was there need for any "duty" to be omitted, or any service to the Lord's people limited. To him you will give the glory for his fathomless grace.

At this conference, one-fifth of the whole attendance was composed of ministers of the gospel; and Mrs. Penn-Lewis had the joy of the co-operation, for two days, of her old friend, Dr. F. B. Meyer. One of the most remarkable features of all the conferences at Swanwick was the attendance, year after year, of numbers of clergy and ministers, many of whom testified that their ministries had been "entirely revolutionized" as a result of the gatherings; and eternity alone will reveal what the impact of these servants of God has been upon the church of Christ as a whole. As one minister, himself a conference speaker, wrote later:

> … her addresses at Swanwick and elsewhere were so Scriptural and sane that I cannot recall ever listening to her without receiving definite blessing… She gave us bedrock teaching of the soundest description. We saw our deep need of the experimental fact of Calvary. Our death-union in Christ was *the only way* to our *life-union in him*. I thank God for his dear child, and for her untiring witness to the blood-stained cross of Calvary in the fullness of its applied power…

* * *

But in the midst of these and other "labors more abundant," the dark cloud of an acute personal trial was creeping up over the horizon in the gradually failing health of Mr. Penn-Lewis. His work for the City of Leicester during the war years had been strenuous and exacting. It was said that by his skillful handling of the finances of the city he had saved its citizens many thousands of pounds, but the long continued strain and responsibility told heavily upon him. Three months' entire rest, ordered by his physician in 1921, gave only temporary relief; and in the year 1924 it became necessary to resign his position as city treasurer and retire, in the hope that his life might thereby be prolonged. Cartref, the house in Leicester to which the thoughts of thousands lovingly turned as the home of *The Overcomer*, was therefore sold; and Mr. and Mrs. Penn-Lewis removed, with their household, to a new home in the Surrey hills, some sixteen miles from London.

In the previous summer God had, by a long train of circumstantial leadings, placed at the disposal of Mrs. Penn-Lewis for her conference and prayer work, the premises in London known as Eccleston Hall, built by the 3rd Lord Radstock forty years before as a place where Christians might meet in the service of God apart from any barriers of sect or denomination. The temporary use of the building as a place of rest and refreshment for the troops passing to and from the continent had dispersed the clientele which had once used it for their meetings, and Lord Radstock's trustees called a day of prayer to seek guidance as to the future of the premises.

Meanwhile, the monthly Overcomer Conference, formerly held at Eccleston Hall, but during and since the War at Sion College, was literally "crowded out," numbers having to stand during the meetings; and it was clear that some change would have to be made. The outcome of it all was that Eccleston Hall was handed over to Mrs. Penn-Lewis for one year in order to "test" the Lord's will concerning it, and was soon in full use as a prayer center for the "mobilizing of the prayer forces" in special days of prayer, prayer conferences, and other activities.

The guiding hand of God in this was manifest when, a few months later, the removal from Leicester to the country home in the south necessitated the separation of the literature work from the private home where it had been carried on for so many years. In the twelve-roomed house adjoining the conference hall there was ample accommodation for the Overcomer Book Room, and secretarial work, and a small flat at the top of the house formed a quiet resting place for Mrs. Penn-Lewis, when conferences or her editorial work and heavy correspondence required her presence in town for a few days at a time.

Here, therefore, the work with its worldwide links was transferred, in July 1924.

But alas, the hope that a more genial climate and release from professional responsibilities would effect a restoration for her beloved husband was not justified, and eight months later, on March 24th, 1925, Mrs. Penn-Lewis was called to hand back to God the precious gift of more than forty years. *The Overcomer* for April was prepared under the very "shadow of death," but with a steady, calm trust in God that left no trace of the shadow upon the magazine; and the editor's "Letter" touchingly opens with this note of Easter triumph:

> Up from the grave he arose
> With a mighty triumph o'er his foes.
> He arose a victor from the dark domain—
> And he lives for ever, with his saints to reign!
> He arose! He arose! Hallelujah, Christ arose!

"Victor" *over death's* "domain" is the word that is full of power to me. "Death's domain" is around us on every hand, but he is victor. "Death" hath no "dominion over him." May we each realize that to the degree we enter into *"his death,"* we rise above the death of nature which is ours in Adam, and share in his victory over it, and his triumphant emergence into life.

Speaking, in the July issue, of the Lord's tender preparation of her spirit for the "translation to glory" of her "fellow-heir of the grace of life" (1 Pet. 3:7), the following striking message on the "reign of life" was given—which will surely speak afresh to other hearts in the "valley of *the shadow* of death":

This preparation began at Cardiff on March 12th, when at the last meeting the Lord gave me a message of victory over death in such a way that I personally broke through in spirit into a sense of triumph over death that I had never conceived to be possible. I saw what the apostle Paul meant when he said that the *"reign"* of death had been *"established"* by the one man [Adam], through the sin of him alone," (Rom. 5:17, c.h.) and I realized as never before how truly "death" was *reigning* in the world in spite of an appearance of "life" which was only possible until "death" again asserted its grip on the fallen creation.

Then I went on to the latter part of the same verse and rang out the glorious message of the gospel of the cross, that although the "reign of death" had become established through the first Adam, *far more shall the reign of life be established* in those who receive the overflowing fullness of the free gift of righteousness, by the one man, Jesus Christ." Much more! Much more! (v. 17, A.V.) Not only just as much, but *"much more"* shall the *"reign of life"* be established" in those who receive the "overflowing fullness" of life through our Lord Jesus Christ.

It was after this that on the Saturday morning—March 14th—I awoke as with a chime of bells ringing in my spirit the Easter hymn I have already told you of. It rang and rang like bells. I did not know what it all meant, more than that the Lord was seeking to tell me that he was victor over death, and that he means us in union with him to share in his triumph. Then the story of Lazarus became alive with power. I saw that Christ had absolute authority over death, even before he went to the cross, and voluntarily submitted to the death which was ours in Adam. How glorious that mighty shout to the dead Lazarus, when he said "Come forth," and "he that was dead came forth." God was speaking to me of victory over death…

The whole story is one of the most remarkable records of the tenderness of God toward one of the frailest of his children. I had known since early February, from a specialist, that there was no human hope for my husband's life; but I had faced "death" so often that I could not take this verdict as final until I had it from the Lord himself. Much prayer was therefore made… but the moment came when the Lord clearly showed me that it was his time to take him… He was laid to rest on March 27th in the Friends' Burial Ground, Reigate, Surrey, with a simple, touching service led by Dr. F. B. Meyer.[1] There was no shadow from "death's domain." It was a foreshadowing of the way in which, in God's time, mortality will be "swallowed up of life" when the Lord comes. I am more than ever deeply convinced that the Lord is seeking to bring us into a

---

1   Dr. Meyer remarked that this quiet garden attached to the Friends' Meeting House was peculiarly appropriate as the last resting place of William Penn-Lewis, as he was a descendant of William Penn, one of the Pilgrim Fathers, the founder of Pennsylvania.

place where we must lay hold of victory over death, *even though it may not mean, individually, immunity from physical death for any one of us.* Blessed be God, it is literally true that to the believer who is "in Christ" there is no death. Death is swallowed up in victory...

There is much I should like to tell you of what the church of God owes to the one who has gone home; for all that the Spirit of God has enabled me for in the Lord's service would never have been possible without the full support of my "fellow-heir" of grace...

Through the home-going of my husband, the veil has now been lifted to you a little upon the strain which has been upon me for quite four years in carrying on the work. Marvelously have I been carried through, in answer to many prayers...

"Now I must be poured out for God as never before," she wrote in a private letter; and this was her attitude throughout those sad days. The monthly conference day falling the following week, she stood on the platform—a delicate and touching figure—and gave such a message of victory in Christ as awed the hearts of her hearers, while "they glorified God in her." Then came the Swanwick Conference in May, and again the enabling of God for full service, though the marks of suffering were patent to all who knew her. The summer was spent almost entirely in the settlement of business matters and the rearrangement of personal affairs necessitated by the loss of her husband, and the physical breakdown, within a few months, of the faithful and devoted Mary, who had relieved her mistress of all household cares since the Richmond days, more than thirty years before. Truly God was stripping his beloved child, so as to leave her "no shadow of anything to cling to or rest upon *outside of himself,*" that she should "flow into God, as water joined to its source blends with it ever deeper and deeper" (Guyon, in *Spiritual Torrents*).

We read in *The Overcomer* for October 1925:

I must frankly say that I do not recollect, in all the deep sufferings of the past, any period of time so full of keen conflict over the work of God committed to me, as the summer months now drawing to a close... And the enemy has not failed to press the battle to the gate and to use every possible advantage to compel me to lay my armor down. Every attitude of the past thirty years, of surrender to God for his uttermost use for the service of his body the church, has been sifted to the foundations, with the enemy's pressure urging the impossibility of my "going on."

But blessed be God, in answer, no doubt, to the upholding of your prayers, I am emerging from the wilderness conflict with faith that has come through fire, that by his grace I shall be enabled to press forward "alone," reverently to say with my Lord, "yet not alone, because the Father is with me" (John 16:32).

At the end of November a brief visit was made to Copenhagen, when, as the guest of Baroness Schaffalitzky, two days were put to full use in drawing-room meetings and important interviews with strategic workers, renewing many links of previous visits. Then on to Stockholm to fulfill a long-promised engagement to give God's message at a conference of the K.M.A. (equivalent of the English Y.W.C.A.). The time of year made such a journey a real venture of faith; but a volume of prayer surrounded her, and every step of the way was hedged about by the God of deliverances. A rich tide of blessing accompanied the meetings— "More, far more than we could ask or think," said the president of the K.M.A. Thus Sweden was both the first and the last of the "regions beyond" the homeland to receive the word of the Lord through this messenger of the cross.

"And they overcame him by the blood of the Lamb, and by the word of their testimony, and they loved not their lives even unto death" (Rev. 12:11).

The shadow of his cross has come upon her, but only a shadow—a "likeness"—for he removed the sting from death as he trod the wine-press alone, drank the bitter cup to its dregs, and made propitiation for the sins of the people.

Nought but a "SHADOW" of death for his redeemed ones, that they might give him the fellowship he seeks, and be conformed to the image of the Lamb.

Chapter 13

Deepening Conformity to the Pattern of the Lamb

1926–1927

The fellowship of his sufferings—The Llandrindod Convention and her last ministry—Death swallowed up in victory

"For those whom he foreknew, he also predestined to be made like to the pattern of his Son," wrote Paul to those "called to be saints" in Rome (Rom. 8:29). *"Like in suffering* seems to be meant,"is Conybeare's footnote to this verse, linking it with the similar word in Phil. 3:10; not vicarious suffering, but better expressed in the law of nature and of grace, "travail," a sharing in the travail of Christ over the birth of his church; not a suffering FOR, but a suffering "together with"Christ over souls "until Christ be formed" in them; leading them on into ever fuller planes of the life in God (cf. Col. 1:28–29; 2:1). This travail must needs come through the outward circumstances of life, or instruments permitted of God, as in the case of Paul himself. The message of this life to the people of God would be incomplete were this phase entirely omitted.

Correspondence and contact with servants of God, not only at home but in many parts of the world, gave Mrs. Penn-Lewis a unique insight into the dangers connected with great spiritual experiences of every kind (even when not shown in supernatural physical manifestations) apart from a continuous surrender of the flesh to the Holy Spirit to be made to die. It was in the light of this wide outlook upon the whole church of God that she knew the "fellowship of his sufferings" and something of what Paul meant by "filling up the afflictions of Christ for his body's sake" (Col. 1:24).

Mellowed by suffering, and with vision cleared by many years of intimate walking with God, she now looked upon the church of God as from some "Pisgah" height very near the gates of the heavenly city; and seeing the peril of all who might be "beguiled" from the "simplicity that is in Christ Jesus," she entered into the deepest prayer ministry of her life, in tender sympathetic understanding and anguish of spirit over the members of the body of Christ, "upon whom the ends of the ages have come" (1 Cor. 10:11).

"There is no doubt," she wrote early in 1927,

> ...that we are increasingly moving on into the shadow, if not having a foretaste, of the great tribulation. God is shaking all that can be shaken, and within our knowledge there is scarcely a leader, or a teacher of spiritual things, or an advancing Christian among the rank and file, who is not being acutely tested, not only circumstantially, but even as to the very foundations of the spiritual life. Such a "shaking" by the hand of God, so that the "things which cannot be shaken" may remain, has meant that the foundations are being laid bare, raising the question as to whether much that has been believed to be real personal knowledge of truth has not been, in some degree, based upon hearsay rather than direct proving of the Word of God...
>
> I am deeply persuaded that never was the message of *The Overcomer* as to the identification aspect of the cross more needed. "Prayer warfare," apart from it, will cease to be effective; for the "old Adam" life will surely spring into action again unless the power of Christ's death is perpetually applied in the very center of our being... Every error that has ever sprung into existence in the history of the church has had its inception in the ignorance of believers concerning this aspect of the cross, or their failing to see the vital necessity *of its continuity*. The message of identification the devil hates and dreads more than any other, for it is the only way whereby the believer escapes from his power. The "flesh" (inclusive of the *psuche*, or soul-life) is the devil's workshop, and that fallen life of

Adam which has come to us through the Fall needs ever deeper to be dealt with at the cross...

Three times during the years 1926–7 was Mrs. Penn-Lewis brought very near the gates of death; and three times, in answer to the prayers of others and her own indomitable faith and courage "for the work's sake," was she brought back as by a miracle, so that her physician remarked on one occasion that he could not say *how* it would go, as Mrs. Penn-Lewis was "a law unto herself." But these attacks left her weaker in body in spite of her buoyant spirit. In order to avoid the long drives between the home in Surrey and the work in London, which now wearied rather than refreshed her, the country home was closed in 1926, and she took up her residence permanently in the flat at Eccleston Place, that her whole remaining strength might be conserved for the service of God. Her list of engagements fulfilled during this period shows very little diminution and includes, in addition to the monthly conference and other gatherings at Eccleston Hall, conferences at Bristol, Liverpool, Cardiff, and other centers.

The Swanwick Conference of 1927—the eighth, the "glory" number—was one of the *happiest* of the series; and though only three weeks had elapsed since her third attack of pneumonia, Mrs. Penn-Lewis presided over all the principal meetings, and on the last day gave a full message on the "endowment of power for service"; the burden of the messages during the week being sustained by the Revs. R. B. Jones, Gordon Watt, and others. From her last "Letter" to the readers of *The Overcomer* (July 1927) we cull the following extracts, only to give a glimpse into the "overweight of joy" which the Lord so lovingly shed upon this last "Swanwick":

> With unspeakable thankfulness I am able this time to tell you that I have, in a great measure, been renewed in bodily strength, in answer to the volumes of prayer which have gone up for me during three attacks of pneumonia which have followed one another since the Swanwick Conference of 1926.

My space will not allow me to write at length and tell you how sore the battle for life has been, and what a miracle it is that I am still spared to continue the service to the church of God which he has graciously given me. Numbers have wondered why the trial has been so prolonged … but they have not known the "fellowship of the sufferings of Christ," in which I have been sharing in the background *for his body's sake, the church,* which made it difficult for the physical frame to respond to the life which the risen Lord was ready to give, in answer to their prayers … Yet, to the glory of God, he enabled me to be at my post at Swanwick—with no ill-effects or relapse …

The atmosphere was crystal clear, and the spirit of love and joy abounding. None of us can ever forget what it meant in this time of strain and suffering to have been bathed, as it were, for even five days in such a tide of life from God …

There is much else I should like to refer to in connection with the conference, which was so manifestly under the hand of God that it ran, as it were, of itself, without a single hitch. The ministers had never had such meetings, in which the unity of the Spirit deepened into a fellowship which swallowed up all the "labels" of denomination and nationality. The praise meeting gave evidence of this, as all magnified the grace of God …

* * *

After forty days of intercession for the people of God, it is recorded of Moses on his return to the camp that "his face shone, though he wist it not"; and more than one who saw Mrs. Penn-Lewis at Keswick in July 1927 remarked upon the light of joy that seemed to shine from within upon her face. Returning to London for one week, she traveled to Llandrindod Wells on July 29th, as one of the speakers of the convention, which that year was celebrating the twenty-fifth anniversary of its inauguration.

Acknowledging the gift of a smiling "snapshot" of Mrs. Penn-Lewis, taken at Llandrindod, a friend who was much with her during that week in close spiritual fellowship, wrote:

> … It shows the peace within and peace without that seemed to characterize that last week … One has more than once noted that

when the Lord is about to take to himself some valiant one, he grants that one at the end a period of unharassed interior comfort—as if to say, "The stormy voyage is nearly over; this is the land-locked harbor; the shore and I are just ahead!"

During the whole of that last week of her active life there was a peculiar mellow sweetness... She seemed to be enjoying herself interiorly. To a comment upon the pace at which she was living, she replied, "Oh, this is life to me!" I believe this was so—a grant of grace from above, that she should have that last week of inward relief and outward joy of filling up the full measure of her ministry.

She was ministering, in one way or another, all the week... Evidently it was all with a keen sense of joy at being able. All her messages were in remarkable lucidity and power. I say power, but not referring to physical strength, which on at least two occasions seemed flagging; but the kind of power which conveys the truth to the hearers.

One evening I remarked that I knew for a certainty that she had hardly drawn breath since dawn. She twinkled over this, and asked how I knew. "Well," I said "I heard you speak to the Porth Bible School students after breakfast... Then I saw you whisked off to a council meeting at ten o'clock. Then you appeared on the platform for the eleven o'clock meeting. Then you had to have a meal; and you said just now you had been driving up to the Elan valley, sixty miles. And I found you now rising from your tea. So that is how I know!"

Moreover, after that she was on the platform at the evening meeting—although with head down in her hands much of the time.

The story of this last public ministry, and of the weekend which followed the convention, we give in the words of the Rev. J. R. Morgan, minister of the church at Treharris in which this "bond servant of Jesus Christ" gave her last message, as follows:

When Mrs. Penn-Lewis arrived at Llandrindod, we saw how weak and frail she was. Many who had the privilege of knowing her will remember what it was to take her little delicate hand into yours and feel your heart go out in deep sympathy and real fear that one so frail should undertake any duty at all. However, her ministry at Llandrindod was really marvelous. I can see her now as she came in to the first meeting, unable to walk from her hotel, but driving in my friend's car, and getting down from it so slowly and walking into the tent. She appeared quite unable for anything; but when she was on the platform and facing the congregation, she seemed strengthened; and later, when she spoke in that meeting, we were amazed to hear how her voice filled the tent so that some twelve hundred people heard her distinctly.

Her message that afternoon was a most striking one. She spoke on *schism in the body of Christ,* and her words were one great intense appeal for sympathy between the members of the body of Christ one for another. She said that the word "schism" came from the same root as the word "sympathy," and emphasized that the cause of all schism was *lack of sympathy and love.* She appealed to all to bear one another upon their hearts in loving sympathy, and especially in view of the days of testing and trial that are coming upon the earth. It seemed to us as we listened to her that she was uttering prophetic words as she spoke of days of persecution which the church will face in the near future, and it humbled us before the Lord.

How she was strengthened by God! In spite of her weakness, she was mighty during that whole week. She spoke altogether in some nine or ten meetings, and she came into very close touch with a company of young people from the South Wales Bible School, staying together in a hotel. On four mornings at 9:30 she came and spoke to about a hundred of us there. Her teaching, her wonderful illumination upon the Scriptures was in God's hands a marvelous ministry to those young students; and today there are many of them who praise and bless God for the privilege of having heard her, many for the first time.

The convention came to a close, and Mrs. Penn-Lewis went to the home of her friends at Maesycwmmer for the weekend, and came to speak at our little church on the Sunday. I stood at the door when I heard the car coming, and as it pulled up I was distressed to see her sitting in it looking more like an invalid than one come to undertake a service; and after the car stopped at the curb, it was fully two minutes before she attempted to get out, because, she said, she wanted to get her breath! I can see her now walking down the aisle, weaker than I had ever seen her before; and she took her place in a corner pew, drawing her fur cloak around her. I wanted her to go through to the vestry, for I felt she could never take part in the service; but she sat there during the introductory part, and when I had led the congregation in a chorus, "There is power in the blood of the Lamb," I saw her stirring! She pulled herself together, and in her characteristic way threw off her cloak and walked up to the platform ...

"Many think of the precious blood as some 'power' coming down *upon them,*" she began. And from that she went on to open out the significance of the blood of our Lord Jesus Christ, and spoke with wonderful power, holding the whole congregation in intense interest. The blood of Christ, she said, in the New Testament, has always a Godward aspect. We are "made nigh by the blood"; we have access to God by the blood; we are redeemed by that precious blood; we enter into the holiest by the blood, and so on. Even where the blood of Christ is spoken of as cleansing, the ultimate purpose of that cleansing is with a Godward view. The operation of the blood of Christ is never earth-ward, man-ward, but heavenward and Godward. The blood cleanses from *sin,* the cross delivers from the *power of sin,* as it is allowed to operate in the life of the believer. The cross of Christ is the instrument God uses to deal with the "flesh," the old nature, the Adam life. *God does not cleanse the flesh,* he condemns it to death ...

She pleaded earnestly that those present would take the message God had given her for them, as it might be the last time they would ever hear her voice. She spoke for over an hour; but for the last quarter of an hour her voice was growing weaker and weaker, until it became almost inaudible. She closed her address and then dismissed the congregation with prayer; but as she prayed her spirit seemed to rise, and she appeared as strong as ever.

When she came off the platform she seemed almost to collapse; but after a moment's rest, she passed into the vestry, where we had refreshment for her. When she was asked why she spoke so long when so weak, she replied: "I had to get through with my message." We shall never forget that visit. To me it has been a new beginning, and I believe that God will manifestly answer her prayer for that church. "So then *death worketh in us,* but LIFE IN YOU" (2 Cor. 4:12). As one friend said to me afterwards: "So you at Treharris received the last drops of the sacrifice!"

To a stranger this last sentence might appear superlative, but to all who were privileged to know this servant of God in the background of her *private life*, this moving story is but the climax of a life continually poured out for many years in selfless service for God and his people, regardless of personal weakness and suffering. Perhaps no one woman has ever called forth so much devoted love from souls all over the world, many of whom never saw her face to face, but to whom she stood as the one who had taught them the way of personal victory and effective service for God. From none, however, did she receive a deeper love and more intense loyalty than from those who lived and worked with her in the personal background of her life. We say "worked *with her*" advisedly, for to serve under her direction was to be actively and consciously in the service of God, a "fellow laborer" with his ambassador. As no sacrifice was too great for the leader, so this privileged co-service demanded the utmost measure of glad and willing toil from others, "poured out" in the same ministry to the Lord.

Mrs. Penn-Lewis traveled back from Wales to London on Tuesday, August 9th. It was clear, to those who received her home with loving anxiety, that she was ill; but it did not appear more serious than on many occasions when she had returned from a series of meetings utterly spent out. As the week went on, however, she became weaker and weaker, though she dealt with her correspondence daily until the Saturday. The doctor said that her heart was over-strained and there was a little pneumonia also.

On Monday, August 15th, God called his beloved servant into his immediate presence, to "go out no more." Like Bunyan's Pilgrim, as she entered the "river," the powers of darkness drew near in an endeavor to trouble her. Then she asked us to repeat "There is a fountain filled with Blood"; and when, after a time, one of us changed it to another hymn, she said, "No, do not alter what God is using!" The dying warrior knew the weapon to select—it was Revelation 12:11—the blood of the Lamb that "destroyed him that had the power of death," to which she appealed for the last time and with triumphant effect.

One whose privilege it was to be beside her throughout that day, and to go with her as far as human love can go, wrote of her entry into glory:

On Monday afternoon, about four o'clock, she appeared to fall asleep. Then her breathing (which had been labored and painful) became easier, and growing more and more gentle, at about nine in the evening it quietly ceased, as she slipped out of the tired body of "fragile clay" into the bosom of the Father.

We who were with her shed no tears as she entered into the glory, for the presence of the Lord with us in the room was something beyond the realm of "faith"—it was almost "sight" in its reality. We proved indeed the truth of the word that "through death" Christ "brought to nought him that had the power of death," for the Prince of Death appeared to have no part or lot in the matter, and death was swallowed up in victory…

A memorable service was held in Eccleston Hall on August 18th, and in spite of the usual August "exodus" from town, the hall was full, many having traveled long distances to pay their loving tribute to her memory. The service was conducted by the Rev. H. Tydeman Chilvers, of Spurgeon's Tabernacle, assisted by the Rev. George Harper. Speaking from Romans 6:5–11, Mr. Chilvers stressed with great power the testimony to the cross of Christ, and the Christ of the cross, which this life had been poured out to proclaim. Of his address we can give but the closing sentences:

All that she received she got from this blessed Book, and the Book is ours. The source of her strength is the source of our strength. The source of her power, the fountain of her light, is our source and fountain today. So we say, under the shadow of death, and yet realizing the glory and magnificence of the life that is now hers *with* Christ as well as in Christ, "Thanks be unto God who giveth us the victory through our Lord Jesus Christ." She is with her Lord, triumphant, truly an overcomer—an overcomer by the blood of the Lamb.

If the lifting of a finger would bring her back we would not lift it. That frail little body! We almost wondered sometimes how the flesh and bones hung together. And yet what a power she was! How she *flamed* for God! Has she flamed out? No, the flame was so mighty for God that he has delivered it from the weak vessel of clay that it might flame to its uttermost in his presence for ever.

And Jesus is coming again! He will soon be here! *Occupy,* "Occupy till I come!"

* * *

And then the outworn "earthly tent" was laid to rest in the little God's Acre at Reigate where, some two years before, she had laid that of her husband; and around the open grave we sang the old hymn, "There is a Fountain filled with Blood," adding the chorus, the last few words of which were almost the last Mrs. Penn-Lewis spoke:

> I do believe I now receive
> The life he offers me,
> And standing on Christ's finished work,
> I claim the victory.

She is not dead. Such a life as hers can never die. Her fruit remains, for it is living seed planted in the hearts and lives of God's children in every corner of the world—it is a host of living souls delivered from the power of the enemy and brought into fellowship and union with God by the testimony of the Holy Spirit through her lips and pen. She has "completed the glorious contest" (2 Tim. 4:7, lit.); she has kept the faith; henceforth… a crown of righteousness from the pierced hand of her beloved Lord.

Books by Mrs. Penn-Lewis

The Story of Job: A glimpse into the mystery of Suffering

The Cross of Calvary and its Message, with preface by the late Dr. Andrew Murray

The Warfare with Satan and the Way of Victory

Thy Hidden Ones: Union with Christ traced in the Song of Songs

The Centrality of the Cross

Soul and Spirit, and "Soul-Force" versus "Spirit-Force": A Glimpse into Bible Psychology

Face to Face: The Inner Life of Moses, the Man of God

The Conquest of Canaan: Sidelights on the Spiritual Battlefield

Life in the Spirit: A glimpse into the heavenly warfare

The Climax of the Risen Life: The path of fellowship with Christ

All Things New: The message of Calvary for the time of the end

The Magna Charta of Woman "According to the Scriptures"

Union with Christ in Death and Resurrection

Abandonment to the Spirit and Ministry to the Lord

The Work of the Holy Spirit

Power for Service and Warfare

The Spiritual Warfare

The "Clinic Hour"

Spiritual Perils of Today as seen in the Pentecostal Movement

The Spirit of Truth, the Power of Pentecost

Much Fruit

Life Out of Death; and Characteristics of Divine Union

Your Intelligent Service

Prayer and Evangelism

The Cross—the Touchstone of Faith

Dying to Live

A Revival of Prayer Needed

Booklets

The Glorious Secret

The Self-Life Unveiled

Change Your Attitude

The Magnificent Christ

The Time of the End

The Battle for the Mind

The Gate to Life

Buy online at our website: **www.KingsleyPress.com**
Also available as an eBook for Kindle, Nook and iBooks.

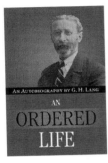

The Revival We Need

by Oswald J. Smith

When Oswald J. Smith wrote this book almost a hundred years ago he felt the most pressing need of the worldwide church was true revival—the kind birthed in desperate prayer and accompanied by deep conviction for sin, godly sorrow, and deep repentance, resulting in a living, victorious faith. If he were alive today he would surely conclude that the need has only become more acute with the passing years.

The author relates how there came a time in his own ministry when he became painfully aware that his efforts were not producing spiritual results. His intense study of the New Testament and past revivals only deepened this conviction. The Word of God, which had proved to be a hammer, a fire and a sword in the hands of apostles and revivalists of bygone days, was powerless in his hands. But as he prayed and sought God in dead earnest for the outpouring of the Holy Spirit, things began to change. Souls came under conviction, repented of their sins, and were lastingly changed.

The earlier chapters of the book contain Smith's heart-stirring messages on the need for authentic revival: how to prepare the way for the Spirit's moving, the tell-tale signs that the work is genuine, and the obstacles that can block up the channels of blessing. These chapters are laced with powerful quotations from revivalists and soul-winners of former times, such as David Brainerd, William Bramwell, John Wesley, Charles Finney, Evan Roberts and many others. The latter chapters detail Smith's own quest for the enduement of power, his soul-travail, and the spiritual fruit that followed.

In his foreword to this book, Jonathan Goforth writes, "Mr. Smith's book, *The Revival We Need,* for its size is the most powerful plea for revival I have ever read. He has truly been led by the Spirit of God in preparing it. To his emphasis for the need of a Holy Spirit revival I can give the heartiest amen. What I saw of revival in Korea and in China is in fullest accord with the revival called for in this book."

Buy online at our website: **www.KingsleyPress.com**
Also available as an eBook for Kindle, Nook and iBooks.

Lord, Teach Us to Pray
By Alexander Whyte

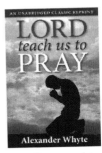

Dr. Alexander Whyte (1836-1921) was widely acknowledged to be the greatest Scottish preacher of his day. He was a mighty pulpit orator who thundered against sin, awakening the consciences of his hearers, and then gently leading them to the Savior. He was also a great teacher, who would teach a class of around 500 young men after Sunday night service, instructing them in the way of the Lord more perfectly.

In the later part of Dr. Whyte's ministry, one of his pet topics was prayer. Luke 11:1 was a favorite text and was often used in conjunction with another text as the basis for his sermons on this subject. The sermons printed here represent only a few of the many delivered. But each one is deeply instructive, powerful and convicting.

Nobody else could have preached these sermons; after much reading and re-reading of them that remains the most vivid impression. There can be few more strongly personal documents in the whole literature of the pulpit. . . . When all is said, there is something here that defies analysis—something titanic, something colossal, which makes ordinary preaching seem to lie a long way below such heights as gave the vision in these words, such forces as shaped their appeal. We are driven back on the mystery of a great soul, dealt with in God's secret ways and given more than the ordinary measure of endowment and grace. His hearers have often wondered at his sustained intensity; as Dr. Joseph Parker once wrote of him: "many would have announced the chaining of Satan for a thousand years with less expenditure of vital force" than Dr. Whyte gave to the mere announcing of a hymn. —*From the Preface*

Buy online at our website: **www.KingsleyPress.com**
Also available as an eBook for Kindle, Nook and iBooks.

The Way of the Cross

by J. Gregory Mantle

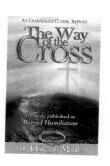

"**D**YING to self is the *one only way* to life in God," writes Dr. Mantle in this classic work on the cross. "The end of self is the one condition of the promised blessing, and he that is not willing to die to things sinful, *yea, and to things lawful,* if they come between the spirit and God, cannot enter that world of light and joy and peace, provided on this side of heaven's gates, where thoughts and wishes, words and works, delivered from the perverting power of self—revolve round Jesus Christ, as the planets revolve around the central sun. . . .

"It is a law of dynamics that two objects cannot occupy the same space at the same time, and if we are ignorant of the crucifixion of the self-life as an experimental experience, we cannot be filled with the Holy Spirit. 'If thy heart,' says Arndt in his *True Christianity,* 'be full of the world, there will be no room for the Spirit of God to enter; for where the one is the other cannot be.' If, on the contrary, we have endorsed our Saviour's work as the destroyer of the works of the devil, and have claimed to the full the benefits of His death and risen life, what hinders the complete and abiding possession of our being by the Holy Spirit but our unbelief?"

Rev. J. Gregory Mantle (1853 - 1925) *had a wide and varied ministry in Great Britain, America, and around the world. For many years he was the well-loved Superintendent of the flourishing Central Hall in Deptford, England, as well as a popular speaker at Keswick and other large conventions for the deepening of spiritual life. He spent the last twelve years of his life in America, where he was associated with Dr. A. B. Simpson and the Christian and Missionary Alliance. He traveled extensively, holding missions and conventions all over the States. He was an avid supporter of foreign missions throughout his entire career. He also edited a missionary paper, and wrote several books.*

GIPSY SMITH
HIS LIFE AND WORK

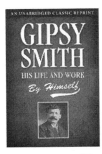

This autobiography of Gipsy Smith (1860-1947) tells the fascinating story of how God's amazing grace reached down into the life of a poor, uneducated gipsy boy and sent him singing and preaching all over Britain and America until he became a household name in many parts and influenced the lives of millions for Christ. He was born and raised in a gipsy tent to parents who made a living selling baskets, tinware and clothes pegs. His father was in and out of jail for various offences, but was gloriously converted during an evangelistic meeting. His mother died when he was only five years old.

Converted at the age of sixteen, Gipsy taught himself to read and write and began to practice preaching. His beautiful singing voice earned him the nickname "the singing gipsy boy," as he sang hymns to the people he met. At age seventeen he became an evangelist with the Christian Mission (which became the Salvation Army) and began to attract large crowds. Leaving the Salvation Army in 1882, he became an itinerant evangelist working with a variety of organizations. It is said that he never had a meeting without conversions. He was a born orator. One of the Boston papers described him as "the greatest of his kind on earth, a spiritual phenomenon, an intellectual prodigy and a musical and oratorical paragon."

His autobiography is full of anedotes and stories from his preaching experiences in many different places. It's a book you won't want to put down until you're finished!

THE AWAKENING
By Marie Monsen

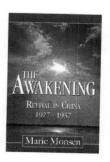

REVIVAL! It was a long time coming. For twenty long years Marie Monsen prayed for revival in China. She had heard reports of how God's Spirit was being poured out in abundance in other countries, particularly in nearby Korea; so she began praying for funds to be able to travel there in order to bring back some of the glowing coals to her own mission field. But that was not God's way. The still, small voice of God seemed to whisper, "What is happening in Korea can happen in China if you will pay the price in prayer." Marie Monsen took up the challenge and gave her solemn promise: "Then I will pray until I receive."

The Awakening is Miss Monsen's own vivid account of the revival that came in answer to prayer. Leslie Lyall calls her the "pioneer" of the revival movement—the handmaiden upon whom the Spirit was first poured out. He writes: "Her surgical skill in exposing the sins hidden within the Church and lurking behind the smiling exterior of many a trusted Christian—even many a trusted Christian leader—and her quiet insistence on a clear-cut experience of the new birth set the pattern for others to follow."

The emphasis in these pages is on the place given to prayer both before and during the revival, as well as on the necessity of self-emptying, confession, and repentance in order to make way for the infilling of the Spirit.

One of the best ways to stir ourselves up to pray for revival in our own generation is to read the accounts of past awakenings, such as those found in the pages of this book. Surely God is looking for those in every generation who will solemnly take up the challenge and say, with Marie Monsen, "I will pray until I receive."

Buy online at our website: **www.KingsleyPress.com**
Also available as an eBook for Kindle, Nook and iBooks.

A Present Help
By Marie Monsen

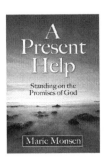

Does your faith in the God of the impossible need reviving? Do you think that stories of walls of fire and hosts of guardian angels protecting God's children are only for Bible times? Then you should read the amazing accounts in this book of how God and His unseen armies protected and guided Marie Monsen, a Norwegian missionary to China, as she traveled through bandit-ridden territory spreading the Gospel of Jesus Christ and standing on the promises of God. You will be amazed as she tells of an invading army of looters who ravaged a whole city, yet were not allowed to come near her mission compound because of angels standing sentry over it. Your heart will thrill as she tells of being held captive on a ship for twenty-three days by pirates whom God did not allow to harm her, but instead were compelled to listen to her message of a loving Savior who died for their sin. As you read the many stories in this small volume your faith will be strengthened by the realization that our God is a living God who can still bring protection and peace in the midst of the storms of distress, confusion and terror—a very present help in trouble.

Buy online at our website: **www.KingsleyPress.com**
Also available as an eBook for Kindle, Nook and iBooks.

ANTHONY NORRIS GROVES
SAINT AND PIONEER
by G. H. Lang

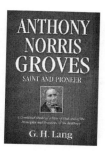

Although his name is little known in Christian cirlces today, Anthony Norris Groves (1795-1853) was, according to the writer of this book, one of the most influential men of the nineteenth century. He was what might be termed a spiritual pioneer, forging a path through unfamiliar territory in order that others might follow. One of those who followed him was George Müller, known to the world as one who in his lifetime cared for over ten thousand orphans without any appeal for human aid, instead trusting God alone to provide for the daily needs of this large enterprise.

In 1825 Groves wrote a booklet called *Christian Devotedness* in which he encouraged fellow believers and especially Christian workers to take literally Jesus' command not to lay up treasures on earth, but rather to give away their savings and possessions toward the spread of the gospel and to embark on a life of faith in God alone for the necessaries of life. Groves himself took this step of faith: he gave away his fortune, left his lucrative dental practice in England, and went to Baghdad to establish the first Protestant mission to Arabic-speaking Muslims. His going was not in connection with any church denomination or missionary society, as he sought to rely on God alone for needed finances. He later went to India also.

His approach to missions was to simplify the task of churches and missions by returning to the methods of Christ and His apostles, and to help indigenous converts form their own churches without dependence on foreign support. His ideas were considered radical at the time but later became widely accepted in evangelical circles.

Groves was a leading figure in the early days of what Robert Govett would later call the mightiest movement of the Spirit of God since Pentecost—a movement that became known simply as the Brethren. In this book G. H. Lang combines a study of the life and influence of Anthony Norris Groves with a survey of the original principles and practices of the Brethren movement.

MEMOIRS OF DAVID STONER

EDITED BY
WILLIAM DAWSON & JOHN HANNAH

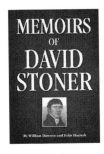

The name of David Stoner (1794-1826) deserves to be ranked alongside those of Robert Murray McCheyne, David Brainerd and Henry Martyn. Like them, he died at a relatively young age; and like them, his life was marked by a profound hunger and thirst for God and intense passion for souls. Stoner was saved at twelve years of age and from that point until his untimely death twenty years later his soul was continually on full stretch for God.

This book tells the story of his short but amazing life: his godly upgringing, his radical conversion, his call to preach, his amazing success as a Wesleyan Methodist preacher, his patience in tribulation and sickness, and his glorious departure to be with Christ forever. Many pages are devoted to extracts from his personal diary which give an amazing glimpse into the heart of one whose desires were all aflame for more of God.

Oswald J. Smith, in his soul-stirring book, *The Revival We Need,* wrote the following: "Have been reading the diary of David Stoner. How I thank God for it! He is another Brainerd. Have been much helped, but how ashamed and humble I feel as I read it! Oh, how he thirsted and searched after God! How he agonized and travailed! And he died at 32."

You, too can be much helped in your spiritual life as you study the life of this youthful saint of a past generation.

"Be instant and constant in prayer. Study, books, eloquence, fine sermons are all nothing without prayer. Prayer brings the Spirit, the life, the power." —*David Stoner*

Buy online at our website: **www.KingsleyPress.com**
Also available as an eBook for Kindle, Nook and iBooks.

The Christian Hero
A Sketch of the Life of Robert Annan

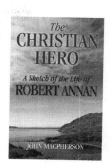

If you've never heard of Robert Annan of Dundee, otherwise known as "the Christian Hero," prepare to be astounded at the amazing grace of God in his life as you turn the pages of this incredible little biography. Its thrilling story will stir you to the depths and almost certainly drive you to your knees with an increased desire to be used for God's glory.

The record of his beginning years reads much like that of John Newton—a life of wandering far from God in the ways of sin and rebellion. At least once he miraculously escaped death through the overruling providence of God. As time passed, he became thoroughly discontented with his sinful life; but he didn't want anything to do with God or Christianity. He thought he could overcome sin and live a morally good life by his own efforts. He soon discovered, however, that he was no match for sin or Satan; and casting himself entirely on God's grace and mercy in Jesus Christ, he was gloriously saved.

From the very first day of his conversion, he became a tireless seeker of lost souls. He worked during the day time as a stone mason, but his evenings and weekends were spent preaching in the streets or in homes. Frequently he would spend whole nights in secret prayer, pleading at the throne of grace for lost sinners. As he went to his employment in the early mornings, he would often write Scripture verses on the pavement for others to read as they passed by on their way to work or school. Thus he was instant in season and out of season, using every opportunity to present to men the claims of Jesus Christ and the reality of heaven, hell, and the judgment that awaits every human soul.

Read his story and be amazed, remembering that what God did for Robert Annan he can and will do for anyone.

Buy online at our website: **www.KingsleyPress.com**
Also available as an eBook for Kindle, Nook and iBooks.